Listening to the Spirit

ACADEMY SERIES

SERIES EDITOR
Margaret D. Kamitsuka

A Publication Series of
The American Academy of Religion
and
Oxford University Press

A POST-PATRIARCHAL CHRISTOLOGY
David W. Odell-Scott

PROSPECTS FOR POST-HOLOCAUST THEOLOGY
Stephen R. Haynes

PROFILE OF THE LAST PURITAN
Jonathan Edwards, Self-Love, and the Dawn of the Beatific
David C. Brand

VICTOR TURNER REVISITED
Ritual as Social Change
Bobby C. Alexander

CHINESE WOMEN AND CHRISTIANITY, 1860–1927
Kwok Pui-Lan

THE MAN IN THE YELLOW HAT
Theology and Psychoanalysis in Child Therapy
Dorothy W. Martyn

THE GRACE OF DIFFERENCE
A Canadian Feminist Theological Ethic
Marilyn J. Legge

THE INTERSUBJECTIVITY OF THE MYSTIC
A Study of Teresa of 'Avila's Interior Castle
Mary Frolich

NARRATING HISTORY, DEVELOPING DOCTRINE
Friedrich Schleiermacher and Johann Sebastian Drey
Bradford E. Hinze

ANALOGICAL POSSIBILITIES
How Words Refer to God
Philip A. Rolnick

WOMANIST JUSTICE, WOMANIST HOPE
Emilie M. Townes

WOMEN DON'T COUNT
The Challenge of Women's Poverty to Christian Ethics
Pamela K. Brubaker

THE EXPLORATION OF THE INNER WOUNDS—HAN
Jae Hoon Lee

COMPREHENDING POWER IN CHRISTIAN SOCIAL ETHICS
Christine Firer Hinze

THE GREENING OF THEOLOGY
The Ecological Models of Rosemary Radford Ruether, Joseph Stiller, and Jürgen Moltmann
Steven Bouma-Prediger

THE SPIRIT AND THE VISION
The Influence of Christian Romanticism on the Development of 19th-Century American Art
Diane Apostolos-Cappadona

THE FREEDOM OF THE SPIRIT
African Indigenous Churches in Kenya
Francis Kimani Githieya

BRIDGE-MAKERS AND CROSS-BEARERS
Korean-American Women and the Church
Jung Ha Kim

GOD BLESS THE CHILD THAT'S GOT ITS OWN
The Economic Rights Debate
Darryl M. Trimiew

ENERGIES OF THE SPIRIT
Trinitarian Models in Eastern Orthodox and Western Theology
Duncan Reid

THE GODDESS LAKṢMĪ
The Divine Consort in South Indian Vaiṣṇava Tradition
P. Pratap Kumar

CREATIVE DWELLING
Empathy and Clarity in God and Self
Lucinda A. Stark Huffaker

HOSPITALITY TO STRANGERS
Empathy and the Physician-Patient Relationship
Dorothy M. Owens

THE BONDS OF FREEDOM
Feminist Theology and Christian Realism
Rebekah L. Miles

THE SPECTER OF SPECIESISM
Buddhist and Christian Views of Animals
Paul Waldau

INCARNATION AND PHYSICS
*Natural Science in the Theology of
Thomas F. Torrance*
Tapio Luoma

OF BORDERS AND MARGINS
Hispanic Disciples in Texas, 1888–1945
Daisy L. Machado

YVES CONGAR'S THEOLOGY OF THE
HOLY SPIRIT
Elizabeth Teresa Groppe

HSIEH LIANG-TSO AND THE *ANALECTS*
OF CONFUCIUS
Humane Learning as a Religious Quest
Thomas W. Selover

GREGORY OF NYSSA AND THE CONCEPT
OF DIVINE PERSONS
Lucian Turcescu

GRAHAM GREENE'S CATHOLIC
IMAGINATION
Mark Bosco, S.J.

COMING TO THE EDGE OF THE CIRCLE
A Wiccan Initiation Ritual
Nikki Bado-Fralick

THE ETHICS OF ANIMAL
EXPERIMENTATION
*A Critical Analysis and Constructive
Christian Proposal*
Donna Yarri

PAUL IN ISRAEL'S STORY
Self and Community at the Cross
John L. Meech

CROSSING THE ETHNIC DIVIDE
The Multiethnic Church on a Mission
Kathleen Garces-Foley

GOD AND THE VICTIM
Traumatic Intrusions on Grace and Freedom
Jennifer Erin Beste

THE CREATIVE SUFFERING OF
THE TRIUNE GOD
An Evolutionary Theology
Gloria L. Schaab

A THEOLOGY OF CRITICISM
*Balthasar, Postmodernism, and the Catholic
Imagination*
Michael P. Murphy

INCARNATION ANYWAY
Arguments for Supralapsarian Christology
Edwin Chr. Van Driel

DISABILITY AND CHRISTIAN
THEOLOGY
*Embodied Limits and Constructive
Possibilities*
Deborah Beth Creamer

MEETING GOD ON THE CROSS
Christ, the Cross, and the Feminist Critique
Arnfríður Guðmundsdóttir

MUSLIMS, SCHOLARS, SOLDIERS
*The Origin and Elaboration of
the Ibāḍī Imāmate Traditions*
Adam R. Gaiser

RACE AND RELIGION IN AMERICAN
BUDDHISM
White Supremacy and Immigrant Adaptation
Joseph Cheah

JOURNEY BACK TO GOD
Origen on the Problem of Evil
Mark S. M. Scott

BEYOND THE WALLS
*Abraham Joshua Heschel and Edith Stein on the
Significance of Empathy for Jewish-Christian
Dialogue*
Joseph Redfield Palmisano, S.J.

TYPES OF PENTECOSTAL THEOLOGY
Method, System, Spirit
Christopher A. Stephenson

OTHER DREAMS OF FREEDOM
Religion, Sex, and Human Trafficking
Yvonne C. Zimmerman

LIBERALISM VERSUS POSTLIBERALISM
The Great Divide in Twentieth-Century Theology
John Allan Knight

IMAGE, IDENTITY, AND THE FORMING
OF THE AUGUSTINIAN SOUL
Matthew Drever

RIGHTEOUS RHETORIC
*Sex, Speech, and the Politics of Concerned
Women for America*
Leslie Durrough Smith

ENFOLDING SILENCE
*The Transformation of Japanese American
Religion and Art under Oppression*
Brett J. Esaki

LONGING AND LETTING GO
*Christian and Hindu Practices of Passionate
Non-Attachment*
Holly Hillgardner

MEANING IN OUR BODIES
Sensory Experience as Constructive Theological Imagination
Heike Peckruhn

INTERPRETING ISLAM IN CHINA
Pilgrimage, Scripture, and Language in the Han Kitab
Kristian Petersen

THE GOODNESS OF HOME
Human and Divine Love and the Making of the Self
Natalia Marandiuc

UNSAYING GOD
Negative Theology in Medieval Islam
Aydogan Kars

TROELTSCH'S ESCHATOLOGICAL ABSOLUTE
Evan F. Kuehn

MONKS IN MOTION
Buddhism and Modernity Across the South China Sea
Jack Meng-Tat Chia

MELVILLE'S WISDOM
Religion, Skepticism, and Literature in Nineteenth-Century America
Damien Schlarb

DRIFTING THROUGH SAMSARA
Tacit Conversion and Disengagement in Goenka's Vipassana Movement
Masoumeh Rahmani

LISTENING TO THE SPIRIT
The Radical Social Gospel, Sacred Value, and Broad-Based Community Organizing
Aaron Stauffer

Listening to the Spirit

The Radical Social Gospel, Sacred Value, and Broad-Based Community Organizing

AARON STAUFFER

Vanderbilt University

OXFORD
UNIVERSITY PRESS

Oxford University Press is a department of the University of Oxford. It furthers
the University's objective of excellence in research, scholarship, and education
by publishing worldwide. Oxford is a registered trade mark of Oxford University
Press in the UK and certain other countries.

Published in the United States of America by Oxford University Press
198 Madison Avenue, New York, NY 10016, United States of America.

© Oxford University Press 2024

All rights reserved. No part of this publication may be reproduced, stored in
a retrieval system, or transmitted, in any form or by any means, without the
prior permission in writing of Oxford University Press, or as expressly permitted
by law, by license, or under terms agreed with the appropriate reproduction
rights organization. Inquiries concerning reproduction outside the scope of the
above should be sent to the Rights Department, Oxford University Press, at the
address above.

You must not circulate this work in any other form
and you must impose this same condition on any acquirer.

Library of Congress Cataloging-in-Publication Data
Names: Stauffer, Aaron, author.
Title: Listening to the spirit : the radical social gospel, sacred value,
and broad-based community organizing / Aaron Stauffer, PhD.
Description: New York, NY, United States of America : Oxford University Press, [2024] |
Includes bibliographical references and index.
Identifiers: LCCN 2023046744 | ISBN 9780197755525 (hardback) |
ISBN 9780197755549 (epub) | ISBN 9780197755556 (ebook)
Subjects: LCSH: Religion and politics. | Community organization. |
Social justice. | Church.
Classification: LCC BL65.P7 S753 2024 | DDC 261.8—dc23/eng/20231103
LC record available at https://lccn.loc.gov/2023046744

DOI: 10.1093/oso/9780197755525.001.0001

Printed by Integrated Books International, United States of America

For those I hold most dear:
Lauren, Julian, and August

Contents

Preface xi
Acknowledgments xxix

PART I. SACRED VALUES AND ORGANIZING FOR POWER

Introduction: Inductive Christian Social Ethics: The Method of the Radical Social Gospel 3

1. Religion, the Secular, and Sacred Value in Counterpublics 17
2. Organizing Religious Practices 48

PART II. WHY SACRED VALUES MATTER

3. Our Political Relationship with Sacred Value 81
4. Radical Democracy and Sacred Value 117

PART III. NOW WHAT? HOW ORGANIZING AND THEOLOGY CAN CHANGE GOING FORWARD

5. On Organizing as Practice 147
6. On Black Organizing: Capitalist Exploitation, Racial Expropriation 168
7. On Churches 186

Bibliography 209
Index 225

Preface

After a months-long intentional process of planning, recruiting, and gathering congregants to listen to one another about their core values and most pressing community issues, the church invited our local council member to hear what we had discovered about our congregation and community. We had come a long way. As a member institution of the local Gamaliel affiliate, Nashville Organized for Action and Hope, the congregation I attended had recently finished a listening campaign and was preparing to present its findings to the council member. The Gamaliel Foundation is one of four national broad-based community organizing (BBCO) networks.[1] Broad-based organizing is a political and religious practice that sits at the heart of this book's argument. So when the pastor at our largely white Protestant church invited the congregation to the meeting, I was surprised to hear him say rather definitively, "Now, this is not a political meeting." I could not believe my ears. "Why did you put it that way?" I later asked him. We were clear on what issues we wanted to present, and more important, we were clear on why those values were so central to our faith. We had built relational power and we wanted to act. We wanted the council member to know we were paying attention. The pastor said in response that some in the congregation were worried that the council member might get the impression we were telling people to vote for a specific party. "That's partisanship," I said, "not politics." More than that, politics is about the goods we hold in common and our life together—Christian faith is deeply concerned about that.

Stories like this are far too common in our religious and political lives. Christians and people of faith are often without clear responses for why it is important for them to bring their fundamental faith commitments to democratic politics. The story in the news today is that such commitments only prevent or frustrate democratic politics rather than make it possible. The United States is so deeply mired in cultural wars, so we're told, that holding something as sacred—human dignity, human life, the right to vote, a land,

---

[1] The other three are Industrial Areas Foundation, Faith in Action (previously Pacific Institute for Community Organization; PICO), and Direct Action Research & Training Center.

or natural resource, for example—only serves to further entrench us in our enclaves. A democratic politics of the common life and common good is atrophying. To many, religion and religious commitments are responsible for putting the brake on our democratic life and gassing up our culture wars. When religion and politics mix, things get heated, democracy stalls, and the economically and politically powerful triumph at its disfunction. Religious commitments are too absolute and comprehensive to allow for compromise or negotiation—strategies necessary for a healthy democratic culture. It's better to just exclude religion and religious attitudes or commitments from political life, so this logic runs.

As many other scholars have argued over the years, however, it's not quite clear why religious commitments are claimed to be so different from secular commitments that have purchase in our political life.[2] Religious reasons look and sound a lot like their supposed secular opposites. When you ask religious people why they are involved in politics, the answers you get have to do with deeply held values and relationships of love and concern. One of the key contributions of this book is to offer an account of the political role of sacred value in broad-based organizing. When I say "sacred value," I mean something separate from (because differently understood from) the "sacred." Sacred values are evaluative attitudes people take up toward goods and people; the sacred is another way of talking about the divine. Values and relationships drive much of our political life. Many of these religious and political attitudes can be captured by what I call in this book "sacred value." An evangelical opposes abortion because it violates the sacred value of life. An Indigenous activist holds a landmark or natural resource as sacred and therefore supports its legal protection because its current recreational use threatens to destroy it. The abolitionist argues that prisons attack the sacred dignity of the incarcerated. Excluding religious commitments from politics is tricky precisely because claims of sacred value can equally capture religious and secular commitments and attitudes and are held by secular and religious political participants. Both secular and religious political participants make claims of sacred value. The term "sacred value" is another way of talking about what people hold most dear. By focusing on the political role of sacred values we can pull back the curtain and expose the richly entangled reality

---

[2] See Wolterstorff, "An Engagement with Rorty." This is not to mention that "the secular" itself presents a whole host of questions involving the claims that secularism and the secular as an ideology exhibit religious qualities, a question I will address throughout this book.

of our political life, revealing aspects of our religious and political lives that have often been ignored or pushed aside.

The recent debate over the role of religion in democratic politics during the past several decades has swung the full arc of the pendulum. One way of telling this recent story is like so: some scholars start off by claiming that religious commitments are inherently polarizing because they are too comprehensive to be reasonable and so are conversation stoppers; thus they need to be excluded from political discourse. Others respond by arguing that religious commitments are equally valid and should take their place among the many other commonly held resources in democratic discourse.[3] As democratic theorist Jeffrey Stout says, "People who claim that religion as such is bad for politics, and should be minimized to the extent possible, have not had an easy time defining what they want to minimize, or explain how the elimination of religion from politics is to be carried out by means that are both realistic and democratic."[4] This trouble of imprecision and ambiguity hasn't stopped some from arguing that religion and politics don't mix, even though such arguments neglect the political role of sacred values. Such ideological arguments made on the basis of excluding religion or including only secular reasons rightly raise suspicions of hidden agendas. Often, arguments for secularism are vague, nefarious attempts to normalize one definition of religion.[5]

Debates about a secular society often go off the rails when one faction acts in bad faith. Secular*ism* as a political doctrine describes a polity where no religion is dominant—and so all religions and philosophical viewpoints are equal players in democratic exchange. This does not guarantee that such arguments will be persuasive to one's peers or assume that all religious and philosophical viewpoints are equally well thought out and reasonable. It just means that such arguments are equally available to members of a democracy.

---

[3] John Rawls made the initial claim that religious reasons in public are to be excluded, along with other comprehensive claims, see Rawls, *A Theory of Justice*. Richard Rorty initially argued that religious claims are conversation stoppers (*Philosophy and Social Hope*, 168–74). Rawls later adjusted his position in *Political Liberalism*; see "Introduction to the Paperback edition," esp. li–liii and "The Idea of Public Reason Revisited," and Rorty adjusted his position in Springs et al., "Pragmatism and Democracy," 418–25. For accounts that argue for the equality of religious reasons in democratic politics, see Stout, *Democracy and Tradition*, ch. 3; Wolterstorff, "An Engagement with Rorty"; Wolterstorff, *Religion in the University*. For a wonderful exchange on these positions, among others, see the entire forum of Springs et al., "Pragmatism and Democracy."

[4] Stout, *Blessed Are the Organized*, 223.

[5] See Scott, *Sex and Secularism*; Fessenden, *Culture and Redemption*; Lloyd, *Religion of the Field Negro*. In chapter 2, I offer an account of how broad-based organizing coalitions trouble political "secular" frames.

But often, what some bad faith actors seek to establish is really a form of secular ideology—let's call this "the secular" or "secular*ization*." As an ideology it baptizes certain expressions of religious and civic culture and practices as normative for public life. The secular in this sense turns out to be a vague form of white heteropatriarchal Protestantism supporting racial capitalism.[6] One quick way of grasping this point is to consider recent debates on religious freedom that in fact function as guises for anti-Muslim bigotry and anti-Semitism.[7] Non-Christian public and political expressions of religion are viewed as existential threats. Separating out secularism—a political doctrine—from the secular as an ideology in real time can be tricky. To some, it's easier to say that religion and politics are better off separate.

Democratic interfaith organizers are not immune to this mindset. When I first started as a broad-based organizer with the Industrial Areas Foundation (IAF), I fell in love with the practice because it engaged faith communities and challenged them to think critically about the relationship between religion and power. I wanted to dig deeper into the theological roots of this relationship. Once, I told a senior IAF organizer that I was leading a congregational core team through this work. "If you want to do theology," the organizer said in response, "go get a theologian. Organizing is about building power." This struck me as an odd thing for an organizer to say, and yet it remains a common attitude among organizers. For example, Richard Wood and Brad Fulton's recent work on the changes in organizing methodology demonstrates how organizers are working hard to address challenges that arise from racial and gender differences in organizing, but little is being done on religious diversity.[8] The relationship between religion and politics is captured by the fraught "religious versus secular" frame.

---

[6] I draw this distinction between "secularism," "the secular," and "secularization" from the work of Alkeel Bilgrami. See Bilgrami, *Secularism, Identity, and Enchantment*, especially ch. 1, "Secularism: Its Content and Context."

[7] See Hurd, *Beyond Religious Freedom*; Sullivan, *The Impossibility of Religious Freedom*; Sullivan, *Church State Corporation*. Hurd's legal analysis stems from the groundbreaking work of Asad, *Genealogies of Religion* and *Formations of the Secular*.

[8] For example, see how Wood and Fulton capture the traditional way of approaching racial difference in organizing (namely, by de-emphasizing it): "That is, PICO—like most of the faith-based organizing field descended from Alinksy's work—often implicitly recognized the racial dimensions of inequity in America, but strategically chose to de-emphasize any explicit discussion of those dimensions in its public narrative about its work or in its internal organizing culture. Faith-based organizing continues to handle *religious* diversity in a similar way, rarely focusing on lines of difference in order to focus on shared ethical commitments and social priorities" (*A Shared Future*, 87, emphasis in original).

What is more, Christian political theologians who may admit some relationships between religion and politics leave the two undisturbed in their analysis, at times for theological reasons (i.e., instrumentalization of worship for political ends).[9] The pages that follow explore how things shift, conceptually and practically, when sacred values are centered in our religious and political lives. One outcome is that our sense of Christian identity—understood as socially constructed as other social norms and practices like race, class, and gender—shifts in interesting and important ways. By exploring the political role of sacred values in the practice of BBCO, the role of theology in organizing becomes clearer and a potentially new political and ecclesiological terrain opens for Christians addressing injustice in a pluralistic world. Democratic organizing is certainly about power, but so is theology. Theology plays a fundamental role in our lived religious and political practices. People organize to protect and fight for what they hold most dear, what they hold sacred. Those "If you want to do theology go get a theologian" organizers—and their ilk who study organizing—stunt our political and religious imaginations and prohibit the practice from improvising and meeting new theological and political challenges. Typically, sacred values are thought to be incommensurate with and allergic to compromise, or, so it is often claimed, sacred values inevitably splinter groups. But things are more complicated than that. The challenges that face organizing today largely have to do with limiting religion's role in the practice, from seeing sacred values as a threat rather than an opportunity for broad-based organizing.

This is a book about the political role of sacred value in democratic organizing and how the practice of organizing can be transformed when organizers and scholars studying organizing center rather than marginalize sacred value in democratic politics. I'm interested in a specific form of political practice, however: the BBCO tradition of politics most often associated with Saul Alinsky. My own religious convictions and my own organizing experience inform my argument, but the lessons learned on the political role of sacred value have purchase beyond Christian readers or those who are unfamiliar with BBCO. I don't attempt to justify BBCO against other forms of organizing and will often call for deep revision of the practice; it is one tradition of organizing among many others. The challenges we face today

---

[9] More will be said on this in chapter 1, but I'm thinking particularly of Luke Bretherton and C. Melissa Snarr here. See Bretherton, *Resurrecting Democracy*, 159–60; Snarr, *All You That Labor*, 134.

from racial capitalism require every political, economic, and theological resource we can summon. BBCO is one of those resources. The book makes a social ethical and political theological case for how Christians can graft their democratic organizing into a long tradition of radical social gospelers whose politics of sacred value led them to the heart of radical and progressive political and economic movements. The influence of the theological and political tradition of the radical social gospel has largely been forgotten in recent accounts of BBCO. Radical social gospelers introduced and made popular powerful arguments for economic and political positions crucial to organizing today: God's cooperative commonwealth, the solidarity of all working people, and biblical critique of capitalism's colonial and racial formation were all high notes in speeches and sermons of the radical social gospelers.

The field of social ethics provided the conceptual framing and methodology for the movements of Black and white radical social gospelers. People and movements rallied around and found deep meaning in such phrases as "God's cooperative commonwealth": they built institutions, informed legislation, published magazines, and turned out in droves to hear speeches and sermons on these topics because they articulated something we know today: that there is power in the politics of sacred value. The Movement for Black Lives and movements for reproductive justice and for climate justice are rocking our social, political, and religious lives and are commonly trading in discourse of sacred value. Building movements from values and relationships, not merely issues, is an important strategic shift in the practice of organizing.

I argue that BBCO is a practice grounded in relationships and values, not merely issue campaigns and platforms. Some of these values are held sacred by their practitioners. People organize to fight for and protect what they hold sacred, and because of the role of sacred values in BBCO some practices can be seen as religious practices, namely the listening campaign and the relational meeting. The relational meeting and the listening campaign are the "bread and butter" of BBCO. A relational meeting is a public, value-directed conversation between two people on what they care most about in their community and what they are willing to do to fight for and protect those values, goods, and people. A listening campaign is a series of relational meetings carried out within a single institution or organization with the aim of identifying the institution's core values and issues. The largest national networks of broad-based organizing are made up of networks of local affiliates, counterpublics, that are collectives of a broad range of local institutions and organizations. BBCO affiliates are best conceptualized as counterpublics and so have a particular power relationship to their broader political and economic landscape. They are dialogical arenas, where discourses are invented and power is built to address goals of the members of these counterpublics. Broad-based organizing begins with local leaders mobilizing other leaders and their institutions, with listening to others by setting up individual relational meetings with potential leaders and by institutions and organizations intentionally committing to listen to their own members. This book makes the case that the practice of organizing begins by listening to the Spirit.[10]

By calling organizing a practice, I mean to position it in the political culture of the BBCO constituency. Too often, scholarly accounts of BBCO by political scientists and Christian ethicists tend to adopt an unarticulated methodological individualism, especially when organizing is imagined as an art or craft. Insofar as organizing is a skill developed over time, under the tutelage of a mentor, and allows for individual expression within an established repertoire of strategies and tactics, capturing the activity of organizing as an art or craft is laudable. But too often, by calling organizing an art scholars and organizers fail to capture how organizing happens in a network of relations that makes possible certain moves and delimits others.[11] Organizing happens in a field of relations in which people are positioned and move. One relational field is in a power relation with other fields. What is politically possible for an organizer is in part determined by their relational position in one field and in regard to other fields. More than this, navigating these relationships takes familiarity with the group's culture, norms, habits, and style of organizing. Organizing is a practice in that it requires practical knowledge of these relationships and an embodied understanding of what is or is not appropriate at a certain point in time in the group's life. Much of organizing has to do with a use of time; a pithy and to-the-point question can agitate people in the right way and therefore strategically move the group to action. A misjudgment and inappropriate action can lead to the dissolution of a campaign. Capturing the relational dynamics that occur within the constituency by the terms "field" and "practice" allows for the combination of

---

[10] I capitalize "Spirit" to signify the emergence of a theological and spiritual bond that is formed through practices of mutual recognition and determinate negation and to draw explicit connections between Hegel's use of "spirit" (*Geist*) and the Christian tradition's use of "Holy Spirit."

[11] For a related critique of contemporary accounts of organizing, see Speer and Han, "Re-engaging Social Relationships and Collective Dimensions of Organizing to Revive Democratic Practice."

agency and structure, intentionality and habit that I have witnessed in my own organizing and have heard confirmed by other organizers.

My argument is more than the claim that organizing is a practice grounded in sacred values and relationships. Once we position the practice of organizing within the larger life of the group and embrace the role of sacred values within the practice, the claim that some of the practices of organizing are lived religious practices becomes clear. Lived religious practices are the kinds of human action that emphasize both the intentional and the habituated character of practice. Lived religious practices in a crucial sense are "unfinished" insofar as they subvert traditional dichotomous views of the world that come with prefabricated notions of "religion" along with opposing "secular" concepts. A lived religious practice is entangled with political and secular (in the nonideological sense) practices and not always spoken about approvingly in the pages that follow. Because religious practices are lived and social, they are open to deformation and twisting to dominating ends. Organizers and scholars need to recognize the political role of sacred values in the practice, and when they do, some of the self-imposed political and theological limits on the practice can be addressed and perhaps surpassed.

The dominant BBCO networks, however, have adopted an organizing methodology that marginalizes sacred values and imposes theological and political limits on the practice. In my conversations with organizers and leaders about sacred values, the unsaid fear is that sacred values are too polarizing and that they threaten to split the affiliate. The dominant logic in BBCO has been to select issues that are "winnable" and to stay away from sacred values that are found in wedge issues. Sacred values are too tightly clung to, and in interfaith constituencies—like BBCO counterpublics—sacred values across traditions only lead to conflict. Here, issues of abortion, the death penalty, and racial and sexual identity (for example) are viewed as "unwinnable" because they are too polarizing and so unwise for organizers to take up. This is one implication of the "If you want to do theology, go get a theologian" mindset. In this frame of organizing, issues take precedence over values. What tends to happen is organizers are taught that power is built by winning issues rather than by building relational power grounded in values. In this framework, my argument never sees the light of day. A primary source of this tension between issues and values might be found in Alinsky's own articulation of the process of organizing in *Rules for Radicals*, but the problem has evolved past Alinsky's influence and now impacts the appropriately perceived role of theology and religion in organizing.[12] Yet important improvisations in the model of BBCO are making my argument more likely to have purchase with organizers currently working in the field and with scholars writing about organizing.[13] In my own organizing and in my conversations with other organizers, the fundamental role of values and theology is being embraced and the model is beginning to push its current political and religious imaginaries. This is good news and makes my argument and the stories I tell all the more relevant to BBCO and its current practice.

This is not to argue that there is consensus or agreement on attitudes of sacred value within a BBCO constituency. Indeed, deep disagreement and animus characterize political matters of sacred value; pluralization abounds. This is because attitudes of sacred value inevitably have to do with a person's or a community's experience and narrative of democratic politics. Democracy is about our common life together and the pursuit and protection of the goods we hold in common. When what we hold most dear is arbitrarily threatened or attacked, we have reason to work with others to build institutions and communities that prevent such arbitrary attack and harm in the future. Sacred values play a particular role in democratic life. Not only do they inspire; they sustain. The goods and people we hold most dear keep us going in the long slog of democratic politics. Organizing is slow and patient work, and so if you're going to get involved, it's best to be clear about why you're in the fight. When we are clear about what we hold most dear, we can personalize abstract political issues. Personalizing the issue places it in a narrative, which helps us get a sense for how it is that things came to be the way they are and what we might do to change them.

When a Christian church engages in the listening campaign, they are discerning the movement of the Spirit in their midst and what the Spirit is calling them to do in their public life. These organizing practices are religious practices that can enliven churches. In my experience, churches that see organizing as an expression of their faith, specifically in the relational

---

[12] See, for example, the relationship between issues and values as it is outlined in Alinsky, *Rules for Radicals*, especially 113–25.

[13] Richard Wood's work has provided an account for how Faith in Action (previously PICO) has transformed its organizing method. More recently, the Gamaliel Foundation has followed suit in the founding of its Race and Power Institute. See, Wood, *Faith in Action*; Wood and Fulton, *A Shared Future*. For the Gamaliel Foundation's Race and Power Institute, see "Race and Power 2019," accessed May 19, 2021, https://raceandpower.org/.

meeting and listening campaign, incorporate these practices into their broader liturgical life. Situating the relational meeting and listening campaign within the collection of liturgical practices germane to the church can lead us to a deeper understanding of the mission and vocation of the church as deeply tied to the work of organizing. The church, then, is more properly defined by its task and its work rather than by beliefs or doctrines. People do church by organizing. When they listen to the movement of the Spirit, it calls them into deeper reciprocal relationships. Spiraling outward, the Spirit weaves relationships within and through congregations, moving the church out into public life and into the work of building economic and political power.

My claim that some organizing practices are lived religious practices depends on an understanding of social practices as repertoires of human activity grounded in fields of ethically significant relationships that collectively make up institutions. These lived religious practices are social practices, and so the values, principles, and norms that guide the practice are shared and based in shared assumptions, patterns of behavior, and goods internal and external to the practice itself. Social practices often become part of broader cultural institutions, which can work to cultivate the goods internal to a practice, thereby fostering and cultivating virtues that serve to realize the internal goods. Here, social structures are collections of practices.

My social practical argument draws deeply from a certain tradition of philosophical theology that is grounded in the ethical and epistemological insights made by G. W. F. Hegel. One of these insights is that what it means to be a self is to be in relations of reciprocal recognition, accountability, and responsibility. Social practices of reciprocal recognition attest that my full selfhood cannot exist without a practical, embodied act of reciprocal recognition demonstrating that the other ethically and politically "counts." Social practices of reciprocal recognition ground broader epistemological points, which help us understand what it means to participate in an ethical community consisting of inferential relations of accountability and responsibility. The term Hegel used to talk about the state of such ethical relationships is "Spirit." For Hegel, practices of recognition are crucial to social practical reasoning. But what "Spirit" means is contested by readers of Hegel, especially those who are interested in what Hegel has to say about religion.

Over the past several decades, however, there has been a recent turn (and then questioning of this turn) by Anglo-American, predominantly analytic philosophers to read Hegel in a "non-metaphysical" fashion.[14] These scholars typically downplay, overlook, or even flat out ignore Hegel's interest in theology and religion.[15] I don't follow this turn. Yet I do find the social pragmatic reading of Hegel's epistemology persuasive, especially in providing a genesis of inferential social practical reasoning. This "non-metaphysical" turn in Hegel scholarship was a response to a reading of Hegel's epistemology and philosophy in equally troublesome ways that read Hegel as a totalizing philosopher whose all-encompassing thought had no space for difference, multiplicity, or the other. And yet, in response, these non-metaphysical readings of Hegel often overlook his writings on religion and theology. Debates about what Hegel meant by which term will most likely not end anytime soon, and so my reading is decidedly post-Hegelian. Those scholars of Hegel who are attuned to the musicality of theology and religion in his works help us grasp the multiple keys of Hegelian terms like "Spirit" and "religion." The argument in this book attempts to learn from both the non-metaphysical and metaphysical readings of Hegel in order to gain clarity in the politics of sacred value in BBCO. I aim to say less about Hegel and more about what can reasonably and responsibly be made clear by his thought.[16]

Listening to the Spirit is a Christian social practice. It is a normative and ethical affair. For my purposes, "Spirit" in Hegel is ethical, social pragmatic, idealist, political, and theological. Reciprocal recognition gets Hegel's conception of individual and collective identity off the ground, but mutual recognition is a *social practice*: the human practice of determining conceptual content is a social, historical one, in which conceptual content is worked out through relationships of authority and accountability.[17] Unless we *count* as a fellow practitioner and mutually recognize others to count as such, the ethical shapes of Spirit are incomplete. Spirit in this sense refers to normative structure and the inferential practice of determining the meaning of our concepts. But mutual recognition can also be an experience of love, of grace,

---

[14] Lumsden, "The Rise of the Non-Metaphysical Hegel."

[15] Robert Brandom's approach here is perhaps enlightening as he admits his work addresses only certain aspects of Hegel's thought. Cf. Brandom, "Some Pragmatist Themes in Hegel's Idealism." I turn to Brandom and others to build a post-Hegelian sense of inferentialism useful for my project. I turn to other thinkers to develop a compatible, religiously musical post-Hegelian account of Spirit. My account then, is *post*-Hegelian.

[16] Those interpreters of Hegel that I find most insightful are Dorrien, *In a Post-Hegelian Spirit*; Farneth, *Hegel's Social Ethics*; Hodgson, *Hegel and Christian Theology*; Lewis, *Freedom and Tradition in Hegel*; Lewis, *Religion, Modernity, and Politics in Hegel*; Williams, *Hegel's Ethics of Recognition*; Williams, *Recognition*.

[17] Cf. Brandom, "Freedom and Constraint by Norms"; Brandom, *Tales of the Mighty Dead*, chs. 6 and 7.

of God's Spirit transforming how it is we are with each other and how we are in the world.

Take, for example, the relational meeting. The one-on-one is a religious practice when a Christian narrates the mutual experience of listening to their conversation partner and being listened to in a theologically and ethically significant way. The relational meeting as a dialogical and co-constructed practice is an example of a social practice of reciprocal recognition insofar as it enacts norms, values, assumptions, and patterns of behavior that are socially grounded to establish an ethical and political relationship of mutual recognition. Truly listening to an other (and being listened to) in a way that honors their story, pain, and vulnerability—and committing to working with them to protect and fight for what we both hold most dear—is a powerful act that expands our religious and political imaginaries. The relational meeting creates the space for Christians to listen to the movements of the Spirit in their everyday life and to then narrate that movement together. The one-on-one involves attending to how an individual Christian's story fits into a larger Christian tradition and narrative. The act of narrating one's own story, while feeling listened to and empathetically cared for, creates space for critical theological and political reflection that can agitate and energize Christians toward political action. Each relational meeting is a moment of narrative work, wherein Christians are asked to do this critical reflective theological and political work that centers on what they hold most dear, what they hold sacred. Everyday Christians are emotionally, theologically, and politically vulnerable in such meetings, opening themselves up to perceive the work of God in their own lives, their collective life as a church, and the BBCO affiliate.

The Plan Ahead

The book is organized into three parts, each can be read separately, but the argument builds throughout the entire book. Part I introduces the argument and its significance in the broader field of religion and politics and concludes with a chapter that makes the book's central claim: seeing the relational meeting and the listening campaign as religious practices. Part I is an encapsulation of the entire book: here is the politics of sacred value in organizing in theory and action.

The introduction clarifies what I mean in terms of the radical social gospel and Christian socialism. It sets out my basic methodology and central analytics in terms of racial capitalism, domination, exploitation, and expropriation. It also offers my account of why social practices and lived religion are central to my social ethical argument.

Chapter 1 argues that broad-based organizing constituencies are counterpublics that have a particular power relationship to the larger economic and political structure. Counterpublics are discursive arenas that contest dominating interpretations of a group's identities but can consist of members from all sectors of society. A basic claim of my argument is that BBCO is a social practice that takes place in counterpublics that themselves refuse a neat distinction between religion and the secular. Black and feminist writers over the past hundred years—at least—have contributed examples that refute this framing, and so I turn to feminists who have troubled the concept of the secular and Black scholars who have read Black churches as counterpublics. Counterpublics like BBCO affiliates and Black churches are made up of people experiencing—or in solidarity with those experiencing—exploitation, expropriation, and domination. This counterpublic framing of BBCO helps make clear the significance of refuting a neat divide between religion and the secular, and it helps to accurately illuminate what is really going on with sacred values, religion, and politics in BBCO constituencies. This chapter ends with an overview of the book's contribution to the scholarly field of BBCO as well as a brief on the nebulous concept of sacred value.

In chapter 2, I delve into the practice of the relational meeting and the listening campaign in order to make the case that these are lived religious practices. In doing so, I draw on the study of lived religion and practice theory. My account of the relational meeting and the listening campaign places agency at the forefront of religious and political practices in order to better analyze political and economic power relations in the practice of organizing. This chapter explores how these two organizing religious practices are deeply embedded in relationships of power and how centering the political role of sacred values can transform the entire practice of BBCO. I offer some brief reflections on the role of agitation in the relational meeting and demonstrate how one congregation incorporated liturgy into their listening campaign and deeply integrated the practice of listening to their sense of how the Holy Spirit was moving and calling their congregation to act in public. These points build up to make the case that the listening campaign and the relational meeting itself are Christian religious practices insofar as churches perceive the practice as fitting into the larger narrative of their life and work as the people of God.

Part II teases apart the relationship between religion and political practices in organizing, religious identity, and sacred values, and the radically democratic politics of sacred value.

Chapter 3 offers my post-Hegelian, social practical account of the role sacred values play in our politics and in our social practical reasoning. The chapter brings philosophical theology into conversation with my own organizing experience. I offer an account of social practical reasoning, sacred value, and the ethical life of Spirit, as I define it. Social practical reasoning requires practices of mutual recognition and determinate negation. Determinate negation is another way of talking about how concept use brings along inferential relationships that include or exclude other concepts. Organizing practices like the relational meeting and listening campaign, when done well, place individuality and reciprocal recognition at the core; they can be seen as religious practices that place evaluative attitudes like sacred value in the broader inferential scene of social practical reasoning. By figuring scared values, mutual recognition, and the ethical life of Spirit in the relational meeting we gain epistemic, practical, and spiritual insight into the practice itself. We see just what is at stake in this organizing practice. Such evaluative attitudes like sacred values stem from larger traditions and narratives; in this way we can speak of Christian sacred value as a socially constructed, fallible social practice that can be leveraged to social ethical ends. What it means to be "Christian" needs to shift to incorporate lessons from feminists, studies of racial capitalism, and class theorists that seek to critically revise dominating norms and values in our practices of reasoning and evaluation.

Chapter 4 elaborates how counterpublics like BBCO affiliates habituate individuals in radically democratic social practices and what political conditions are required for individuals and groups to engage in an ethical way of life free of domination and exploitation. Certain political conditions are required for individuals and groups to freely engage in such social practices, political conditions that John Dewey spoke of as an ethical way of life free of domination and arbitrary influence. To be radical, democracy must start at the root of our associational life, asking questions about the kind of persons and power formed within groups. But there are particular problematics that exist in Dewey's thinking of the political, namely with regard to stark challenges posed by the role of power in democracy and the dangers white supremacy poses for radical democracy. Sheldon Wolin's democratic theory might be one source to address these problematics, but his notions of democratic fugitivity and his politics of tending ultimately fall short, too. My reading of Cornel West's work helps to address these shortcomings in Dewey and Wolin and in so doing come to terms with the way everyday patient work of BBCO recasts Dewey's and Wolin's theories of radical democracy. My attention here is not only to a particular kind of radical democratic theory in Dewey, Wolin, and West, but also what results when radical democracy is in dialogue with BBCO, namely, a Christian democratic socialist account of interfaith BBCO.

Part III is a collection of shorter chapters, grounded in experiences from my own organizing, that take up three topics: the practice of organizing, racial expropriation, and organizing churches. Each of these chapters is meant to critically reflect on the practice of BBCO in a way that demonstrates what changes in organizing when sacred values are centered, why that matters for organizers and scholars studying it, and how and why Christians and their congregations should pick up this work as central to the mission and vocation of churches.

Chapter 5 argues that framing organizing as a practice—rather than a craft or art—matters for organizers, scholars who study organizing, and for my broader Christian social ethical argument. Most accounts of broad-based organizing tend to frame it as an activity by single individuals. The lone professional organizer has become the emblem of BBCO, a single stand-in for a collective practice. The activity of organizing can be best understood by following the action itself rather than focusing on individual actors or actor organizations. What results is a richer description of the role of sacred values in the life of BBCO counterpublics and a truer account of the feel of the practice of BBCO.

Some religious scholars and theologians are less convinced that BBCO is the right example for the kind of radical democracy I am after. Most recently, Vincent Lloyd and Charlene Sinclair have challenged and invited BBCO to seriously consider how it wrestles with white supremacy and racial expropriation in racial capitalism. Lloyd's and Sinclair's critiques of BBCO get right to the heart of one of my main concerns with BBCO by forcefully raising the question: Can BBCO actualize the radically democratic power it purports to build in the face of racial capitalism? Both Lloyd and Sinclair offer an invitation, and in chapter 6 I find deep convergences with BBCO as I've experienced it and the sort of organizing they are calling for. Lloyd's and Sinclair's work invites us to image how BBCO might look if it adequately contends with not only the violent reality of racial capitalism's exploitation but also the conditions of possibility that expropriate peoples, lands, and societies. The chapter makes a case that by centering the political role of sacred value, in this specific case the sacred value of Black life, BBCO can more adequately build relational power that grasps the role of race expropriation and class exploitation in contemporary racial capitalism.

Radical democracy would be weaker without churches, and so the final chapter offers a counterpublic political ecclesiology for local churches to join BBCOs. To make this case, I draw from a historical example of the radical social gospel: the life and work of Rev. George Washington Woodbey. Woodbey was formed and shaped in Black counterpublics. Long before he joined the Socialist Party of America as its first Black organizer, and for many years after he left the Party, he was a committed churchman. I draw out from his life and work key themes and principles of a counterpublic political ecclesiology: cooperation, dialogue, and agitation. Each of these principles leads to a deep entanglement between religion, politics, and economics. For Woodbey, socialist politics were enactments of biblical principles. Today we can read Woodbey's works and about his life and construct our own counterpublic political ecclesiology. As I make constructive claims I build on the social practical reasoning and socially constructed conception of religious identity I advanced in chapter 4. A church's identity is deeply connected to its task, which I understand to be a specific sort of work: Christians are gathered by God and sent into the world to do the Spirit's work of establishing relationships of liberation and love.

Relations of liberation and love consist positively in political conditions of radical democracy and mutual recognition as an intersubjective Spirit that characterizes our ethical and political life. Spirit in this sense refers to normative structure and the inferential practice of determining the meaning of our concepts. But mutual recognition can also be a loving experience that welcomes one into a community of grace and liberation, sending us out into the world to build relational power to protect and fight for what we hold most dear. God's Spirit beckons us, moves us toward ethical practices that more accurately live out this sense of liberation and love. This is another way of saying that the radical social gospel is a movement, an ethical, Spirit-filled way of life. Being brought together by God's Spirit, the life of Christians is distinct insofar as their lives and relational bonds are transformed in the Spirit's grace and love. Churches can again pick up this work of the radical social gospel through broad-based organizing.

These ecclesial and theological claims bring the book's argument full circle, yielding a richer description of the role of sacred values in BBCO and a more accurate account of the feel of the practice of BBCO. By paying attention to sacred values in the social practice of organizing, some organizing practices can be seen as lived religious practices. Woodbey believed there was power in the churches to build the cooperative commonwealth. That power is still there in the people of God. Christian churches are called to this particular work of building relational power for radical democracy against racial capitalism and do so by listening to the Spirit's graceful movement in the world.

Acknowledgments

I first began thinking seriously about religion and community organizing many years ago in San Antonio, Texas, as I organized with COPS/Metro Alliance. Jorge Montiel was my first true mentor of organizing. Later, organizing with Religions for Peace and the Faith and Culture Center, I refined those skills in a different context on different issues. This book uses examples and experiences I gained through that work and with Nashville Organized for Action and Hope. Through it all the lessons remained the same. People organize to protect and fight for what they hold most dear. Issues fade, values don't.

Gary Dorrien was the best doctoral advisor for a project like this. He remains a mentor and brilliant teacher who has deep experience organizing. Charlene Sinclair and Peter Laarman have become wise conversation partners and collaborators. At Vanderbilt Divinity School, Melissa Snarr is a dear colleague, co-teacher, and friend, who has seen this project from its earliest days. Joerg Rieger has been a welcome conversation partner and generously made space for me at the Wendland-Cook Program in Religion and Justice. Jonathan Tran read several chapters and provided crucial feedback and encouragement as we talked pragmatism, theology, and racial capitalism. Molly Farneth graciously waded into the Hegelian waters and helped me track a course. Toni Alimi, Luke Bretherton, David C. Chao, and Nicholas Hayes-Mota have been steadfast friends and interlocutors. Margaret Kamitsuka is an excellent editor of the American Academy of Religion series and skillfully helped shepherd this book through the editorial process. Much of what is in this book stems from conversations that began with friends in classes at Union with Gary and then in Princeton with Jeff Stout, Cornel West, and Eric Gregory. Their generosity of spirit and attention to getting things right stays with me today.

PART I
SACRED VALUES AND ORGANIZING FOR POWER

Introduction: Inductive Christian Social Ethics

The Method of the Radical Social Gospel

This book is a work of Christian social ethics in the tradition of the radical social gospel. I should say a word or two about my own position in social ethics, and the field itself, along with such terms as "radical social gospel" and "Christian democratic socialism," because such terms are not self-evidently clear.

Christian social ethics is a distinct field of Christian ethical reflection that finds its roots in the inductive methodology pioneered by Francis Greenwood Peabody.[1] Social ethics came to be along with the arrival of sociology, the social gospel movement, Christian socialism, and the trade union movements.[2] That Christian ethical principles could address problems of economic, social, and political injustice was a distinctly modern idea.[3] Social ethics is a movement and a discourse—a way of responding to and addressing modern social problems. Christian social ethicists did their work out of the conviction that Christian principles had an important bearing on social structures and a role in transforming those structures away from social sin to social justice. Social salvation was the novel idea that the social gospelers shouted from the mountaintop: salvation had to be personal *and* social to be real.[4] The founders of the field believed that social ethics had to have a distinct social scientific method. Peabody's method started by throwing his students into the current social movements of the day. His basic methodology can be summed up in three steps: observation, generalization, and correlation.[5] The radical social gospeler Harry Ward, who learned social ethics

---

[1] For the definitive account of social ethics, see Dorrien, *Social Ethics in the Making*.
[2] Ibid., 1.
[3] Dorrien, *Economy, Difference, Empire*, xi.
[4] See Luker, "Interpreting the Social Gospel"; Evans, "Historical Integrity and Theological Recovery."
[5] Dorrien, *Social Ethics in the Making*, 20.

from Peabody at Harvard in the late 1890s, later simplified this method to three questions: What are the facts? What do they mean? What should be done?[6] This basic inductive methodology is crucial to my own account as I seek to tease out the significance and role of sacred values in democratic politics of broad-based organizing constituencies in a way that makes sense to the participants themselves.

Nowadays, questions about an inductive social scientific method in social ethics are more likely to be found in conversations regarding "everyday ethics" and ethnography in Christian ethics. Take, for example, a recent book by Michael Banner, *The Ethics of Everyday Life*. Banner's book is a helpful reflection point not because of its argument—which is not necessarily unique—but because it has served as a sort of conversation starter on the relationship between Christian ethics, social sciences, and theology. Banner's argument is motivated by a two-pronged claim: (1) Christian ethics, as it is predominantly practiced today, is an ethics of "hard cases" or "quandary ethics," and (2) because of this Christian ethics fails to adequately attend to and narrate the social context of the morally good and bad in the lived reality of ordinary Christians.[7] Christian ethics as quandary ethics stands aghast at "unfathomable" decisions such as gender reassignment, abortion, or pursuing in vitro fertilization despite huge economic and personal burdens.[8] Banner proposes an ethics of everyday life, which turns to tools like ethnography and social anthropology to help ethicists understand morality as a social practice that can help ethicists narrate Christian character and virtue to and situate it in contemporary life.

A range of scholars has responded to Banner by contextualizing, historicizing, and extending his argument.[9] Luke Bretherton, Eric Gregory, and Jennifer Herdt published their responses from a conference focusing on Banner's book; their work also joins many other scholars who have addressed the turn to culture and practice: Sheila Green Davaney, Vincent Lloyd, Richard Miller, Ted Smith, and Kathryn Tanner, are other notable

---

[6] Ibid., 126.
[7] Banner, *The Ethics of Everyday Life*, 24, 203. Banner uses "moral theology" and "Christian ethics" interchangeably.
[8] Ibid., 9, 16.
[9] Lamb and Williams, *Everyday Ethics*. For a list of the conferences and volumes that take up the topic of ethnography, ecclesiology, social anthropology, moral theology, and Christian ethics in response to Banner's book, see 15–16. For attention to those works that precede Banner's argument in *The Ethics of Everyday Life*. see chapters 1, 2, 5, 6, 11, and 13. None of these accounts, however, mentions Christian socialism, and only Eric Gregory briefly mentions the social gospel movement as a forerunner of Banner.

ethicists taking up culture and practice as ethically and theologically laden points for reflection.[10] This is not to mention the long history of womanist, Black theology, Latin American, *mujerista*, Asian American, Pacific Islander, and Indigenous peoples' work in Christian ethics and theology that has long turned to culture, narrative, social practices, and social movements as theological and ethical resources.[11] For my purposes, however, it is important to remember that Christian socialists and the radical social gospelers turned to these resources at the turn of the twentieth century in response to the advent of social problems and the question of social justice.

Banner's argument is not—or at least not *only*—about the challenge that quandary ethics poses to Christian ethics. The problem fundamentally lies in Christian ethical responses to unique problems first posed by modernity. As Banner says:

> We need a different moral theology. Not a moral theology of hard cases, nor one which simply names the good and denounces the bad. Somehow, if the seeming paradox can be excused, we need a moral theology which can fathom what we may casually refer to as the "unfathomable" choices and wishes of contemporary life. But there is no real paradox, of course, in fathoming these unfathomable cases, just because the forms of life lived out amongst us are not really unfathomable in practice, but only unfathomable from where we may currently stand, with our particular limitations of experience and knowledge and failures of imagination and insight.[12]

Contemporary life poses particular challenges to Banner's singular "Christian imagination."[13] These challenges force theologians and Christian ethicists to give an account of how Christian theology can adequately speak to contemporary life in its current forms. For example, Banner examines Pope John Paul II's encyclical *Evangelium Vitate* as an example of Christian ethics that is held back by the predominant ethical method of hard cases and therefore is

---

[10] Bretherton, "Coming to Judgment"; Davaney, "Theology and the Turn to Cultural Analysis"; Gregory, "Social Anthropology, Neighbor-Love, and the Ethics of Humanitarianism"; Herdt, *Forming Humanity*; Lloyd, *Black Natural Law*; Smith, "Theories of Practice"; Tanner, *Theories of Culture*.

[11] The resources here are too many to list, but as a representative sample, see Williams, *Sisters in the Wilderness*; Cone, *A Black Theology of Liberation*; Gutiérrez, *Essential Writings*; Isasi-Díaz, *La Lucha Continues*; Kao and Ahn, *Asian American Christian Ethics*; Deloria, *God Is Red*.

[12] Banner, *The Ethics of Everyday Life*, 16.

[13] One important critique here is the singular "imagination" in Banner's argument. It is important to attend to the diversity within the Christian tradition, as Molly Farneth points out in her response to Banner: *Everyday Ethics*.

unable to "fathom the unfathomable."[14] Christian ethics, as Banner imagines it, can benefit from the rise of social anthropology in solving these questions. Turning from hard cases to everyday ethics can help Christian ethics articulate its sense of the human to a world that seems foreign to it. An ethics of hard cases is unable to address "the character and form of Christian life" and is instead left to sounding "silent" trumpets from our enclaves.[15]

Ethics as it is lived in the everyday is a social practice. In everyday life, According to Banner, humans enact and sustain ethical social practices in a manner similar to how they uphold grammatical practices. We may not be able to articulate the precise reasons *why* we do what we do, but such ethical practices are shared and grounded in social norms, values, patterns of behavior, and attitudes. This doesn't mean that our ethical social practices are unreasonable or without reason, but instead that, as Banner says, "ethics—like grammar—often goes without saying."[16] Christian ethics of hard cases cannot participate in this game because it doesn't study the basic, quotidian moves of everyday life.

The turn to social practices is a helpful one, in my mind. Grounding Christian ethical reflection in communities' social practices harks back to the inductive methodology of social gospel social ethics. The social gospel movement and the field of social ethics developed in direct response to these sorts of questions. "The simultaneous rise of the social gospel and social ethics was not coincidental," writes Gary Dorrien, "nor the fact that sociology, 'social justice,' social Darwinism, corporate capitalism, modern socialism, and the trade unions arose at the same time."[17] The underlying problematic that gives rise to a Christian ethics of hard cases is the question of how the Christian imagination can articulate its sense of Christian character and Christian life to contemporary life. But, as I pointed out above—and others have pointed out to Banner himself—there are rich Christian ethical traditions that have already responded and continue to respond to this problematic.

Christian socialists and the radical social gospel, this book argues, is one tradition that has been overlooked in contributing to this discussion on Christian ethics, social anthropology, social practices, and the turn

---

[14] Banner, *The Ethics of Everyday Life*, 14–16.
[15] "In engagement with social anthropology, moral theology can learn the better to display and explicate the character and form of the Christian life—and to engage constructively and therapeutically with other forms of human being, fathoming the unfathomable choices against which that silent trumpet sounds so ineffectively" (ibid., 23).
[16] Ibid., 201.
[17] Dorrien, *Social Ethics in the Making*, 1.

to culture. Social ethics is a broad movement that gave birth to three large schools: the social gospel, Christian realism, and liberation theology. It was the social gospelers who argued that social structures should be transformed in the direction of social justice, but the Christian socialists were a small, though crucial flank of the social gospel school and imagined a particular strategy of this transformation. Grafting this book's argument into the tradition of Christian socialism and the radical social gospel connects the argument into an ethical and theological history of communities organizing and struggling for democratic transformations in the social, economic, and political realms.

The relationship between Christianity and socialism from the late nineteenth century up to today is a dramatic and diverse one. At the turn of the twentieth century, social gospelers made arguments for and against explicitly joining socialist organizations—and many of these organizations, like the Knights of Labor, the Social Democracy of America, the Christian Socialist Fellowship, or even the Socialist Party of America (SP), had such meteoric rises and catastrophic falls that in the end official membership mattered little in comparison to what one said, practiced, or preached. Christian pastors, academics, activists, and organizers were at the heart of the socialist movement. The Christian socialist message then, and still today, is a deep and abiding commitment to economic democracy, but not *only* to economic democracy.

Christian socialists disagreed on class warfare language, Marxist philosophy, the labor theory of value, and nationalization of industries, but nearly all championed socialism and economic democracy as the way to end capitalist domination of workers and prizing profit over people. They disagreed on how closely socialism was tied to unions, and specifically the American Federation of Labor, some splitting off to help form the scrappy, militant Industrial Workers of the World (IWW) and their one big union. But after watching the federal government step in to crush strike after strike and side with corporations, even the most stouthearted of socialist politicians recognized that electoral politics wasn't enough: unions and labor were key to winning socialism. Issues of immigration, gender, and race were consistent points of conflict at the 1908 and 1912 annual conventions of the SP and in the broader movement. Everyone agreed that socialism offered the promise of democracy to the world—disagreement remained on just *how* economic democracy might benefit the feminist, immigration, and racial justice cause. Nearly all Christian socialists and social gospelers were theological liberals, and many Christian socialists successfully brought the socialist message to middle-class churches. Theological liberalism itself was radicalized and transformed by its relationship to the social gospel, where some radicals struggled mightily to push it beyond middle-class Victorian white supremacy and imperialism. For those who orbited socialist circles, socialism and socialist platforms offered the surest way to bring democracy, liberty, equality, and freedom to all humankind. The coming socialist transformation would be possible only by bringing democracy to industry—and to some, the two were indistinguishable.

But at the turn of the twentieth century, Christians were both attracted to and repelled by the socialist label because of the ethical drive for economic democracy, but also because socialism was not enough.[18] The boundary drawing of the socialist identity worked to include and exclude, and Christians used that to their advantage in their own organizing.[19] During and after the First World War, when the SP purged itself of its radical left wing, those figures leading the loosely held Christian socialist movement feared what the label "socialist" could do to their professional and social standing. The same could be said today. In the first half of the twentieth century, socialists were ransacked, dominated, and crushed by the federal government's breaking strikes and investigating their organizations, which fed a culture of hysteria and red-baiting. Jim Crow capitalism entrenched itself in the South and the North, while radical white supremacist groups grew in numbers and struck out against feminist, pro-immigration, racial justice, and antiwar movements.[20] In the long wake of the failure of Reconstruction, capitalist investors and boosters tore down forests and feasted on the land in the New Cotton South through tenant farming and sharecropping, while poor white and Black farmers languished under plantation capitalism.[21] Some Christians fighting for economic democracy outwardly identified as socialist; others never officially joined a party organization or instead donned older political identities like that of "producerism"; still others operated covertly, while often claiming that they could bring more

---

[18] W. E. B. Du Bois's brief membership in 1911–12 in the Socialist Party of America is a good example here. See Marable, *W. E. B. Du Bois*, esp. introduction.
[19] For an excellent account of how the Knights of Labor and the Populist Party organized around and through race and class boundaries, see Gerteis, *Class and the Color Line*.
[20] Kelley, *Hammer and Hoe*. See also Kelley, "The Roots of Anti-Racist, Anti-Fascist Resistance in the US."
[21] Greene, "Southern Christian Work Camps and a Cold War Campaign for Racial and Economic Justice"; Roll, *Spirit of Rebellion*.

nonsocialists to socialism by remaining unaffiliated and instead working in churches.[22]

Christians organized themselves to fight for economic, racial, gender, and social justice in, alongside, and apart from official socialist parties.[23] Radical organizing wasn't beholden to specific political or industrial movements like the SP or union organizing, especially for African Americans, who were so often explicitly excluded from such settings. (Only the Knights of Labor and the IWW explicitly organized across the color line in the early twentieth century.) Black churches nurtured and fed the Black radical tradition and New Abolitionist movement and eventually led to the birth of the civil rights and Black freedom movements.[24] Black churches in the late nineteenth century were one of the few institutional and financial supports for Black farms and Black schools; such "sabbath schools" were places where young Black people, recently emancipated from their slaveholders, could grasp the meaning of freedom for themselves and begin to cleave a life out of a culture in which plantation capitalism was deeply sedimented. Churches were resources for mutual aid and for education and were one of the earliest and most important spaces of cooperative economics.[25] This tradition is a deep well of ethical commitment to economic democracy and the neo-abolitionist fight against capitalism's racial and heteropatriarchal formation, and it feeds my argument in this book. Today, one figure who carries this mantel is Cornel West, who features largely in chapter 5.

Christian socialists were a small but important part of the white and Black social gospel movements, and many of their insights are shared today in various fields of liberation theology, especially the preferential option for the poor, the solidarity among the oppressed, and the attention to the interlocking nature of capitalism's exploiting and expropriating reality. Many white Christian socialists in the early twentieth century were horrible on race and gender issues, but those Christian socialists in the Black social gospel tradition made radical critiques of capitalism that are still seldom heard

---

[22] Up until he joined the party in 1911, W. P. D. Bliss was an excellent example of the "I can bring more to Socialism without being a socialist" point of view. See Dressner, "William Dwight Porter Bliss's Christian Socialism." Methodist pastor and radical social gospeler Howard Kester always identified as socialist; see Dunbar, *Against the Grain*. The Baptist pastor and professor of church history Walter Rauschenbusch and the Methodist pastor and professor of social ethics Harry Ward are good examples of those who never joined a party but always fought for socialist, anticapitalist causes.
[23] Dunbar, *Against the Grain*.
[24] Ali, *In the Balance of Power*; Payne, *I've Got the Light of Freedom*; Dorrien, *The New Abolition*.
[25] See esp. Gordon Nembhard, *Collective Courage*; Du Bois, *Economic Co-operation among Negro Americans*; Curl, *For All the People*.

today in progressive theological circles.[26] This tradition, led by theologians, pastors, church leaders, organizers, and activists, goes to the root of the social gospel message. That social ethical message, which these figures *radicalized*, is that "Christianity has a social-ethical mission to transform the structures of society in the direction of social justice."[27] This tradition's core message is reiterated in my argument, and I draw inspiration from its key figures and founders.

I have a few things in mind when I say these figures "radicalized" this social ethical mission at the heart of the social gospel.[28] To be a radical requires, on the one hand, a specific analysis of the problems our society is facing; it means one's analysis goes to the root of the problems. A sketch of this sort of analysis could be the following: (1) that there are some issues that lie at the root of other issues, (2) and these issues have to be dealt with before other issues can be addressed and before our most important relationships can be qualified as just, and finally (3) the political action we take to address these root issues should be directed toward the ideas, practices, and institutions that support and sustain them.

Now, I think that there is broad agreement among many figures in the social gospel movement (white and Black) with this (1)–(3) analysis. Take, for example, how Shailer Mathews and Harry Ward might agree on (1)–(3). Mathews is a great example of the mainline liberal and reformist wing of the social gospel.[29] As a Baptist theologian and New Testament scholar at the University of Chicago, Mathews's evangelical, moral idealism funded his vision of moral progress. Christianity created good individuals, who then created a good society—not the other way around.[30] Ward, a Methodist pastor, social ethicist, church leader, and "anti-capitalist revolutionary," represents the white radical social gospel. Ward's anticapitalism put him far to the left of Mathews's reformist position, but he had a loner streak and so never identified as a socialist.[31] Both would agree with the broad points of

---

[26] See Dorrien, *The New Abolition*, *Breaking White Supremacy*, and *A Darkly Radiant Vision*.
[27] Dorrien, *Social Ethics in the Making*, 1.
[28] My sense of "radical" takes leave from Dunbar's use of the term "radical social gospel" in Dunbar, *Against the Grain*, vii.
[29] Dorrien, *Soul in Society*, 23–25
[30] Ibid., 36–37.
[31] "Anti-capitalist revolutionary" in Dorrien, *Social Ethics in the Making*, 113. Dorrien and a number of Ward's biographers, however, have explored how Ward's inability to critique Russian communism, even when one of his own students was killed by Stalin's police, tarnished his career and unfortunately relegated his legacy to near obscurity for many years. See Duke, *In the Trenches with Jesus and Marx*; Link, *Labor-Religion Prophet*.

(1)–(3). But some important divergences begin to emerge between Mathews and Ward when we speak about strategy and tactical approaches to remedy these root issues.

For some early Christian socialists, going to the root of the matter means identifying the economic basis of racial and gender oppression; bringing about socialism will solve the race and gender problems. That position is reductionistic. For my account, to be radical requires that we identify the intersectional, overlapping, and interlocking nature of oppressions, so that race, class, gender, and sex are always analyzed together. Those arguments of the radical social gospelers and Christian socialists that are most worthwhile returning to today affirm similar positions found in studies of liberation theology, racial capitalism, and Black radicalism. The Christian socialist and radical social gospel message needed today is that we cannot do without unyielding ethical commitment to economic democracy because capitalism infects our raced, sexed, gendered, political, and social lives. To be radical on my account means (4) the problems we confront are *intersectional* and *interlocking*: going to the root of one issue means going to the root of all of the racial, gender, sex, economic, and political problems confronted in contemporary society and (5) focusing on the relational, social, and shared basis of the ideas, practices, and institutions that uphold and sustain the root problems. The Christian socialists and radical social gospelers radicalized the social ethical message of the social gospel in order to transform the structures of society in the direction of social justice. My sense is that many of the positions they held can be faithfully adjusted to meet (4) and (5). Today we continue that work of radicalizing the social ethical message to meet late modern capitalism's changing circumstances.

There is much to learn from the radical social gospel, especially in its analysis of class and racial power in capitalism.[32] As scholars of the Black radical tradition, settler colonialism, and racial capitalism have shown, like Lisa Lowe's and Jennifer Morgan's recent work and as W. E. B. Du Bois pointed out in *Black Reconstruction*, histories of difference and histories of value develop together.[33] Explanatory strategies that provide foundational accounts

---

[32] Cf. Evans, "Historical Integrity and Theological Recovery": "This basically theological premise for the social gospel—that Christianity must be rooted in faith-based communities committed to social transformation—is worthy of reassessment and fleshing out considering the complexities that confront churches at the beginning of the twenty-first century" (2). Twenty-odd years later, the theological premise of the social gospel, and how Christian socialists radicalized this premise, is still worthy of reassessment and what Evans later calls "critical reappropriation" (10).

[33] Morgan, *Reckoning with Slavery*, 8. For example, Du Bois's analysis of the "doctrine of Negro inferiority" is particularly apt here: "The espousal of the doctrine of Negro inferiority by the South was

12 SACRED VALUES AND ORGANIZING FOR POWER

by pitting racial domination in class dynamics or class exploitation in racial domination is a strategy that occludes how the very human practice of capitalist economics requires racial concepts and vice versa. Production of knowledge is deeply connected to material systems of domination, exploitation, and expropriation. Afterlives of settler colonialism, the Atlantic slave trade, coercive immigration from Asia of indentured labor, and the displacement and genocide of native peoples ripple through our current late modern capitalist society.[34] One of the important lessons that the radical social gospel teaches us is that race and class are not static concepts but relational ones that capture material dynamics of power. As such, they must be examined and explained together. Throughout the pages that follow, I will deploy the analytic of racial capitalism as a way to capture these power dynamics. I will speak primarily of domination, exploitation, and expropriation. These concepts help track how racial capitalism works. Domination exists when someone is in a position to arbitrarily exercise their will over others. Exploitation is a labor relationship wherein workers do not have control over the surplus profit of their own labor. Expropriation is accumulation by other means, outside the labor relationship and the market. This collection of terms helps me track how race, class, and gender oppression work in racial capitalism.

Recently some religious ethicists, theologians, and social ethicists have turned to racial capitalism's exploitation and expropriation and (in some instances, the separate matter of) domination in their work.[35] This is a welcome turn, in my mind, as it joins scholars in the wider humanities and social sciences who have expanded and deepened the field of racial capitalism beyond Cedric Robinson's exemplary work and back to Du Bois's classic *Black*

---

primarily because of economic motives and the inter-connected political urge necessary to support slave industry; but to the watching world it sounded like the carefully thought out result of experience and reason; and because of this it was singularly disastrous for modern civilization in science and religion, in art and government, as well as in industry" (Du Bois, *Black Reconstruction in America*, 39). The literature in the Black radical tradition is extensive, but see Du Bois, *Black Reconstruction in America*; Kelley, *Hammer and Hoe*; Lowe, *The Intimacies of Four Continents*, esp. chs. 1 and 5; Robinson, *Black Marxism*.

[34] Lowe, *The Intimacies of Four Continents*, "racial barrier" (24); Jung, *Coolies and Cane*: "The construction of coolies, moreover, formed a crucial ingredient in redefining blackness and whiteness—and Americanness—when equality under the law (Reconstruction) and wage labor (industrialization) seemed to erode their meanings" (9).

[35] Day, *Azusa Reimagined*; Tran, *Asian Americans and the Spirit of Racial Capitalism*; Lloyd, *Black Dignity*. Tran's work is exemplary here for his unique contribution in carrying to the work of theology and religious ethics the lessons from the field of racial capitalism. Lloyd's most recent work, *Black Dignity*, was published too recently for me to consider it forthrightly in the rest of this book, yet his analysis of domination, prototypically captured in the master-slave relationship, is notable and deserves further engagement.

Reconstruction in America.³⁶ What tends to happen, however, is that terms and discourse stand in and take over, muddling our grasp of how racial capitalism is an institutionalized social order, sustained through institutionalized social practices that teach us, among other things, how to properly love, hate, and profit.³⁷ My account here of racial capitalism balances intentionality and habit, structure and agency, by attending to relationships of domination, exploitation, and expropriation. For some, however, my account will not be explicit enough. They may ask for an ordered relationship among domination, exploitation, and expropriation. Yet this often leads to a one-size-fits-all power analysis. Furthermore, such explanatory strategies and power analyses often neatly provide organizers or counterpublics with practical strategies for theories of social, political, and economic change. I find things to be more complicated than this power analysis and theory of change. Organizing is not a straightforward affair; building power at times involves negotiation, compromise, and even losses on individual issue campaigns that in turn strengthen the relational power of the counterpublic. Throughout the pages that follow, I have attempted to think with organizers, holding myself accountable as we collectively think and imagine how to build radically democratic power to counter racial capitalist domination, exploitation, and expropriation. I find the radical social gospelers and Christian socialists to be crucial in this work.

My own reading of the Christian socialist tradition and the radical social gospel is informed by my subject position as a white scholar in the early twenty-first century far removed from the experience of slavery and Jim Crow, which many Black radical thinkers return to as context and resource in making their own ethical critiques.³⁸ Reading across such historical and cultural distances in order to recuperate a tradition in new contexts and arguments today raises the prickly, yet necessary, reflexive question of how my own world obscures and prevents me from hearing what Black radical critiques are really saying. The danger is not only that of inserting my own political, social, and economic visions into the past in order to construct a useful history for the present. Though anachronism and Whig histories are

---

[36] Robinson, *Black Marxism*. See footnotes 50 and 51 for relevant sources in humanities and social sciences on racial capitalism.
[37] "Institutionalized social order" in Fraser, "Behind Marx's Hidden Abode." Note that "profit" is not always a dirty word, so to speak. As many radical social gospelers understood and argued, economic democracy encourages democratically controlled and worker-owned profit.
[38] Kelley, "Winston Whiteside and the Politics of the Possible."

important to avoid. Generally, the question here addresses the proper relationship between intellectual history and social ethical criticism.

For some, this is the question of political theology. For me, it is about properly recuperating the social ethical school of the radical social gospel. As one scholar of political theology writes, "Political theology as a form of inquiry is compelling only to the degree that it helps us recognize that our political practices remain embedded in forms of belief and practice that touch upon the sacred."[39] When doing intellectual history—or even in focusing on local examples of democratic organizing—the temptation might be to focus so intently on getting a specific local situation right that we fail to see how an example brings to light theological and political resonances in our own practices, and thus helps us select what is worthy of our emulation in the examples.

As we explore the politics of sacred value in democratic organizing, there will be many examples—some of which seem too foreign and of their local context to be relevant to a particular reader's context; some, on the other hand, may seem too familiar. Good social ethical criticism balances observation of the relevant theological, political, economic facts of an example with generalization of those facts to other contexts (thus exploring their theological, political, and economic significance and meaning). Then the tricky question arises: What should be done? The hope is that the scholar balances reflexivity with the work of observing, generalizing, and drawing correlations. But throughout, we attend to the lived nature of theology through our political and economic lives in order to have the presence of the past break open new theological, political, and economic imaginings.[40] Emulation of the exemplary is a normative practice of social ethical criticism.

By asking a writer (and reader) to reflect on our theological commitments as lived, enacted, and persistently a part of our political practices, we return to the recent calls in Christian ethics like Banner's for an ethics of everyday life.[41] Here, my inductive social ethical method is meant to position the relevant relationships so that beliefs, commitments, and actions can conceivably

---

[39] Kahn, *Political Theology*, 3.
[40] Here I take note from Kahn's own political theological method and his reading of Karl Schmidt's text, *Political Theology*: "My aim here is not to elaborate the meaning of *Political Theology* as [Schmidt] understood it. Rather, it is to engage his work as a point from which to illuminate our own political experience" (Kahn, *Political Theology*, 8).
[41] See also Oliver O'Donovan's recent three-volume theological ethics of which the first task is to ground Christian ethics in practical reasoning and the "lived experience of practical deliberation" (*Self, World, and Time*, ix).

be made comprehensible in a particular time and place. It also provides intellectual tools to attend to lived religious practices in our contemporary lives. Readers interested in the politics of sacred value might emulate the examples that follow in their own context, in their own organizing. In this way, my inductive methodology attends to the reflexive question by listening and watching: listening and watching for the enactment and construction of a politics of sacred value in our social practices of BBCO. To listen with some examples in mind can help guide our normative critique.

Across the white and Black social gospel and Christian socialist movements, radical social gospelers understood Christianity as a *life* to be lived—not a doctrine to be claimed—and that this life propelled them into contemporary social, economic, gender, and racial justice fights. So it is with us today. But this point—that Christianity is a lived reality—raises important questions for Christians today as they actively *construct* and live into their Christian identity. These are questions I'll attend to in chapter 3.

My inductive social ethical methodology dovetails with my social practical inferentialism. By "inferentialism" I mean a particular sort of philosophical thought that argues that moral action and ethical judgments are made based on inferences reasoners make about their fellow reasoners.[42] This is just how social norms get established, by reasoners making certain inferences of and about the world and others in it, and by having their fellow reasoners hold them accountable to and responsible for such inferences. I develop an account of social practical reasoning that embraces normative critique, and so in the pages that follow I use interviews and personal experiences of organizing along with philosophical theology and social theory. Social practices are not enough to secure social justice—we need to make sure we get our concepts clear and right. But philosophical or social criticism abstracted from everyday life will inevitably make incorrect judgments about social justice at the very least; at the most, it can encourage or excuse conditions of domination. My Christian social ethical methodology engages in philosophical critique in order to question the norms and standards of our democratic political social practices. To do this, clarity is needed on what a "social practice" is in the first place, and we need deeper insight on how the normative nature of practices like gender, race, and religious identity sustain

---

[42] Robert Brandom has done the most to further this line of philosophical thought, but Jeffrey Stout and Molly Farneth are the relevant scholars in religion. Cf. Brandom, *Making It Explicit*; Stout, *Democracy and Tradition*, esp. part 3; Farneth, "Constructivism in Ethics."

our social practices. Such insight will help guide our radical revisions of social structures, institutions, and practices that are socially constructed yet very real. A Christian social ethics that picks up the inductive methodology of Peabody and Ward can pair philosophical normative critique with analysis of contemporary social practices.

Religious ethicist Eric Gregory once provided a fourfold scheme of political theology and named an emerging field of political theology that this book is closest to.[43] In this emerging form of political theology, "[i]ntellectual history or formal theory need not compete for attention with social practices—indeed, the best of each learn from the other—but this approach tells the story of religion and democracy less in terms of 'big ideas' and more in terms of the micro-history of democratic habits, dispositions, and movements. . . . [D]emocratic practices are taken to be part of God's work of redemption through dense webs of institutions and movements."[44] My inductive method of Christian social ethics fits squarely within this emerging model of political theology, but I'm keen to be explicit about the influential role of Christian social ethics, Christian socialism, and the radical social gospel in my account. Rather than negotiating how politics and theology fit together as big concepts, this book offers a social practical account of the politics of sacred value in the lived religious practices of broad-based organizing today inspired by the tradition of Christian socialism and radical social gospel.

---

[43] Gregory, "Christianity and the Rise of the Democratic State."
[44] Ibid., 101.

1
Religion, the Secular, and Sacred Value in Counterpublics

Over the past twenty years, BBCO has made a name for itself. With the election of President Barack Obama and the telling of his organizing story in *Dreams from My Father*, the U.S. public began to turn again to the life and work of that radical Saul Alinsky, who founded the Industrial Areas Foundation (IAF) in Chicago's Back of the Yards neighborhood in 1939. For years it seemed that no one was interested in writing about organizing except Alinksy and his protégés. Things have changed: an interdisciplinary field has emerged that spans religious studies, theology, sociology, and politics. Even so, problems still plague the public conversation on organizing: the largest of which might be the arbitrary separation between religion and politics, based on an unfortunately rigid distinction between religion and secularism.

This book's argument reconfigures the popular and presupposed distinctions between religion, politics, and the secular, which are often taken to be static terms, when in fact each concept stands for human social practices that exist in relational fields pervaded by power. This book makes an argument about the political role of sacred value in BBCO. I argue that people organize to protect and fight for what they hold most dear and that some practices, like the relational meeting and the listening campaign, attune Christian churches to the movements of the Spirit in ways that blur boundaries between religious and political practices. Due to the political role of sacred value in our social practical reasoning and in practices of recognition like the relational meeting and listening campaign, some organizing practices can be seen as religious practices. In my argument, religion and politics are social practices humans take up and enliven. Much of the emerging literature on BBCO too often adopts an unarticulated methodological individualism, where organizing is primarily viewed as an activity performed by one individual: the expert organizer. Part of my purpose in this chapter is to introduce the reader to how my larger argument engages with the emerging field on BBCO. I need to set up the chessboard and introduce you to the

Listening to the Spirit. Aaron Stauffer, Oxford University Press. © Oxford University Press 2024.
DOI: 10.1093/oso/9780197755525.003.0002

pieces and familiar moves, so to speak. I mean to carry out this chapter in a way that reconfigures the board, however. It might be too much to say that I'm going to change the rules of the game, but I broadly lay out the argumentative moves that are to come in the following chapters and begin to make a case for why these moves are justified in light of the current state of the field.

In the chapter's first section, I'll introduce the types of political groups that are BBCO constituencies by starting with a vignette from my own experience. Typically, writers of religion and politics incorporate a distinction between secular and religious groups, and then they complicate the way that a "religious" group is or is not political. To my mind, however, such a beginning already has things confused. A basic claim of my argument is that BBCO is a social practice that takes place in *counterpublics* that themselves refuse a neat distinction between religion and the secular. I'm not alone in this argument, of course. Scores of Black and feminist writers over the past hundred years—at least—have contributed examples that refute this framing. So, in this first section, I turn to feminist thinkers to contextualize and historicize the category of "secular."

Black churches are a more intimate example of how this "religious versus secular" framing is ill suited for books on organizing. I say "intimate" because, as I argue in chapter 7, a key historical figure for my argument who helps me thematically lay out my ecclesiology, Rev. George Washington Woodbey, learned much of his economic and political views in Black churches. That story will come later, but lessons from Black religious thought are crucial to my larger argument. In the second section, I turn to scholars who have read Black churches as counterpublics: groups that have a particular economic and political power relationship with the broader society. Counterpublics like BBCO affiliates and Black churches are made up of people experiencing—or in solidarity with those experiencing—exploitation, expropriation, and domination. Counterpublics are distinct dialogical and social arenas where discourses are created that contest the reigning racialized economic and political order of racial capitalism. This counterpublic framing of BBCO helps make clear the significance of calling BBCO a counterpublic, insofar as it refutes a neat divide between religious and secular, and it helps to accurately illuminate what is really going on with religion, politics, and practice in BBCO constituencies.

The upshot of this counterpublic framing is that it can expand our political theological imaginary of BBCO. In the third section, I briefly offer my reading of the scholarly field of BBCO and address why my argument is distinct and valuable. At the heart of my argument is the concept of sacred value. This concept itself refutes clear divides between religion and secularism. People organize to protect and fight for what they hold most dear. As they do, they build relational power in their efforts to organize around people's sacred values. The fourth section is an overview of this nebulous concept. In the concluding section, the chessboard will be set, the game explained, and the moves to come will be clear.

The Religious and Secular Politics of Counterpublics

It is mid-August in Nashville, and I have just arrived a few minutes early to the monthly board meeting of Nashville Organized for Action and Hope (NOAH). BBCO is one of the oldest models of community organizing, with roots in an institutionally based model first pioneered by Alinsky and later adapted by his successors Ed Chambers and Ernesto Cortes.[1] National organizing networks help set up local affiliates and support their organizing work in various ways, such as through a mutually beneficial financial arrangement, training organizers and leaders, and offering campaign and media support. Local affiliates primarily include institutional membership of churches, schools, unions, or other organizations working in the public sector. In 2010, I was an organizer with the San Antonio, Texas, IAF affiliate that Cortes helped start in the 1970s, Communities Organized for Public Service, which has an important role in developing the strategy of BBCO, because, according to Cortes, it was the first IAF affiliate where congregations were dues-paying members.[2] Something else Ernie said to me when we first met has stuck with me since those early days: Organizing is about values, not issues; because issues fade, values don't.

About fifty NOAH leaders sit in the large open sanctuary in August, and we don't even take up a quarter of the sonorous room. Halfway through the meeting the group is asked to break out into task forces. I link up with the affordable housing task force in the back of the sanctuary, well under the second-floor balcony. A middle-aged white woman asks us to go around and introduce ourselves. She is a longtime member of NOAH and a leader

---

[1] Sanford Horwitt's biography, *Let Them Call Me Rebel*, is still the authoritative account of Saul Alinksy and the birth of the IAF.
[2] Elmer, "Community Organizer Genealogy Project."

in a Jewish synagogue. After introductions, she wants to know why we care about this issue. Most in the group share a similar story: people either know someone who has or have themselves experienced the squeeze of rising home costs. That is what I say, noting that my neighborhood has seen drastic gentrification. Others are discouraged by the lack of change and leadership from the metro council on this issue; they cannot imagine what it must be like trying to find an affordable home or apartment. One of the first to share says she believes the issue of affordable housing is a "moral issue," and that phrase gets repeated more than any other. That is, until we come to one middle-aged white man who says, "A lot of us have said that this is a moral issue. But I don't think it is a moral issue. It is a damn political issue! And the city government and mayor aren't going to do a thing about it!" Exasperated and despondent, he sits back down.

"Unless what?" The organizer, Tim, asks.[3] Surprised and a bit stirred, the older man picks up on Tim's point: "Unless we do something about it!" People laugh and smile at Tim's quick thinking. But a Black male pastor, whose turn is next, picks up on this exchange: "Like my friend here, I think this is a political issue, but it is a political issue with a moral imperative. The political issue has to be driven by a moral imperative."[4] Later, when the entire group has reconvened and each task force is asked to report back, the Jewish woman who ran the affordable housing task force meeting points to this three-person exchange. She says with a smile, "This is a damn political issue driven by a moral imperative." The work of NOAH, she says proudly, is fundamentally about the question "What kind of city do we want to be?"

Counterpublics like NOAH establish their political culture collectively and dialogically. Through exchanges like this one, individual members of NOAH—and the larger group itself—enact, embody, and live into the individual and collective public sense of self. Through discursive and embodied practices of reciprocal recognition, BBCO affiliates like NOAH constitute counterpublics that contest the status quo.

BBCO constituencies are counterpublics that have a particular power relationship to a larger economic and political structure. Counterpublics are discursive arenas that contest dominating interpretations of a subjugated group's identities but can consist of members from across society; in this sense BBCO as a counterpublic is truly broadly based. In *The Public and Its*

---

[3] Names are changed to provide anonymity.
[4] Reconstructed from field notes, August 8, 2017.

Problems, philosopher John Dewey argues that democracy is grounded in a theory of publics making judgments about and taking action on interests that concern them. Dewey dismisses the idea that there might be one singular thing called "the public." Publics "consist of all those who are affected by the indirect consequences of transactions to such an extent that it is deemed necessary to have those consequences systemically cared for."[5] Dewey's political theory of publics will be crucial in chapter 4 in helping me draw out the sort of radical democracy present in the political culture of BBCO. For now, his basic sense of publics as groups formed around consequences and interests is central to my claim that BBCO constituencies are counterpublics, with one amendment: BBCO constituencies are counterpublics whose members' faith and values are a vital part of that group's lived reality.

The term "counterpublic" is traditionally associated with philosopher Jürgen Habermas's work on the public sphere. Feminist social theorist Nancy Fraser's critical engagement with Habermas's work illustrates how he failed to account for subaltern and radical movements that were "nonliberal, nonbourgeois, and competing public spheres."[6] Fraser proposes that Habermas's liberal, bourgeois notion of the public sphere be adjusted to include revisionist historical research that posits the reality of "*subaltern counterpublics.*"[7] "[W]omen, workers, peoples of color, and gays and lesbians . . . have repeatedly found it advantageous to constitute alternative publics," which are "parallel discursive arenas where members of subordinated social groups invent and circulate counter discourses to formulate oppositional interpretations of their identities, interests, and needs."[8] I take Fraser to be correct in her critiques of Habermas. But I follow Dewey's analysis of publics rather than Habermas's notion of the public sphere. Publics are groups formed around concern for and interest in "extensive" and "enduring" consequences by people directly and indirectly impacted by them.[9] BBCO constituencies are a specific sort of counterpublic insofar as they cannot be accurately classified as either separately a "secular" or a "religious" public.

NOAH's collective identity is worked out over time across many discussions and embodied exchanges that take place within a web of relationships. No single opinion dominates. NOAH's collective identity doesn't fit neatly into

---

[5] Dewey, *The Public and Its Problems*, 69.
[6] Fraser, "Rethinking the Public Sphere," 115.
[7] Ibid., 123, emphasis in original.
[8] Ibid.
[9] Dewey, *The Public and Its Problems*, 69, 87.

"secular" and "religious" categories, in part because those categories are disingenuous descriptors of what's going on. It doesn't quite fit to classify the NOAH exchange as solely "religious" or "secular." Though it took place in a church, the talk of the participants was devoid of overtly "religious" matters, except for vague terms like "moral imperatives." But their talk definitely involved goods and people they hold sacred. This is in part what I hear in the Black pastor's addition to the conversation: this is not just politics, but a politics infused with sacred values. The relationship between religion and the secular in BBCO is anything but simple. Too often, we approach scenes like this one with reified concepts that occlude important realities about the lived religious practice of BBCO. As a counterpublic, BBCO affiliates complicate our go-to categories when talking about religion and politics.

Was the NOAH exchange "religious" or "secular"? Not long ago, many declared the triumph of the secularization thesis; now we are not so sure.[10] Some are claiming the return of "public" religions,[11] while others are proclaiming that we live in a secular age that is primarily constituted by an immanent frame, where religious belief is no longer an unproblematic standpoint in modern Western North Atlantic societies and our sense of self is buffered.[12] Meanings exist primarily in the head; values may exist in the world, but they certainly don't press upon us in any enchanted way. Still others argue instead that our categories of religion and the secular are mutually informing, mutually constructing. This point—that what is "secular" and what is "religious" are connected in an intimate way—resonates with my own account in this chapter.[13] The conceptual boundaries between what is "religious" and what is "secular" are porous and the definitional centers migratory.[14] These are important insights, but they largely avoid a rich tradition of Black and feminist scholars who have long been pointing out that organizing movements blur the line between what is religious and what is secular. Important work by Black and feminist scholars demonstrates how the "secular" is itself constructed of religious, racial, and gender supersessionisms;

---

[10] In a review of Charles Taylor's *A Secular Age*, John Patrick Diggins summed up the secularization thesis: "[T]he idea that as modernity, science and democracy have advanced, concern with God and spirituality has retreated to the margins of life" ("The Godless Delusion").
[11] Casanova, *Public Religions in the Modern World*.
[12] Taylor, *A Secular Age*.
[13] Casanova, *Public Religions in the Modern World*; Casanova, "Rethinking Secularization." For relevant work on this topic, see Asad, *Formations of the Secular*; Asad, *Genealogies of Religion*; Mahmood, *Politics of Piety*.
[14] Casanova, "Rethinking Secularization," 45–52.

the "secular," it turns out, is another way of silencing, erasing, or "overcoming" difference by the heteronormative, racial capitalist status quo.

Contrary to popular assumptions, secularization is not an inevitable march beyond partial and polarizing religious bias into a future of universal reason, equality, and democracy. In *Sex and Secularism*, Joan Wallach Scott shows how gender inequality and a hierarchical racial and religious ideology are baked into the discourse of the secular. The problem is that the secular is conceived as a reified entity synonymous with gender equality; Scott challenges such claims "and the racism associated with that equation."[15]

When secularist logic turns to political emancipation, the binary of religion/secularism, public/private is cemented by narratives of the religious "other" being inherently violent, unreasonable, and misogynistic. A white Christian society is a democratic, secular society, so the narrative goes. As Scott puts it, at the turn of the twentieth century, "[t]he power of the secularist discourse prevailed; citizenship and femininity were taken to be antithetical, a violation not only of a gendered division of labor but also of the necessary identification with power."[16] The extension of the vote to women came only with the emergence of the "social" sphere, which served to insulate the "political" sphere from femininity, religion, and passion.[17] Ann Taves makes a similar and compelling case by arguing that the "feminization" of the Protestant church was a manufactured crisis arising out of the politics of gender in the early twentieth century. Movements that sought to establish "muscular Christianity" responded to a rereading of the historical record, a rereading that arose from contemporaneous concerns, not actual trends in the church.[18] The political emancipation of women welcomed them into a social sphere that equated the political with the masculine. As Fraser and Joan Landes respectively argue, the birth of a new bourgeois public sphere was accompanied by an "austere," "rational," "manly," and "virtuous" public discourse that was "political." This led to the formal exclusion of women from political discourse and political life; such an ideology became so entrenched

---

[15] Scott, *Sex and Secularism*, 3, 4, 27.
[16] Ibid., 104.
[17] For a comparative account of differing organizing styles that are rooted in the "public" (masculine) and "private" (feminine) spheres, see Stall and Stoecker, "Community Organizing or Organizing Community?" Though I agree with Stall and Stoecker's emphasis on the need for feminist methodologies in BBCO, I think their approach reifies the public and private distinction that Scott and Fessenden work so hard to dislodge (all the while illustrating the crucial role of religion in entrenching the secularist public sphere as a white Christian male space). My point is that feminist approaches to organizing need not be rooted in "private" spaces.
[18] Taves, "Feminization Revisited."

that femininity and publicity appeared oxymoronic.[19] Religion and women were relegated to the work of the "social," which was first represented in the early twentieth century by social workers, factory inspectors, reformers, and philanthropists.[20] The narrative that relegated women and the feminine to the social sphere depended on a reified concept of the secular and on the fundamentally indeterminate (and thus self-constituting) politics of gender and race.

Secular progressive narratives, with their odious gender and racial hierarchies, also exhibit religious supersessionism. White feminists of the nineteenth century like Caroline Gilman, Catharine Beecher, and Harriet Beecher Stowe made claims for women's rights in the name of Christianity as inherently superior to "backward" and other "savage" religions. As Tracy Fessenden notes, such claims were signaled by their treatment of non-Christian women in terms like "the harem, the seraglio, foot-binding, child-marriage, sutee."[21] Current feminists should recognize and criticize such religious supersessionisms in the past, but the reaction should not be to evacuate religious discourse altogether from feminist scholarship today in the hope of turning to a wholly secularized discourse.[22] Fessenden argues against attempts to construct a "rupture" between a narrative wherein white Protestant Christianity is superior—signaled by its treatment of women—and a narrative that is "genuinely" progressive because it is not grounded in religion. Such a "rupture" obscures the continuity between the narratives based on racial hierarchies. "Rupture" narratives are often predicated upon religion as suffocating, where the true "white" light of reason is the liberating breath of fresh air, freeing societies from their savage (religious) pasts.

Racial and religious progressivisms still pervade feminist politics, Fessenden writes, as a "self-righting, self-transcending mechanism."[23] Scott argues that the discourse of the secular has "organized our vision of the world" so as to make the identification of "women with/as religion" appear as "a timeless religious teaching."[24] Feminist scholarship, Fessenden claims, has

---

[19] Fraser, "Rethinking the Public Sphere," 113–14. See also Landes, *Women and the Public Sphere in the Age of the French Revolution*. For a more recent take on the suffrage movement as a broad-based democratic movement, see Teele, *Forging the Franchise*.
[20] Scott, *Sex and Secularism*, 109. See also Ryan, "Gender and Public Access."
[21] Fessenden, *Culture and Redemption*, 161.
[22] Cf. ibid., 162: [T]he terrain on which white, middle-class women managed most successfully to enlarge their political and social authority in the nineteenth century—evangelical Christianity—is also the terrain from which American feminism in its second and third waves has most concertedly retreated in its efforts to constitute itself as genuinely progressive."
[23] Ibid., 173.
[24] Scott, *Sex and Secularism*, 59.

rejected religion as a category of analysis because of its antifeminist and racist connotations. Yet supersessionisms of religion "fail to rankle" in the same way as racial supersessionisms. This is in part, Fessenden thinks, because religion has become conflated with internal, personal belief, itself a Protestant concept, whereas racial identity has been naturalized in the public's mind. Religion is personal, not public, interior rather than social or historical—so the logic goes.[25] The heterogeneity of religion and religious belief is reduced in the traditional secularization narrative so as to erase any meaningful presence of religious difference. Protestantism is rendered continuous with democracy and America. This is a political form of supersessionism, not merely a theological one. To Fessenden and Scott the political supersession is more significant: eventually, in the secularization narrative, Protestantism falls away completely into a vague humanism. Fessenden shakes her head at the supposed superiority of secular progressive narratives, saying, "In being 'democratized' Christianity is rewritten *as* democracy, shuttling its specificity while retaining its normative power."[26] All those who are represented as outside of the sphere of Protestantism supposedly reject "the extension of community on democratic terms."[27] Secularization narratives fail to wrestle with the "ideological contradictions" of our history, and worse still, such narratives "hid[e] the violence and coercion that have attended the formation of American democratic space in the guise of the neutrality and universality of the secular."[28] Through secular eyes religious and racial differences are to be overcome, not something to be engaged as a potential source of dissent.[29]

"The secular" is an ideologically laden construct. I diagnose it as deeply tied to racial, religious, and gender supersessionist narratives as outlined in the work of Fessenden and Scott. "The secular" looks different in different spaces and times. It is not one thing. We are better off paying attention to the various ends to which such a discourse is deployed and asking questions like "Who benefits from the use of such a category?" and "What are the justifying reasons?"

---

[25] Fessenden, *Culture and Redemption*, 178: "And when religion is seen as interior, spiritual and subjective and not also as social, embodied, and historical there is little more to be said, not least because the constitution of religion as belief seems to make religion a matter of individual choice in ways that race, for example, appears not to be."
[26] Ibid., 94.
[27] Ibid., 100.
[28] Ibid., 217.
[29] For a related argument, see Lloyd, *Religion of the Field Negro*.

In the preface, I made the distinction between "the secular" as an ideologically laden category and "secularism." Secularism, as I am using the term, describes a polity where no religion is dominant. Secularism requires certain discursive conditions of democratic exchange.[30] This does not mean that we turn our gaze away from how "the secular" is constructed in a way that privileges racial, gender, and religious hierarchies. We need to hold these two points together. In this sense, secularism refers to the discursive conditions in a counterpublic; however, a certain counterpublic may be more or less "secularist" in the sense that it privileges one racial, gender, or religious hierarchy—a secularist counterpublic might be one that reduces Christianity into a vague sense of democratic humanism that privileges white men as the prototypical political actor.

My account of secularism as a political doctrine characterizing the political conditions of discourse within and between publics also avoids the difficulties that some theological camps face in explaining the rise and fall of the secularization thesis: secularization was a bad thing that needed to be beaten back, and yet today we are somehow seeing the rise of "public" religions. At one point sociologists and political theorists championed the death of religion in the North Atlantic Western world and with it welcomed the rise of the secular as the exclusion of religion. But almost no one embraces that theory now.[31] Some theologians who trade in an ideologically laden sense of "the secular" often underhandedly (or explicitly) embrace the secularization thesis—that theology is a discourse besieged and under attack by a single bureaucratic, rationalistic, and disenchanting force of modernization.[32] The social practical account of sacred values offered in this book allows theology a richer and broader vocabulary (because it can be described as both "secular" and "religious") and does not fear the specter of the political doctrine of secularism. The state of the field of BBCO is dominated by presuppositions about religion and secularism, so this a necessary first point to clear up and can help position the arguments to come.

---

[30] For an astute account of this form of secularization in regard to debates surrounding the discourse of ritual and ritualism, see Lofton, *Consuming Religion*, ch. 4.
[31] Cf. Douglas, "The Effects of Modernization on Religious Change"; Casanova, *Public Religions in the Modern World*; Casanova, "Rethinking Secularization."
[32] Cf. Milbank, *Theology and Social Theory*.

Black Churches as Counterpublics

Upholding a hard and fast boundary between "religion" and "secularism" in the life of Black churches in a white supremacist society is equally fraught with difficulties. NOAH is not unique in its refuting such clean distinctions. In a way, however, the relatively recent scholarly concern with "the secular" is late to the game: not only have feminists been writing about the invention of the "social" sphere as a way of maintaining a gender divide that maps onto a religious versus political divide for decades, but scholars on Black churches have long been writing about how these institutions thwart neat distinctions between religion and secularism. Among those writers of the Black church, however, are those who highlight how Black churches are distinct dialogical and social arenas where discourses are crafted that contest the reigning racialized economic and political order. It's these writers—those who think of Black churches as counterpublics—that I want to focus on here, for their insights help make clear the significance of calling BBCO a counterpublic that refutes a divide between religion and secularism. Studying Black churches as counterpublics helps illuminate what is really going on with religion, politics, and practice in BBCO constituencies.

Postbellum Black churches provided a moral and spiritual form and "vision," scholar of African American religion Eddie Glaude tells us, which shaped the "secular" concerns of Black Christians.[33] To this extent, postbellum Black churches constituted publics in the sense that their members were directly and indirectly impacted by and concerned about their status as humans in a society that had previously racially classified them as "property." Glaude writes, "Put simply, the existence of slavery and the reality of race affected all persons physically marked as black, slave or free!"[34] Black churches functioned as and still are discursive arenas where new discourses are invented to address concerns and interests of its members.[35] Glaude notes that the "cooperation" among Black people to organize communities that could "address the common ills of their lives contributed to the construction of what would become a 'national' community, for the conjoint activity of African Americans would not remain simply a reaction to white prescription."[36] Black churches as counterpublics are organized publics that are a

---

[33] Glaude, "Of the Black Church and the Making of a Black Public," 345.
[34] Ibid., 342.
[35] This is a point that Henry Louis Gates Jr. also makes in his most recent study on the Black church (*The Black Church*, esp. ch. 1, "The Freedom Faith")
[36] Glaude, "Of the Black Church and the Making of a Black Public," 342.

part of the national, heterogeneous, and contentious Black counterpublic consisting of a number of institutional bases and ideologies.[37] It's important to note that this historical and contemporary Black cooperation is both political and economic.

The work of political economist Jessica Gordon Nembhard deepens Glaude's point by highlighting how the cooperative organizing of Black churches led to the emergence and growth of the Black cooperative movement.[38] Gordon Nembhard makes clear throughout her work that political power requires economic power: "Early on African Americans realized that without economic justice—without economic equality, independence and stability (if not also economic prosperity)—social and political rights were hollow, or actually not achievable."[39] The political freedom sought by Black people at the turn of the century needed economic freedom. The economic and political concerns of Black people contributed to the formation of the Black counterpublic. And in turn, Black churches contributed in significant ways to economic and political power-building efforts. Highlighting the work of W. E. B. Du Bois, Gordon Nembhard states that at the turn of the twentieth century, "religious camaraderie was the basis for African American economic cooperation, and churches, secret societies, and mutual-aid societies among enslaved and free alike created the beginnings of economic cooperation."[40] The Black counterpublic today depends on institutions like Black churches that build economic and political power to protect their people from enduring and extensive consequences they face as Black people in a white supremacist society and racialized economic order.[41] The economic and political role of Black churches in the Black community and the faith of Black Christians deeply shaped the economic and political "secular" life of Black people in the United States.

Such a story of the emergence of Black churches as counterpublics need not deny the fact that race—and gender and class, for that matter—are

---

[37] I say "heterogeneous" and "contested" because there is no single ideological platform that dominates what Michael Dawson calls "the black agenda." Dawson outlines six ideologies that are important to the Black counterpublic: radical egalitarianism, disillusioned liberalism, Black Marxism, Black conservatism, Black feminism, and Black nationalism. (*Black Visions*, 15–23).

[38] Gordon Nembhard, *Collective Courage*.

[39] Gordon Nembhard, "Economic Justice as a Necessary Component of Racial Justice."

[40] Gordon Nembhard, *Collective Courage*, 34; see also 41–42.

[41] As Dawson writes, "Similarly, throughout black history numerous black institutions have formed the material basis for a subaltern counterpublic. An independent black press, the production and circulation of socially and politically acute popular black music, and *the social and political activists of the black church* have produced consistent institutional bases for the black counterpublic since the Civil War" (*Black Visions*, 35, 37, emphasis added). See also Gates, *The Black Church*, ch. 1.

socially constructed, yet material realities.[42] Black counterpublics, Michael Dawson instructs us, like Black churches are sites for "criticism of existing American democratic institutions and practices" in part because of the oppression and exploitation Black people face by the larger white society.[43] Importantly, the formation of Black counterpublics is not only a response to white society but emerges from an ever evolving sense of community and autonomy of people marked as Black. The point that autonomy and oppression are equally important forces in the formation of Black counterpublics is something that Dawson and Glaude emphasize.

Postbellum Black Baptist churches, for historian James M. Washington, have a distinct political culture that has a certain kind of discourse available to it whose content is the faith of its members.[44] As counterpublics, Black churches invented discourses that were constructed, in part, from their religious lives. Theology in this situation is deeply political and economic because it has to do with the very survival of a people. For Washington, to divide Black Baptist discourse into religious and secular discourses would be to rip apart the fabric of this tradition.

It was thanks to the unique and hard work of Black women in the late nineteenth and early twentieth centuries that helped make Black churches distinct counterpublics. Evelyn Brooks Higginbotham writes of Black churches as arenas that "blur the spiritual and the secular, the eschatological and the political, and the private and public."[45] Black churches constitute a counterpublic political tradition that "precludes attempts to bifurcate Black women's activities neatly into dichotomous categories such as religious versus secular, private versus public, accommodation versus resistance."[46] As Glaude and Washington have similarly pointed out, Black churches play a historical role in the political and religious life of Black Americans, but Higginbotham's work makes clear the crucial role of Black women in creating these institutions.[47] The point is not that Black counterpublics are bastions of the political left, but that these counterpublics are social arenas where discourses are invented that help Black people build economic and political power in spite of white supremacy. As Higginbotham states, Black churches

---

[42] Dawson, *Black Visions*, 4: "[T]he fact that race is socially constructed does not negate the fact that systematically different patterns of outcomes are produced within a racially stratified society."
[43] Ibid., 29.
[44] Washington, *Frustrated Fellowship*, xiv.
[45] Higginbotham, *Righteous Discontent*, 16.
[46] Ibid., 17, 221.
[47] Ibid., 17.

and Black women's role in constructing this dialogical social arena consisted in both "a conservative and a radical impulse," one that "appropriated and reinterpreted" the broader values of white society as a strategy for structural reform of gender and racial hierarchies in a white supremacist society.[48]

Attention to gender and race in the historical narratives of religion and politics helps to disrupt the dominant narrative championing the march of secular, reasonable democracy hand in hand with white Protestant Christianity. The "unheralded" work of Black women "enriches" the history of "American social reform" in a way that blurs the line between secular and religious work, while adding important racial and gender dimensions that correct the gendered and racist secularization narrative. One point of the ecclesiology put forward in chapter 7 that is thematically built from the work and life of Woodbey is to contribute to this enriching of our historical narratives of religion and politics. The work of these scholars on Black churches as counterpublics helps us see Black churches as a certain sort of public: as dialogical social arenas where discourses are invented to contest dominating interpretations of exploited and expropriated groups' identities.

Black churches are dialogical counterpublics because discursive practices contest and challenge each other within the group; relationships are woven within the public as a constituency is built while the group strives for collective goals and builds economic and political power. As a dialogical social arena, a counterpublic through which Black people have attempted to realize power in the actualization of collective goals, Black churches blur neat distinctions between religion and the secular.

To call Black churches and BBCO affiliates counterpublics is to put them in a particular economic and political power relationship with the broader society. Counterpublics like BBCO affiliates and Black churches are made up of people experiencing—or in solidarity with those experiencing—exploitation, expropriation, and domination. Counterpublics, as Fraser, Glaude, Dawson, Higginbotham, and Washington imagine them, are dialogical and collective arenas. Few scholars—as I will shortly show—who have addressed BBCO have explicitly drawn out the connection between BBCO affiliates and the concept of counterpublics.[49] The concept is essential to this book's argument not only due to its focus on social practices but also due to the fact that insofar as counterpublics are groups that draw identity

---

[48] Ibid., 187. Higginbotham classifies this radical and conservative impulse under the "politics of respectability" in a masterful essay at the end of *Righteous Discontent* (185–229).
[49] Gary Dorrien is a notable and exemplary exception. See his *The New Abolition*.

boundaries, their establishment of social identities is narrative-based and relational.[50]

Groups like NOAH seek to build economic and political power because they have a stake in improving economics and politics that exploit, expropriate, and dominate people. Fraser illustrates this by noting how feminist counterpublics organized to shift the discourse toward feminist agendas on domestic violence, which was at one time viewed as a "private" matter of the home. Fraser's point is that "what will count as a matter of common concern will be decided precisely through discursive contestation."[51] If political decision-makers are out of touch with NOAH's narrative of Nashville, NOAH organizers and leaders act with authority to hold the politically powerful accountable to alternative, more just and equitable visions and narratives of Nashville. For NOAH, this means getting involved in political issues because their religious traditions provide moral, ethical, theological, and political urgency: they hold certain things to be sacred, and to violate or desecrate things we revere is a horrendous act that needs to be prevented. These sacred values guide their sense of self and community. Sacred values are vital evaluative attitudes to the discursive social practices of BBCO.

Counterpublics and the Study of BBCO

The previous sections laid out some of the more powerful moves in the field: the proverbial divide between "religion" and "secularism" and how counterpublics like BBCO complicate this binary and thus open to us new political theological imaginaries. Now I need to focus a bit more precisely on BBCO literature and how it has approached such topics. In the process, I'll demonstrate how my project differs from some of the most successful and recent contributions. The dominant moves in the field seem to depend on particular relations between religion and secularism and a certain classification of groups as religious or political. My counterpublic framing of BBCO and the centering of sacred value help reconfigure these arguments in ways that more accurately illuminate what is actually going on for religious participants in BBCO and how that can help us organize and theorize better.

---

[50] For more on group social identities as relational and narrative, see Lichterman, *Elusive Togetherness*.
[51] Fraser, "Rethinking the Public Sphere," 129.

The field of literature that is emerging around BBCO can arguably be broken up into three camps. The first camp includes social theorists and sociologists exemplified in the work of Mark R. Warren, Richard Wood, Brad Fulton, Ruth Braunstein, and Stephen Hart that largely focuses on the relationship between social capital, political cultures and practices, and BBCO.[52] A second, more theologically interested group of scholars addresses the role of religious activists and religious practices and the specific role of churches in organizing; here we find thinkers like Luke Bretherton, Melissa Snarr, Dennis Jacobsen, Alexia Salvatierra and Peter Heltzel, and Dan Rhodes and Tim Conder.[53] The final group consists of those religious, philosophical, and political theorists who see BBCO as examples of grassroots or radical democracy, like Jeffrey Stout, Romand Coles, and Paul Osterman.[54] Overall in this field there are few thinkers who critically engage in depicting BBCO affiliates as counterpublics. The most well-developed approach is Bretherton's, and so I will say a few words about his work here. Even fewer thinkers in these camps draw attention to the important role of the radical social gospel and Christian socialism in the economic and political tradition of BBCO. As this chapter and my introduction establish, both the radical social gospel and Christian socialism and grasping the counterpublic character of BBCO affiliates are crucial to my argument.

For Bretherton, BBCO is an example of democratic politics that mediates multiple religious and secular traditions and thus gives birth to a "faithful secularity" out of which emerges proper political judgments. As Bretherton puts it, "BBCO can be read as forging a faithful and pluralist kind of secularity through enabling the formation of shared speech and action that forms a public arena of communication between diverse traditions."[55] This is a "postsecular" account of religion and democratic politics as experienced in BBCO.

For Bretherton, the postsecular space is defined by many distinct traditions converging and engaging in contests over the goods at stake as conceptualized in their own particular vision of the common good.[56]

---

[52] Warren, *Dry Bones Rattling*; Wood, *Faith in Action*; Wood, and Fulton. *A Shared Future*; Braunstein, *Prophets and Patriots*; Hart, *Cultural Dilemmas of Progressive Politics*.

[53] Bretherton, *Christianity and Contemporary Politics*; Bretherton, *Resurrecting Democracy*; Snarr, *All You That Labor*; Jacobsen, *Doing Justice*; Salvatierra, and Heltzel, *Faith-Rooted Organizing*; Conder and Rhodes, *Organizing Church*.

[54] Stout, *Blessed Are the Organized*; Hauerwas and Coles, *Christianity, Democracy, and the Radical Ordinary*; Coles, *Beyond Gated Politics*; Osterman, *Gathering Power*.

[55] Bretherton, *Resurrecting Democracy*, 192.

[56] Ibid., 101.

Establishing "common objects of love" and pursuing a politics of the common life is a "necessary condition of faithful witness to the Lordship of Christ over all things."[57] Organizing practices are crucial to the establishment of an appropriate balance between these discourses and their conceptualizations of the goods at stake. Organizing practices mediate these various linguistic practices and help create a postsecular "complex space." When Bretherton speaks of "complex space," he refers to a plurality of institutions with "hazy" boundaries between the ecclesial and nonecclesial institutions (including the church and state) so as to keep at bay idolatrous and monopolistic tendencies.[58] In this postsecular complex space a diversity of groups make alliances and take oppositional stances in their effort to build political power as they pursue penultimate goods. Pursuing these penultimate goods through organizing requires Christian *phronesis*, or "wily wisdom": "Wily wisdom is needed in order to navigate this ambiguous and ever-changing environment."[59] Christian *phronesis* is not a formula but emerges out of the mutually divulging and co-constituting categories of theology and politics.[60] The dyad (not *binary*) between theology and politics sets up a relational ontology that pervades nearly all of Bretherton's work.

Bretherton's vision of the democratic practice of community organizing is "postsecularist" in the sense that "linguistic practices" of religion and politics exist side-by-side.[61] His postsecularist vision sees many distinct traditions converging in the civil sphere, engaging in contests over the goods at stake as conceptualized in their own particular vision of the common good. It takes the mediating work of BBCO to create a "common life" between conflicting and contentious "moral visions," which constructs an "alternative community of interpretation" that is the BBCO affiliate. Bretherton's relational ontology comes through full-tilt here. He consistently draws conceptual distinctions and then works to demonstrate how community organizing "mediates" these distinctions; community organizing is a "middle ground" between various groups pursuing a common life.[62] It is here that Bretherton's

---

[57] Bretherton, *Christianity and Contemporary Politics*, 84.
[58] Bretherton, *Christianity and Contemporary Politics*. See also Milbank, "On Complex Space."
[59] Bretherton, *Resurrecting Democracy*, 213. See also Bretherton, *Christianity and Contemporary Politics*, 57.
[60] Bretherton, "Coming to Judgement," 169
[61] Bretherton, *Resurrecting Democracy*, 101. Cf. Bretherton, *Christianity and Contemporary Politics*, 10–16.
[62] "Mediatory practice" in Bretherton, *Resurrecting Democracy*, 91–96; "middle ground" (190).

postsecularist account of BBCO draws nearest to—and yet clearly steers away from—framing BBCO affiliates as counterpublics.

Drawing from Jeffrey Alexander's work on the civil sphere, Bretherton depicts the democratic politics of counterpublics as tied to the rise of "cultural politics" that are limited to single-issue campaign and identity politics. Broad-based organizing is broad-based and so presents a difference in kind of democratic politics from counterpublics: "Forms of cultural politics are different in kind, if not necessarily in intent, to the repertoires deployed in BBCO.... The communities of interpretation constructed by cultural politics are necessarily less broad-based and tend to be focused on single issues."[63] Bretherton fears that the cultural politics of counterpublics like the feminist, LGBTQ, and Black freedom movements focus too much on what might be called an assimilationist strategy of politics of excluded groups: making space at the proverbial table for those excluded groups. In-group and out-group identities dominate the political practices of counterpublics, Bretherton states. BBCO is more broadly based: those excluded from and included in the civil sphere are a part of the political strategy of BBCO. Broad-based organizing riffs on the established "rulebook" of city hall: "[BBCO] then draws from the existing 'rulebook' within the civil sphere to hold those with power to account but does so by stepping outside of what is considered legitimate behavior through its agitation tactics and outré discourses of power, self-interest, and anger thereby pushing participants into a liminal in-/out-group zone that confuses established boundaries."[64] One way of framing Bretherton's understanding of the difference between the cultural politics of counterpublics and BBCO is to say the following: Counterpublics want to change the bodies in the seats at the table—or perhaps add a few seats or even a new leaf to the table—while BBCO focuses on changing the menu and on how it comes together. Democratic politics in broad-based organizing, for Bretherton, is about forming a common life that enables proper shared political judgments, by the ruled for the ruled through the rulers.[65]

Bretherton's account of the emergence of "alternative communities of interpretation" is a rich one and accurately describes my own experience

---

[63] Ibid., 187.
[64] Ibid.
[65] As Bretherton says, "The practices of community organizing are a means through which to enable shared political judgements to be made by those with the power to rule and those who are ruled. And it is the power of the ruled to demand political judgement by rulers and represent their interests in the process of deliberation and decision making that is a core feature of democratic politics" (ibid., 188).

organizing. It is one way of capturing the NOAH exchange that I told at the beginning of this chapter. I also resonate with Bretherton's hesitancy toward accommodationism, assimilationism, or a politics of recognition, as do others who study BBCO.[66] But broad-based organizing affiliates form in part because dominated and exploited people (and those in solidarity with them) come together to take action on issues that matter deeply to them. Publics like BBCO affiliates, following Dewey's understanding here, are already broad-based in the sense that members have a concern and interest in consequences that directly and indirectly impact them. People and institutions who join BBCO affiliates do so out of direct and indirect concerns. Solidarity and self-interest, as we will explore in chapter 4, are deeply related. This is so in part because what we hold most dear, what we hold sacred, may be directly or indirectly attacked or threatened by the consequences that brought the public together. Black churches function similarly to BBCO affiliates, in that they both blur the boundaries between "secular" and "religious." Black churches, like other counterpublics, stand in a particular economic and political relationship to the broader society and organize in order to build greater economic and political power. For these reasons, I depart from Bretherton and others who have studied BBCO; instead I adopt the language of counterpublics when describing the religious and political life of BBCO affiliates.

I have two additional reasons for not following Bretherton in characterizing BBCO as a *postsecular* political practice. First, it implies that there is (or was) a domain called "the secular," and that our body politic has surpassed it.[67] Bretherton might immediately object to this claim, saying that the body politic is postsecular in precisely the sense that religious and secular linguistic practices can equally be bearers of democratic politics in the civil sphere or body politic. Postsecularity is, as Ola Sigurdson tells us, a *reflexive* secularism.[68] This framing does gesture toward the messy and unpredictable nature of religious practices that guides my account. Fair enough. But does the term "postsecular" accurately capture the reality that the body politic is distinctly formed by racial capitalism? Perhaps Bretherton might say that the

---

[66] Charlene Sinclair's recent dissertation, "Let the Dead Speak!," is a good example of confronting the accommodationist form of democratic politics that is often found in politics of recognition.

[67] It's important to note that both Bretherton and Milbank are right to separate in their work the Augustinian sense of *saeculum* from our modern concept of "the secular."

[68] "Post-secularity means a secularity that has come to be reflexive, and thus as one that is not to be interpreted as 'non-secularity,' but rather as one that affirms the kind of political discussion coming after secularity—secularity understood as a reaction against religion and therefore as also dialectically dependent on religion" (Sigurdson, "Beyond Secularism?," 191).

value of postsecular discourse is to highlight how the ideology of the secular cooperates with capitalism to envelop claims of sacred value in its totalizing commodifying logic. My sense is that Bretherton would worry my account fails to see that Christianity has its own polity, its own social theory. My social, economic, and political analysis, in following radical social gospel and Black radical thought, is too informed by Marxist social theory, which he finds an odd bedfellow with theology. If that is the case, then our disagreement would have more to do with the role of social sciences in theology and not with the term "postsecular."

A second reason is that within the domain of "the postsecular" operates a series of isolatable linguistic practices. In postsecular spaces, religion as a tradition and category is isolatable from the "secular." As the following chapters will show, I find this conceptually and empirically hard to maintain: politics and economics are theological matters; liberation is not only a theological concept; the social sciences can lend historical concreteness to liberation that is theologically valuable.[69] Moreover, I take it as a basic aspect of the human practice of theology that my religious language is deeply informed by my broader cultural environment, so it becomes extremely difficult to concretely separate religion from secular linguistic practices. Things are more entangled.

Indeed, it seems that Bretherton himself has found the language of postsecularism problematic, as he has recently turned toward a notion of secularity similar to the concept that I endorsed above (secularism). In Bretherton's most recent work he has made a shift from advancing postsecularism to a version of secularity without secularism. Here he moves away from an image of a shower, where religion and politics are separate streams, to a jacuzzi, where religion and politics bubble up together.[70] Such a move is funded by the implicit Pentecostal pneumatology in his earlier work; this more recent turn to Pentecostalism breaks open "western rationalist epistemologies" to the free movement of the Holy Spirit.[71] Everyday life is "resignified" in a new "spatiotemporal register," and political agency is offered a "truly emancipatory" power.[72] In earlier writings Bretherton considers the way that BBCO mediates the appropriate relationship between ecclesial and nonecclesial institutions and facilitates Christian political

---

[69] Gutiérrez, *Essential Writings*, ch. 1.
[70] Bretherton, *Christ and the Common Life*, 249.
[71] Ibid., 124.
[72] Ibid., 125.

judgment as Christians pursue a common life politics with our neighbors. In his more recent work, Bretherton considers how the personal God as Spirit "enables frail flesh to both be itself and become something more than itself," thus successfully maintaining the tension of the church-world dyad and not disintegrating into a binary.[73]

When it comes to ordinary life, the various threads of our discursive practices feed into one another in ways that are complex and difficult to separate. In a later chapter, I'll explore Bretherton's rich characterization of ecclesiology and politics as mutually divulging and argue that he is making a similar point. Religious institutions can be effective political bodies. But in his account the spheres of religion and the state, for example, need to maintain a degree of autonomy. For Bretherton, such autonomy is a question of "investment" made clear only by Christian political judgment. My sense is that Bretherton is too influenced by the ideological sense of "the secular" as an ideology and antitheology, and the ecclesia as its own polis and social science, and so misses useful and important theopolitical examples for BBCO like that of Woodbey in chapter 7, and radical democrats like Cornel West in chapter 4. The politics of sacred value refuses neat distinctions between our religious and secular lives, in part because the social practices of sacred value are embedded in both.

Sacred Values, Not "the Sacred": Ronald Dworkin, Robert M. Adams, and Jeffrey Stout

At this point, we've set the chessboard that is the field of BBCO, explained some of the major moves and key pieces. What is left is to focus on my distinct claim of the role of sacred value in BBCO. To do this, it helps to have some familiarity with the concept. To start, we have to be able to think of sacred values separately from the notion of "the sacred." Sacred value as a philosophical concept was made famous by Ronald Dworkin's formidable argument regarding the politics of life and death in his book *Life's Dominion: An Argument about Abortion, Euthanasia, and Individual Freedom*. But today the best thinking on the topic can arguably be attributed to the moral philosopher Robert Adams. Jeffrey Stout has also recently written about the topic in relation to BBCO, though Stout's work is largely indebted to Adams's.

---

[73] Ibid., 133.

Dworkin famously introduced a broader public to the importance of and urgency behind the politics of sacred value, but he didn't invent it. Sacred value has long been an operative concept in organizing movements, even before Dworkin, Adams, and Stout explicated its philosophical and theological contours. To close this chapter, I give a short overview of Dworkin's, Adams's, and Stout's work. I turn to Adams's account for his attention to the sorts of reasons we have to value the good as God. Resembling God is one way of talking about how we experience sacred values. Though the concept "sacred value" can accurately secular attitudes, Adams's account demonstrates the fruitfulness of connecting language of sacred value to thought about God. But Stout's work influences my own account in terms of how it brings talk of sacred value into the heart of politics.

For Dworkin, sacred value is an evaluative attitude distinguished by a good's or person's *intrinsic, objective,* and *inviolable* value.[74] Dworkin thinks people intuitively understand what it means to say that sacred value is intrinsic.[75] The Grand Canyon has intrinsic value; so does great art. If I hold something *intrinsically* valuable, I value it in itself, aside from my (current or future) wants and needs and regardless of whether there is currently less or more of it available to me. Dworkin also contrasts the notion of something being intrinsically valuable with a thing's *instrumental* or *incremental* value. This move will serve to direct Dworkin's whole account, but it's premised on a mistake. In chapter 4 I contrast the mistaken dichotomy between intrinsic and instrumental value with the more appropriate distinction between intrinsic and extrinsic value. Money has instrumental and incremental value. Sacred values don't work like that, Dworkin says—they are *non-incremental*. We treasure a Rembrandt painting, for example, regardless of our instrumental wants and needs, and we would not value the paintings we have now less if we were to suddenly discover several more hidden away. In this way, sacred values are intrinsic; we do not value them instrumentally or with incremental logic.[76]

Dworkin's example of a Rembrandt painting is a good one because it illustrates the *objectivity* of sacred value. Dworkin wants to avoid abstracting and simplifying the concept of sacred value into the concept of "the

---

[74] My account of these three elements of Dworkin's sense of sacred value is informed by Kamm, "Ronald Dworkin's Views on Abortion and Assisted Suicide." See Dworkin's replies to Kamm, in Burley, *Dworkin and His Critics*, 370–73.
[75] "Intuitively" (Dworkin, *Life's Dominion*, 69); "commonplace" (70).
[76] Ibid., 70–72.

sacred"—he is interested in our evaluative attitudes. Let's return to the Grand Canyon as an example. It is awe-inspiring, and I feel it is owed reverence because it exists as an instance of wonder and beauty. Its wonder is independent of my recognizing it.[77] The objectivity of a sacred value is related to its intrinsic value. Neither of these properties is completely determinative; both are relevant.

Dworkin has less to say about *inviolability*, however. But that does not mean its role is any less important. He often speaks of our reactions of "horror" and "shame" at the violation or destruction of something we hold sacred. We strive to "respect," "honor," and "protect" sacred values.[78] Dworkin says that we hold each individual human life sacred in itself because it is a representation of the image of God, and the destruction, waste, or violation of a human life causes "horror."[79] Dworkin later admitted that the connection between inviolability and intrinsic and objective value could have been clearer.[80] As later thinkers will illustrate, the condition of inviolability is an important consideration in discerning our evaluative attitudes of sacred value.

Dworkin's account is not without its flaws; I highlight it here because of its renown. For example, something can have intrinsic value without being non-incremental, but still not be held sacred; likewise, something can be held sacred and not have intrinsic value. Take the American flag as an example of the latter. People hold it sacred because of what it *represents*. Or consider knowledge as a case of the former. We often think knowledge has intrinsic value and we value it objectively, apart from my wants, needs, and desires, but we do not accord knowledge sacred value. These examples illustrate the importance of Dworkin's providing rough outlines of our sense of sacred value, which Dworkin thinks mainly have to do with intrinsic value, objectivity, and inviolability.

What is more, Dworkin makes clear that he thinks people do sacrifice things they hold sacred for other values or in certain choice conditions.[81] But he is not clear on the significance of sacrificing sacred values in our larger ethical and political life together; my account in chapters 3 and 4 will address this point. Second, Dworkin's formulation of sacred value in the abortion debates leads him to separate questions of the good from questions of

---

[77] For more on Dworkin's meaning of objectivity, see his "Objectivity and Truth," esp. 127–29.
[78] See Dworkin, *Life's Dominion*, 72, 73, 74, 75, 78, 80.
[79] Ibid., 84.
[80] Dworkin, "The Concept of the Sacred," 162.
[81] See Dworkin, *Life's Dominion*, 91, 248n9.

justice.[82] He thinks the courts ought to secure the freedom for persons to act with dignity on matters of life and death and so should not impose one conception of sacred value over against others, nor restrict or prescribe behavior based on one interpretation of sacred value.[83] The separation of determinations of value and social justice is one important implication that leads to problems that I seek to correct in chapters 3 and 4. Wherever one lands in regard to Dworkin's claims about abortion's legality, it is to his credit that his conception of sacred value can be critically examined apart from that debate.

For Adams, the sacred is best contrasted by the horrendous—something I take up in greater detail in chapter 3. His account of sacred value largely agrees with Dworkin's claims on the intrinsic, inviolable, and objective character of sacred value, but Adams emphasizes that the intrinsic value of a thing has to do with its ontology. To get to his account of sacred value, we need to understand what he means by *resembling God*. For it is Adams's account of how finite things resemble the Good as God that explains his account of sacred value.

To be intrinsically valuable, according to Adams, means that what one is does not arise from extrinsic relations or instrumental values. Adams's Platonic and theistic account in *Finite and Infinite Goods* builds on groundbreaking work in analytic philosophy on *semantics* and *metaphysics*.[84] Semantics has to do with meaning of a kind; metaphysics is concerned with its nature. Adams imports this distinction into his ethical framework to make the distinction between the meaning of the Good and the nature of the Good. Arguing from theistic premises, he tells us the Good is God, and when we use "good" in the relevant sense, we mean a kind's *excellence*.[85] Excellence is the kind of goodness "which is worthy of love or admiration," intrinsically, in-itself.[86] Finite instances of this sort of excellence resemble God. To help get a sense of what he means by these distinctions and the role excellence

---

[82] The way I have put this is informed by Timothy Jackson's account of Dworkin's argument. This specific formulation of Dworkin's larger argument doesn't mean that I follow Jackson in his own argument in "A House Divided, Again: Dworkin and Singer on Sanctity and Dignity," in Jackson, *Political Agape*, 186–213.

[83] Dworkin, *Life's Dominion*, 239.

[84] The key figures here are Putnam, *Mind, Language, and Reality*, esp. 196–271 and Kripke, *Naming and Necessity*.

[85] This move helps clarify the use and meaning of a particular kind in varying contexts. Adams's theory does not claim a universalistic import in all contexts and every use of the good. He is interested in "good" when we mean "excellence."

[86] Adams, *Finite and Infinite Goods*, 15–16.

plays in his ethics, consider the relation between "water" and "H_2O." Adams thinks that the metaphysical aspect of ethical theory—investigating the nature of the good—is analogous to the scientific investigation of natural kinds.

The sort of scientific investigation of natural kinds that Adams is interested in distinguishes between the *nature* of a kind and its *meaning*. H_2O is the chemical substance that constitutes water; H_2O is water's nature insofar as it accounts for the causal relations between the various concrete samples of "water." But water has an identity and meaning that surpasses its chemical and physical properties.[87] Even before people understood the nature of water, they could master the concept. Before modern chemistry told us that dihydrogen monoxide predominantly constitutes one instance and other varying samples of water, people were quick to tell you the color of water, that it is not a solid, that it turns into a solid when it freezes, a vapor when it enters a gaseous state, and so on. Studying the *meaning* of a natural kind involves grasping its identity—its meaning for competent users of the term. By contrast, studying the *nature* of a natural kind involves investigation into what constitutes it, what "account[s] causally for the observable common properties" among varying samples of the substance.[88] In this way Adams can say that "water does not *mean* H_2O."[89] All competent users of "water" are able to "fix the reference" of the term and thus pick out its identity. Competent users of the concept "water" may understand that its natural properties are H_2O, but they also understand that the *meaning* of "water" surpasses the properties that constitute its nature.[90]

The metaphysical aspect of ethical theory proceeds analogously to the scientific investigation of natural kinds.[91] The *meaning* points out the "role" the *nature* of the ethical concept is to play.[92] Semantics helps signify relevant metaphysical properties. To grasp the meaning of a concept such as "good" is to be capable of making reasonable judgments and taking "good" actions based on our judgments about the meaning and nature of the term.[93] The

---

[87] The distinction between constitution and identity which I have added is taken from the work of Mark Johnston, especially "Manifest Kinds" and "Constitution Is Not Identity." Later I will return to Johnston's helpful distinction between these terms, along with "chemical kinds" and "manifest kinds." See also Jeff Stout's insightful chapter "Adams on the Nature of Obligation," esp. 370–72.
[88] Adams, *Finite and Infinite Goods*, 16
[89] Ibid., 15.
[90] Ibid.
[91] Ibid., 16.
[92] Ibid.
[93] The role of evaluation in our ethical thought will become clear below, in Adams's responses to skeptical challenges on the realism of value.

metaphysical aspect of ethical theory is composed of hypotheses about what constitutes the nature of the good, what properties best fit the role suggested by the meaning. Our moral judgments are rough estimations of the nature of the Good. This roughness of judgment between the finite instance of the good and the infinite Good itself is hedged by Adams's conception of *resemblance*. Adams proposes that any finite account of excellence consists in resemblance to God.[94] As in the case with "water," Adams recognizes that "'good' does not *mean* the same as 'resembles God.'" But he does argue that the role for the nature of the excellent (picked out by our sense of the meaning) is most plausibly filled by God.[95]

What makes the difference between resemblance and parody depends on the *importance* and the *faithfulness* of the sharing of properties. It is not enough for a thing to share certain excellences with God. The sharing of certain properties in the nature of the thing must resemble God in their importance. Resemblances can be "distorted" if they feature too much of one property over another, or resemble one property in the wrong way. The importance of resemblance turns on a judgment of the "way in which the original has the features shared or represented."[96] Importance is guided by the faithfulness of a thing's resemblance of God. Resemblance, then, at least consists in (1) a kind's excellently sharing properties with God, where "excellently sharing" reflects importance and faithfulness in the resemblance.

My evaluations of excellence pervade my judgments of excellence: resembling the excellent in an excellent way is a *good* thing. Adams will wholeheartedly affirm that it is good to value the excellent. But it does not follow that such internal motivations preclude external justifying reasons for loving the Good and reasons that God might have for loving the finite resemblances. This is a crucial second point in Adam's argument regarding resemblance. In addition to (1), resemblance also (2) provides reasons for God to love finite instances of the excellent (that excellently resemble God). This is so because resemblance is grounded in natural properties of the thing itself.[97] Excellence consists in the intrinsic goodness of a thing—it is

---

[94] Adams, *Finite and Infinite Goods*, 15

[95] For further reading on resemblance and the difference between metaphysics and semantics in Adams, see Stout, "Adams on the Nature of Obligation"; on resemblance, see O'Donovan, *Finding and Seeking*. esp. ch. 4, "The Good of Man"; Decosimo, "Intrinsic Goodness and Contingency, Resemblance and Particularity"; Decosimo, "Killing and the Wrongness of Torture"; Bush, "Horribly Wrong."

[96] Adams, *Finite and Infinite Goods*, 33.

[97] Adams is fighting off antirealist claims of internal skepticism on motives and justifying reasons (ibid., 28–38).

an ontological property. God has reasons for loving the excellences that are grounded in a thing's nature; those reasons are the thing's resemblance of God.[98] Taken together the two aspects of resemblance capture the metaphysical aspect of Adams's ethical framework.

Adams's challenging account of resemblance does two crucial things for his broader project. First, it explains what excellence consists in (excellently resembling God), and, second, it provides—in a noncircular fashion—reasons for why God loves the excellent.[99]

Our sense of the meaning of excellence picks out a role for the nature of the Good, but we cannot identify the nature of Goodness (even finite instances of excellence) in our concepts. Our norms guide our evaluative judgments, and instances of resemblance of the excellent also provide us reasons to love the excellent. Adams thinks his metaphysical account not only better explains the "role" of the excellent; it also provides a metaphysical foundation for all value.[100] The excellence of a thing is its resembling God (expressing importance and faithfulness), which also provides God reasons to love the good. This is not simply a rational argument but one that depends on the ontology of excellence in things. Because resemblance is grounded in the nature of finite instances of the Good, Adams provides a robust account of the objectivity of excellence. Resemblance swings completely free of our social practices.

Adams's work is one of the more sophisticated accounts of why humans have reason to value the excellent in their lives and in their social practices. We have good theological reasons to value what it is we hold most dear and to protect it from violation. His metaphysical realism offers theological language about our social practices and in some ways is inspiration for my own account. The metaphysical aspect of ethical theory works in ways similar to my own post-Hegelian account of social practical reasoning. Adams and Dworkin largely speak about sacred values in regard to matters of killing, torture, abortion, and euthanasia. Speaking broadly, Dworkin's and Adams's conceptions of sacred value can largely be considered as dealing with the margins of life. Stout, in contrast, brings the concept of sacred value into the heart of politics.

---

[98] David Decosimo sums up the two aspects of resemblance: "A thing is excellent just in virtue of those features that are its excellence(s), and those features of a thing that are its excellence(s) are just those that resemble God and are such that he has reason to love them" ("Intrinsic Goodness and Contingency, Resemblance and Particularity," 424).
[99] Adams, *Finite and Infinite Goods*, 36–37.
[100] Wolf, "A World of Goods."

Stout introduces his conception of sacred value by distinguishing between a politics of preference and a politics of passion and concern. A politics of preference is best exemplified by the voting ballot, the survey instrument, and the focus group. Where political interests are preselected, all that's left for citizens to do is choose, or vote. In this kind of politics individual and group participation becomes "perfunctory."[101] A politics of passion is grounded in concern and ultimately is connected to "what I care about so deeply that I count its violation or destruction as horrendous."[102] Sacred value plays a crucial role in illustrating how some of the deepest divisions in the U.S. political culture do not involve preferences, but instead involve and express what we deem sacred.[103]

Stout follows Adams's account that the sacred is best opposed to the horrendous, but not because he sides with Adams's metaphysical account on finite instances resembling God. Additionally, he takes notes from Steven Lukes in adding that sacred value is that which "does not fall on a scale" and is not open to trade-offs.[104] He adds that the sacred has to do "with what we treasure for its own sake." The sacred is what we deem "worthy of reverence." Sacred values are both noninstrumental and noncomparative evaluative attitudes.[105] Stout tells us that it is appropriate to celebrate the "existence" and "excellence" of what we hold sacred. What is more, he points out that we respond to sacred values or even threats of horrendous evils by seeking to protect those things and persons by "instituting prohibitions of certain kinds." As long as people continue to trade in these kinds of passionate and concerned responses to sacred values and the horrendous, our political life will deal with religious considerations and theology.[106]

Building power in and through a politics of passion means we will have to cultivate virtues and habits that appropriately express passions such as anger and grief. These habits of passionate expression have to do with our concern of what we hold sacred. Preventing passionate expressions cuts a healthy democratic culture off at the root of what we care most deeply about, leaving only preferences and interests narrowly conceived. Stout argues that conceptions of sacred value and the associated passionate expressions are an essential part of grassroots democracy. Avoiding talk of sacred value is

---

[101] Stout, *Blessed Are the Organized*, 210–11.
[102] Ibid., 211.
[103] Ibid., 215–16.
[104] Cf. Lukes, "Comparing the Incomparable."
[105] Stout, *Blessed Are the Organized*, 211.
[106] Ibid., 210–15.

often a move by those who want to evacuate any talk of religion in politics. As I have argued throughout this chapter, sacred value is a concept that refuses such an arbitrary distinction between religion and secular politics.

Stout is interested in the political role of sacred value insofar as it contributes to a kind of politics that is deeply informed by passion and concern. The relevant form of democratic culture assigns different roles to citizens and is grounded in a deeper *spirit* than a political culture driven by interests and preferences. By "spirit" Stout means the shared habits, practices, and norms of mutual recognition, accountability, and leadership as earned entitlement grounded in social practices of reasoning and acting together with appropriate passionate expression. Take, for example, the role of passion and sacred value in the debates over slavery and women's rights. Stout says they "were in a large part about sacred value and divine authority," and that "grassroots democracy in all its forms—in the Alinsky tradition, as well as in the great democratic reform movements—has self-consciously made room for reference to sacred value in the public square."[107] This is because grassroots democrats understand a politics of common life and the common good to be intertwined with our passionate concerns. Grassroots democracy, as Stout imagines it, is a political tradition that surpasses the paradigmatic instance of citizenship as found in the ballot box, survey instrument, and focus group. Politics of a common life is deeply connected to what its citizens hold sacred.

Stout's conception of sacred value goes against the political economy that has grown up and become sedimented around a narrow capitalist conception of interest. Capitalist political ideology submits everything to "cost-benefit reasoning," which can tend to "dominate the culture as a whole."[108] Grassroots democrats fear that such a commodifying logic is corrosive and corrupting of the social practices that "express" and "cultivate" our deepest concerns. A capitalist culture tends to form citizens and societies that cannot hold the breadth of a politics of passion. "To attribute sacred value to something," Stout offers in contrast, "is to imply that its value can neither be measured exhaustively in quantitative terms, nor reduced to utility, nor subjected to someone's whim to trade-offs of the sort that markets are designed to facilitate."[109] The reigning political-economic ideology only has a language of value that submits everything to the scale of capital.

---

[107] Ibid., 214.
[108] Ibid., 220.
[109] Ibid., 219.

My account of the political role of sacred value in BBCO is closest to Stout's conception of grassroots democracy, especially in the shared concern for domination in our political and economic relationships. My claim that some organizing practices can be seen as religious practices is distinct from Stout, however. Situating my argument in the theological, political, economic tradition of the radical social gospel, taking insights from Black radical thought on racial capitalism, and framing my account of BBCO as a counterpublic similar to Black churches all yield a distinct account of the political role of sacred value. Rather than focusing on a politics of passion, my account offers a unique story of the role of religion and theology in community organizing—one that is more theologically robust yet no less grounded in social practice than Stout's. Still, Stout's and Adams's accounts of sacred value are deeply influential to my own.

Sacred Value at the Heart of Organizing

There are some important lessons that we need to take with us as we move into the following chapters. First, none of the scholars I have considered contrasts "the sacred" with a notion of "the profane." The relevant insight here is Adams's and Stout's pairing of sacred value and moral horror. Dworkin, Adams, and Stout are concerned with our evaluative attitudes and their bearing on politics. Second, in different ways, all three of these thinkers seek to illustrate how the political role of sacred value in democratic common life depends on practical reasoning. Appropriate expression of such reasons are *public*; their meaning is contestable. BBCO affiliates are counterpublics that have a particular economic and political relationship to the broader society, and that position is of a public being exploited, expropriated, and dominated by the status quo. When counterpublics engage in democratic "open-ended discussion," they create room for passionate expressions related to sacred value that are either more or less convincing to the group and in the process may invent new discourses. This means that the social practice of reasoning and evaluating such reason-giving activity cannot be dominated by any one evaluative logic.

Third, Adams and Stout do spend time illustrating how our conceptions of sacred value are fallible and give examples of how abolitionist movements and feminist movements pointed out this societal failure in order to adequately recognize certain humans as sacred and thus worthy of equal rights as citizens. My own conception of the political role of sacred value will be duly concerned with nondomination and fallibilism. A conception of the political role of sacred value that takes leave from feminist and Black radical thinkers, however, will be qualitatively different from those surveyed here and in a way that addresses the economic and political domination counterpublics seek to address in our current society that is deeply characterized by racial capitalism.

The final lesson that we might take from this overview of Dworkin, Adams, and Stout returns us to the first half of this chapter. Attention to the political role of sacred value blurs neat distinctions between "religion" and "secular." The concept of sacred value is meant to be expansive enough so as to be relevant for members of religious traditions and those who identify outside of such groups. What is more, the kinds of reverence due to what we deem sacred or the sorts of prohibitions we set up to protect what we hold most dear are contested within these groups as much as they are between them. The social practices of contestation, discussion, and giving and asking for reasons pervades the culture of democratic counterpublics like BBCO affiliates.

These are the main moves in the game. My argument reconfigures how it is we talk about religion, politics, and practice in broad-based organizing that refutes easy distinctions between religion and the secular in counterpublics. Sacred values are at the heart of organizing—they pull people in, keep them there, and yet are often marginalized due to the fear that they will splinter the group. By centering them in our accounts of organizing, we can expand our political theological imaginary of organizing and in ways that help organizers do their work better and scholars study this lived religious practice in ways that more clearly depict the role of religion and theology in the practice of organizing.

2
Organizing Religious Practices

It is a cool December morning in Nashville and I am setting up for a feedback session at one of the larger Presbyterian churches in town. For the past several months, I have led the congregation through a listening campaign: a series of one-on-one conversations to identify interests and values people care deeply about that merit urgent action. After three years of working on the issues of affordable housing, criminal justice, and economic equity and jobs, NOAH decided it was time to reorganize its base. Saul Alinsky, the founder of the IAF in Chicago in the late 1930s, once wrote that all organizing begins with disorganizing.[1] When Ed Chambers took over the helm at the IAF, he placed the listening campaign and the relational meeting at the heart of the organizing strategy.[2] BBCO is a relational and value-driven practice. A listening campaign is the perfect example of this organizing strategy because broad-based organizing begins here, with listening to our neighbors tell us what they care most about and what they are willing to fight for. It is here, too—in the relational practice of the one-on-one and the listening campaign—that we can see most clearly how some organizing practices are lived religious practices.

The week before this December morning, I held a similar feedback session at the same congregation. There, I reported on the fifty-some relational meetings that ten leaders of the congregation held. We identified core values of the congregation, and I shared specific stories that concretized these values in human flesh and emotion. As might be expected, there was overlap within the congregation on areas of concern. Some of the values and issues might not surprise a regular attendee of a progressive, predominantly white church outside of Nashville: issues of the environment and racial justice were named. Other, more concrete (because relationally grounded) concerns were unique to this congregation and deeply connected to its sense of identity. At the first feedback session several congregants voiced a sense of gratitude for

---

[1] Alinsky, *Rules for Radicals*, 116. See also Cortes, "All Organizing Is Constant Re-organizing."
[2] Chambers and Cowan, *Roots for Radicals*, esp. ch. 2.

this work; this was once a congregation profiled as a church that prays as it protests, and some felt it had lost that social justice bite. At these feedback sessions, congregants expressed their concerns, hopes, and anxieties about taking public action on the values and issues that surfaced through the listening campaign.

Every action in BBCO—from the first one-on-one to the height of BBCO's political repertoire, the public action—is meant to stir a particular reaction. This general rule—of action and reaction—holds true for the listening campaign: once the congregation or institution finishes its series of relational meetings, a process of deciding what to act upon begins. The feedback sessions were part of that process; the organizing committee called the meetings so as to include as many congregants as possible in deciding how the congregation should move forward. Once people gathered and store-bought cookies were passed around, I launched into the review of the core values and issues identified in the relational meetings. There were about twenty of us present, and a vast majority had been a part of the listening campaign in some fashion (either holding their own relational meetings with their fellow congregants or being invited to participate in one). Several of those leaders shared stories about the significance of this practice and what they learned about themselves and their congregation. In the middle of the meeting, however, a middle-aged white woman voiced a sentiment that made me pause: she failed to see how the values provided by her faith could guide her action in the office on Monday morning—they were separate, and rightly so. Instead of responding to her directly, I asked the group to reflect on her comment: "What do we think? What does our Christian faith have to do with our political life?"

Perhaps a few other comments were made in response, but the most powerful was shared with me by another middle-aged white woman via email later that afternoon: "It struck me that I feel completely different. For me those things are all connected—my core values guide everything I do and part of those core values is my faith. I think we have a responsibility to live our faith and demonstrate that not all 'church' is the same. I really think our church needs to be more public. I think we need to take stands on things as a church—I really feel that God calls us to do that." This is another way of voicing the argument of this book: our political lives are deeply entangled with our religious lives. What we care most about, what we hold sacred, shows up in our political lives in important ways. Paying attention to the political role of sacred values can improve our organizing and help us be clearer about the role of religion in politics. What is more, paying attention to the complicated political role of sacred values helps me as a Christian social ethicist be a better Christian and participate more faithfully in the rich tradition of radical social gospelers who believed their faith called them to transform the structures of society in the direction of social justice. The practice of the listening campaign and the relational meeting are two BBCO practices that can be seen as religious practices, illustrating how the church can live into, protect, and fight for those things radical social gospel Christians hold most dear.

This chapter will delve into the practice of the relational meeting and the listening campaign as I have taught it in my own organizing and witnessed it in the organizing of others. In making the case that these are lived religious practices, I draw on two recent trends in scholarly literature by historians, sociologists, anthropologists, and some Christian theologians and ethicists: lived religion and practice theory. The first section sets out what I mean by "lived religion" and "religious practices."[3] In the second section, I turn to the relational meeting and the listening campaign themselves, where I make the case that they can be seen as lived religious practices. In the final section, I explore how these two organizing religious practices are deeply embedded in relationships of power and how centering the political role of sacred values can transform the entire practice of BBCO. The following chapter delves deeper into the philosophical theology that grounds many of the claims I make here.

Lived Religious Practices in the Study of Religion

In the early 1990s scholars of religion began to do away with the secularization thesis.[4] Religion, they realized, was not going away, but neither was the discourse associated with the "secular." As we saw in the previous chapter, for feminist scholars like Joan W. Scott and Tracy Fessenden, the challenge is not to do away with the category "secular" but to analyze its origins and use, to unearth presumptive political and discursive connections between the

---

[3] I should note that traditionally liberation theologians focus on the *praxis* of a community; practical theologians have developed their own responses to the role of "practice" in theology; the difference stems primarily from the role of social science, primarily Marxist social science, in the two fields.

[4] For a more detailed discussion of the secularization thesis and the discourse of the "secular," including my analysis of Joan Scott's and Tracy Fessenden's writing on the topic, see my introduction.

secular and white Protestantism.[5] For some, the failure of the secularization thesis turned scholars of religion to religion as it is lived. If there is no single essence to "religion" and its secular opposite, then scholars can embrace the ambiguity and porousness of such categories, while paying attention to human experience in relations of power. Sociologist of religion Courtney Bender sums up some of the new questions made possible by this scholarly turn when she asks readers to consider religion's "entangled effects." What if, Bender continues, we need to focus on how "the religious . . . is not only lived but produced within nonreligious 'sectors' or 'fields.'"[6]

Who decides what "religion" is depends on the power to classify. Historians like David A. Hall, R. Marie Griffith, Colleen McDannell, and Robert Orsi were some of the first to develop this field of "lived religion."[7] Sharing in an ethnographic approach, sociologists like Bender and Omri Elisha and anthropologists like Charles Hirschkind, Saba Mahmood, and Noah Salomon all followed this general trend toward the connection between religion, practice, and politics.[8] Such scholars probe deeply into religion as it is lived, thereby exploring the new political-theological imaginaries that emerge once the secularization thesis is dropped along with the presuppositions about religion as white liberal Protestantism that are towed along. This scholarship builds on a previous generation's work in practice theory insofar as it investigates how people "do" and create "religion" and "religious" spaces. The stories that I share in this chapter and in the entire book are siblings to those recounted in this broad array of academic literature.[9]

Lived religious practices are the kinds of human actions that emphasize both the intentional and the habituated character of practice. Lived religious practices in a crucial sense are "unfinished" insofar as they subvert traditional dichotomous views of the world that come with prefabricated notions of "religion" along with opposing "secular" concepts. "The challenge is to study religion dialectically," Orsi says, "on the levels both of the self and of culture, tracking back and forth between structure and agency, tradition

---

[5] Kathryn Lofton also makes a similar point in *Consuming Religion*, esp. ch. 4.
[6] Bender, "Things in Their Entanglements," 51, 68.
[7] See Hall, *Lived Religion in America*; Griffith, *God's Daughters*; Orsi, *The Madonna of 115th Street*; Orsi, *Between Heaven and Earth*; Orsi, *History and Presence*; McDannell, *Material Christianity*.
[8] Bender, *Heaven's Kitchen* and *The New Metaphysicals*; Elisha, *Moral Ambition*; Hirschkind, *The Ethical Soundscape*; Mahmood, *Politics of Piety*; Salomon, *For Love of the Prophet*.
[9] A recent collection of Christian scholars led by Charles Marsh at the University of Virginia has also contributed to this broader question of theology as it is "lived," but I do not engage with that project here: my project shares deeper similarity with the field of lived religion as I outline it above. Cf. Marsh, Slade, and Azaransky, *Lived Theology*.

and act, imagination and reality, and in the process dissolving the solidity of such dichotomies."[10] For scholars like LeRhonda S. Manigault-Bryant, who turns to womanist theology as a resource for her own work, lived religion centers the voices—as "creative agents in their theological development"—of those who have been traditionally marginalized as mere subjects of academic studies of religion and theology.[11] Often, this means that those scholars considering religious practices as they are lived thwart preconceived notions of what is traditionally classified as "Christian" or "religious."[12] This is where our conversation on organizing practices as religious practices becomes extremely relevant to the study of lived religion. To consider some organizing practices as religious practices means we must take the religious practitioners as creative agents in their own religious worlds. Theological and ecclesiological reflections in this project start from below and must attend to relations of power, rather than starting with preconceived notions of church or religion, only to then descend to lived reality.[13]

Typically, those theologians or ethicists who write on practice do so in an approbative manner. The practices they explore are meant to be emulated; seldom are examples chosen that illustrate how practice itself might be deformed. I do not mean to speak of practice only in glowing terms. Practice theorists who follow Pierre Bourdieu highlight the historicity and relationality of our actions and so pay attention to power structures that are historically sedimented within traditions while attending to individual subversion and radical revision within given regularities.[14] Others have turned to the concept of practice to illustrate the political relevance of the sacraments.[15] These

---

[10] Orsi, *The Madonna of 115th Street*, xli–xlii.
[11] Manigault-Bryant, *Talking to the Dead*, 18.
[12] This is a point that Manigault-Bryant makes in her introduction about lived religious practices of storytelling and sweetgrass basketry by Gullah-Geechee women in South Carolina, but also something that Hirschkind is keen to highlight in his own study of Egyptians listening to cassette-tape sermons.
[13] In a study on the Gullah-Geechee women in South Carolina, Manigault-Bryant makes a similar point about her own methodological approach: "Central to my analysis is the understanding that religion and religious expression are deeply embedded in our social contexts. One cannot examine religion or religious experience without understanding the powerful social forces that the women of this study find themselves dealing with" (*Talking to the Dead*, 19). In chapter 7, I adopt and advance an "ecclesiology from below" approach to BBCO.
[14] Many scholars of religion studying practice have turned to Michel de Certeau's *The Practice of Everyday Life*, especially ch. 7, "Walking in the City." While I appreciate Certeau's distinction between strategies and tactics—tactics being individual subversive actions that individuals take up within broader social strategies—I find that Bourdieu's account of social power in habituated individual action is a more apt analysis of BBCO.
[15] I am thinking particularly of Cavanaugh, *Torture and Eucharist* and Hauerwas, *After Christendom?*

theological accounts turn to the moral theory and philosophy of Alasdair MacIntyre and Ludwig Wittgenstein, and so their practice-talk quickly loops into virtue-talk. Lauren Winner, however, has powerfully illustrated how Christian practices of eucharist, baptism, and prayer can themselves be characteristically deformed. The point of turning to Bourdieu as a thinker of practice, rather than Wittgenstein or MacIntyre, is precisely for this attention to power, domination, and deformation. Winner puts her critique of the too often positive sense of practice like so: "[T]here is a significant gap between, on the one hand, Bourdieu's contention that practices often function as 'officializing strategies, the object of which is to transmute "egoistic," private particular interests . . . into disinterested, collective, publicly avowable, legitimate interests' and, on the other hand, practical theologians Dorothy Bass and Craig Dykstra's assurances that 'practices, therefore, have practical purposes: to heal, to shape communities, to discern.'"[16] As I consider the practices of the listening campaign and the relational meeting as Christian lived religious practices, I will continually draw attention to the potential for deformation and domination. But such an account is possible only because the practice of organizing is relational, social, and historical.

The work of Bass and Dykstra is noteworthy for more reasons than their approbative reading of practice: they exemplify a concentrated turn in theology to take seriously the practical theological wisdom that exists within normative Christian social practices.[17] Winner's critiques are for the most part accurate, however. As Dykstra and Bass define their sense of practice, they write, "[O]ur descriptions of Christian practices contain within them normative understandings of what God wills for us and for the whole creation and of what God expects of us in response to God's call to be faithful."[18] Certainly, as Christian theologians, Dykstra and Bass situate their understanding of practice in relation to Christian theological understandings of the fall and redemption, but their sense of Christian practices emphasizes God's redemptive activity: "Christian practices share in the mysterious dynamic of fall and redemption, sin and grace. . . . Within the history of any given practice, there have been points at which the social forms of the practice became unjust. . . . Even practices that are in modest disrepair can provide

---

[16] Winner, *The Dangers of Christian Practice*, 168.
[17] In "Theories of Practice," Ted Smith outlines the broad range of practical theological approaches to practice (that includes scholars who do not necessarily identify as practical theologians—Kathryn Tanner, Serene Jones, and Joan M. Martin, for example) by situating this scholarly trend in response to the broader philosophical turn to culture.
[18] Dykstra and Bass, "A Theological Understanding of Christian Practices," 22.

the space within which selves made new by God can respond to God's grace by extending it to others."[19] Taking seriously Winner's caution that Christian practices themselves can be deformed is a serious challenge to all who consider practice as theologically relevant for the Christian tradition.[20]

But Dykstra and Bass's argument makes an essential point that is crucial to my larger argument in the book: Our social practices and the concomitant evaluative attitudes are normatively and theologically freighted. Christian practices are also a consideration of the construction and formation of such theoethical norms. To assert, as Dykstra and Bass do, that Christian practices contain Christian practical wisdom—knowledge of what God wills for us and our world—needs to be supplemented with some account of how practical reasoning in the Christian tradition is a socially constructed practice and how such a claim does not detract from such Christian practical theological wisdom. This will be the work of the following chapter; as I will argue there, constructivist accounts of Christian social norms, ideals, and sacred value is just part of engaging in the social practice of practical reasoning within the broader Christian tradition. Our evaluative attitudes are guided by ideals and norms that train and shape our behavior; the social practice is pervaded by social power, meaning, and experience.[21] Consideration of Christian practices requires attention to the dynamics of classification of such practices as "Christian"; the pluralist political conditions of such practices require radical democracy and an ecclesiology from below.[22] In this chapter, I continue to attend to such power dynamics by calling attention to the role of narratives in the social construction of such social practices.

---

[19] Ibid., 27–28.

[20] Winner's book, and my comments here, have less to do with the *intrinsic* violence of a practice, but as Winner writes, her book is about "deformations of Christian practices that are characteristic of the practices themselves; deformations that are somehow *about* the practices . . . a practice's propensity for violence, for curvature, for being exploited for the perpetuation of damage rather than received for its redress" (*The Dangers of Christian Practice*, 14). For example, looking at the deformation of petitionary prayer by white women about their slaves, Winner writes, "Christianity became slavery's grammar; slavery ventriloquized Christianity so fluently that many didn't see the impersonation going on. . . . In fact, slavery colluded with Christianity to produce this particular deformation—the deformation of commandeering petitionary prayer as if it were a neutral technology, usable in the service of anything" (79).

[21] For a recent volume on the role of each (meaning, experience, power) of these in various approach to the study of religion, see Bush, *Visions of Religion*.

[22] All of this to say that, if practical theologians have been calling for deeper attention to their own valuable insights into Christian practices, one of the complications my argument introduces to their account is that any consideration of practice needs to attend to philosophical, ethical, and political questions like those that I attend to in Cchapters 3 and 4. Too few practical theologians clarify what they mean by practical reason and how their practice might be socially constructed in the way that I have in chapter 3.

Work like Bender's and Winner's helps us understand what it means to claim that people forge religious spaces by taking up and participating in practices in our everyday lives. Characteristic damage is a reality; practices are bent to violent ends and used for domination. It is naive, however, to imagine that a tradition might be scrubbed free of violent practices. Violence and domination are human, political, and theological problems, not intrinsic or ontological. Winner encourages us to recognize that Christian practices like baptism, the eucharist, and prayer are gifts. They are a vital part of the Christian tradition.[23] Similarly, my claim that organizing practices are lived religious practices is not a call to abandon other practices in favor of the listening campaign and relational meeting. Instead, in the same moment that we recognize the constructedness of the Christian tradition, we open the tradition to new movements, explained within the Christian tradition as the movement of the Spirit. Attending to an ecclesiology from below trains our eyes to what some Christians are claiming as God's presence and calls us to attend to new practices, in new spaces, that question rigid boundaries between religion and politics, religious and secular.[24]

Listening to the Spirit

The practice of organizing is grounded in social practical reasoning. Practical reasoning as a social practice means that the values, principles, and norms that guide the practice are shared and are based in shared assumptions, patterns of behavior, and goods internal and external to the practice itself. Often, social practices become part of broader cultural institutions, which can work to cultivate the goods internal to a practice, thereby fostering and cultivating virtues that serve to realize the internal goods. Here, social structures are collections of practices. Habit and intentionality can and do go together in this account, where social practical reasoning takes place in time and makes possible the critique of our practices based on normative analysis

---

[23] See Winner, *The Dangers of Christian Practice*, "Damaged Gifts," 137–66.

[24] For a similar example of the expansion of tradition, or inclusion of new practices not traditionally deemed religious, see Manigault-Bryant's work on how practices of "talking to the dead" are found in "cultural activities" that Manigault-Bryant (rightly, in my view) deems religious: "While some of these activities may not be considered 'religious' in a traditional sense, these activities—which are at the center of these women's lives—are tightly interwoven by religious imagery and concepts.... Whether described as 'religious' or 'cultural,' all of these practices are understood as religious because these women interpret them as such" (*Talking to the Dead*, 105).

of that very practice. Our social practices, the institutions that hold them, and the very practice of social practical reasoning are not naturally immune from criticism. A Christian practice may be exploitative, racist, misogynistic, or dominating, and so we can critique such a practice on its own Christian terms and norms of justice and love.

Evaluative attitudes like sacred value are a part of this social endeavor of BBCO. Individuals practice organizing differently in different settings, and so the action itself is characterized by style and urgency. To try to exclude sacred values from the practice of organizing asks participants to lop off a critical part of their sense of self, thereby maiming the narrative unity that is often sought for in our religious and political lives. Because sacred values are a kind of evaluative attitude, they are subjected to the social construction process undergone by all social kinds that are subjected to our judgments in social practical reasoning. Those who are concerned about questions of religion and politics at the center of BBCO need to pay attention to the role of such valuations in our practice of organizing and how people understand such practices in the broader narrative of their religious tradition. Interfaith coalitions like BBCO affiliates need not limit their organizing domain to consensus issues, which, in fact, just shrinks the political imagination of the affiliate. Instead, sacred values need to be engaged in lived religious practices that, yes, have the potential to stir up intense conflict within the affiliate, but such tension can be generative of deeper relationships and provide insight into how individuals live out their religious tradition through their organizing practice.

BBCO is about organizing the relationships and values of working people for greater democratic power in their communities. When organizing forgets its value and relational basis, it becomes twisted into a practice of building economic and political power for power's sake. But each action in the practice of BBCO is geared toward developing stronger leaders for stronger institutions to ensure more powerful affiliates. When it forgets its focus on power-building, it becomes sentimental. The best organizers I've known and witnessed ground their power-building in their own and their fellow leaders' sacred values. It is in the relational meeting—and specifically when organizers seek to agitate others—where a tension between values and power-building can erupt and where the practice can be melded to ends of domination over others.[25] As a human practice, the relational meeting and

---

[25] In the literature on BBCO, those who have devoted chapters or stand-alone articles to the relational meeting include Chambers and Cowan, *Roots for Radicals*, ch. 2; Jacobsen, *Doing Justice*, ch.

agitation often are twisted awry to evil ends—organizers end up bullying, shaming, berating, or breaking down leaders in a way that deforms the practice of organizing and the Christian sacred value of the human individual. Then the work of organizing is hobbled by its affinities to forms of antidemocratic mastery predominant in U.S. heteropatriarchal racial capitalist society; figures of the boss, bully, or strongman come to dominate the organizing imagination. The relational meeting and agitation need to be grounded in sacred values or else the practice becomes deformed and myopic. Couched in a democratic culture and grounded in sacred values, the practice of the relational meeting can be seen as a Christian practice wherein individual Christians narrate their own experience of suffering and loss together with others as they organize for greater democratic power.

Consider the NOAH listening campaign. From September to December 2018, I led a single congregation through NOAH's listening campaign. In May 2019, during election season, the congregation invited the candidate for Metropolitan Council to Sunday worship and to a forum held afterward where several leaders reported on the issues and values identified during the listening campaign. The practice of the listening campaign is more than a series of relational meetings within the congregation: importantly, it also includes the congregation taking action on the issues and values in a way that enacts those values. When I speak about the listening campaign, I am referring to this entire process of intentional listening, discernment, and action, whereby the congregation acts publicly in a way that announces its public identity to its political representatives. The meeting with the Metropolitan Council candidate was a small action, but it made clear to him what the congregation cares about and also that this congregation was paying attention to his work as their representative. However small, it was a statement of public witness by the congregation and demonstrates how the listening campaign itself is a religious practice grounded in what values the congregation holds most dear. But to make this case, I want to start at the beginning, with the training of leaders in how to hold a relational meeting.

In late August 2018, I gathered fifteen members of the congregation for a relational meeting training with a fellow organizer; let's call him

---

7; Stout, *Blessed Are the Organized*, ch. 12; and Coles, "Moving Democracy." Others have mentioned the importance of the one-on-one but not extrapolated its practical role in the entire organizing process: Bretherton, *Resurrecting Democracy*, esp. 122–23; Hart, *Cultural Dilemmas of Progressive Politics*, 105–7; Osterman, *Gathering Power*, 44–46; Snarr, *All You That Labor*, esp. ch. 3; Warren, *Dry Bones Rattling*.

Tim. Because institutional membership is constantly under pressure and undergoing change, the relational meeting is a crucial part of any institution's organizing process: families grow and responsibilities shift; jobs change and people move to follow them; once-strong leaders burn out. In the cycle of organizing, disorganizing, and reorganizing, the relational meeting is a crucial tool to help institutions identify new leaders, core values, and concerns of their membership, while reweaving the relational fabric of the institution.

After our dinner of pizza and salad in the fellowship hall, I started the training by exploring the scriptural roots of the relational meeting. The Hebrew Bible and the Christian New Testament are littered with examples of frank conversations between humans or between God and a priest, prophet, or individual that skip small talk and jump right into concerns or issues that really matter. Consider Moses's encounter with God at the burning bush (Exodus 3) or Jethro's confrontation with Moses during those early days in the wilderness (Exodus 18); consider Jesus's conversation with the woman at the well (John 4) or his encountering two disciples after his resurrection as they walk to Emmaus (Luke 24); consider Saul's conversion experience on the road to the Damascus (Acts 9; Galatians 1–2).[26] In this training I spent a fair amount of time extrapolating details from Moses's encounter with God at the burning bush.

Although I was not attempting an exegesis of Exodus 3, much of what I presented to the group was intellectual and heady. The group seemed uninspired. Tim suggested that we mock out a relational meeting, where I would illustrate the role of the leader initiating the one-on-one. I began by asking him about the experiences that propelled him to organizing. He shared a story of a Black neighbor who organized her own neighborhood and won infrastructure improvements. She was so energized by this that she started organizing a white community to do the same. He shared stories of neighborhoods coming together and building power. This went on for several minutes, before I cut him off: "Tim, all of this is interesting and inspiring, but you aren't in it. Where are you in these stories?" That question made Tim pause, but he never really responded. We ended that section of the training, and the night went on.

Relational meetings are *intentional* individual meetings. They are *public* meetings, not focused on private chitchat or gossip, and so the conversation

---

[26] For a more detailed account of seeing Jesus as an organizer, including some of the above mentioned passages, see Lambelet, "A One-to-One on the Road to Emmaus."

has a time-limit—the IAF notoriously trains leaders to keep their relational meetings to thirty minutes. The relational meeting is meant to form a public relationship, and the conversation should focus on public matters. This does not mean that the conversation is heartless or that it avoids personal issues; indeed, the conversation needs to be *value-directed*. Leaders holding a one-on-one should be interested in personal stories that focus on one's *self-interest*. We identify one's self-interest by locating one's values and relationships held most dear; when what we hold most dear is threatened, we have a self-interest in protecting and fighting for it. Self-interest is not selfishness. One's self-interest is the value-laden and relational stake one has in organizing. Self-interest is deeply connected to one's values.

Leaders who initiate the relational meeting should ask *probing* questions in the hope of unearthing formative *stories* that help explain why a person cares and values certain things. A relational meeting is typically set up with the intention of forming a public relationship of solidarity in the collective work of BBCO. One needs to be genuinely *curious* about someone in order to unearth these stories, but curiosity and probing are distinct from an illicit intrusion into someone's story. This means that the questions are directed with care and concern: often, these stories involve experiences of loss, trauma, and vulnerability. This is the deeply countercultural aspect of the relational meeting. We are not used to being vulnerable in public about the things we hold most dear. A good one-on-one includes questions that *agitate* us, that stir up in us a sense of cold anger to fight for and protect those things and people we value as sacred.

Often, accounts of the relational meeting fail to capture much of the practical lived style and urgency that are part of the practice of organizing. Following my gut and intuition, I intentionally interrupted Tim when he began telling me stories about other people. I was looking for Tim's self-interest, not stories about the self-interest of others. I interrupted him and asked him a short, snappy question because I wanted to agitate him. I wanted to wake him up. I found Tim's stories to be the "helping" experiences that are often shared in liberal social justice circles, but such stories lack self-interest and failed to explain the values that guide Tim's work. I was curious to hear Tim reflect on his own experience. So I probed deeper.

There is more going on here than curiosity and probing, however. The relational meeting challenges people to give an account of their lives—to explore their self-interest—and to make meaning out of experiences of personal suffering, love, loss, regret, and grief and transform them into publicly actionable issues. The relational meeting provides a chance for someone to see their life in a different way, to consider their position in the all too often unacknowledged relations of power that make up our society. Such questions require reflection on any number of social identities. I was curious to hear Tim reflect on the significance of this work to his larger story as a father, as a Christian, as a middle-aged white man living in a midsize city in the U.S. South. Such questions require vulnerability from Tim and require me to tend to him, to attend to his feelings and emotions, to listen—at times intuitively—to his story. Such vulnerability is a unique space in which to engage in the mutual and co-constructive work of building democratic relationships of solidarity.

Self-interest is not selfishness. Identifying one's self-interest is possible only when one explores the core values in one's life. Self-interest and values are two sides of the same coin.[27] Often, this relational, value-laden nature of self-interest is lost, and instead self-interest is reduced to one's pecuniary or political "interest" in the shallow sense. This tends to miss the relational, historical, and value-laden nature of the practice of organizing. The Exodus 3 passage is especially apt for a one-on-one training because it helps illustrate why it is that organizers often speak of self-interest as the fire that burns inside: What is your burning bush that you can't turn away from? Who has confronted you in your life, calling you back to your family and values you hold most dear—and have you listened to them? By paying attention to these stories that illustrate the values that people hold most dear, relational meetings stir up leaders in a congregation, agitating them by building relationships with others in their congregation who are asking tough questions about weighty matters.

Dykstra writes that Christian practice "is a lot more physical than we usually recognize or let on. It is a body faith—an embodied faith—that involves gestures, moves, going certain places (where people are hungry and thirsty, for example; where suffering occurs), and doing certain things."[28] The relational meeting is an embodied practice. There are seldom moments in our daily life when we sit face to face with someone in public and tell our story. Being asked questions that unearth our sacred values stirs up physical responses in us; such questions can make us uncomfortable and our body language shows our experience of vulnerability in public. We feel differently in these conversations because the values and issues we are talking

[27] Hart, *Cultural Dilemmas of Progressive Politics*, 76–77.
[28] Dykstra, *Growing in the Life of Faith*, 71.

about matter to us in a qualitative, experiential sense. Such probing questions aren't scripted, but drawn from attending to our story, driven more by intuition and a sense of the habitus (and potential to revise it). Dykstra says that Christian practices involve going to places of suffering. The radical social gospelers and liberation theologians remind us that our theological concepts are fully understood only when we grasp their application to our social situation.[29] Though the relational meeting is a conversation, it involves a form of listening that is attentive to people's suffering, to their vulnerability, and for Christians it inevitably involves the question of what God has to say about such suffering and pain.

The one-on-one involves attending to how an individual Christian's story fits into a larger Christian tradition and narrative. In reflecting on my own story, I can invite others to do the same. In the one-on-one I am listening for the values behind the issues; I am actively engaging the story being crafted before me, and I seek to honor that story and the other stories to which it is connected.[30] I pay attention to body language and the physical presence of the individual responding to my questions. The practice of the relational meeting asks people to embody and feel formative experiences they are sharing again. Story work is hard work. As I ask questions, I am reflexively aware of my own self, monitoring how the story is impacting me and how this mutual story-work contributes to the relational work of building a democratic culture. Such narrative work is political and religious because it asks people to critically and collectively reflect on experiences of power in their lives, what they are willing to do to protect those things and people they hold most dear from arbitrary exercises of power, and what the Christian faith might have to say about such political relationships.[31] Such narrative work is guided by social practical reasoning and, insofar as it engages in the social practice of a tradition's right expression of care and concern, engages in revision of traditions within certain limits. Such narrative work is part of what it means to say that religious identities are socially constructed. Being a member of a tradition is to improvise within particular limits, to tell familiar stories anew.

---

[29] "One cannot really understand liberation theology's theological categories until their implications for the way we relate to each other and the way society is organized are developed" (Petrella, *The Future of Liberation Theology*, 36–37).

[30] In the literature on BBCO by political theorists, Romand Coles is the best on "listening"; see his *Visionary Pragmatism*, esp. the introduction.

[31] For more on the role of narrative identity construction in the BBCO, see Oyakawa, "'Turning Private Pain into Public Action.'"

Asking such probing questions with care and concern creates the spaces for Christians to listen to the movements of the Spirit in their everyday life and to then narrate that movement together. The practice of listening and stirring people up—agitating them—opens space for expansion of our theological and political imaginations; it is religiously and politically powerful and generative. The act of narrating one's own story, while feeling listened to and empathetically cared for, creates space for critical theological and political reflection that can agitate and energize Christians toward political action.

But often it takes *agitation* to get to action. Agitation is tricky, as it can devolve into abrasive questioning or offensive pretension. A lot depends on a leader's style of agitation.[32] Organizers agitate to, among others things, unearth the sacred values in people's lives.[33] Inviting a leader to reflect on what they hold most dear and how they can act with others to protect and fight for those persons or things provides a value and relational basis for BBCO. Crucially, however, the organizer can only democratically agitate in and amid relationships of trust and accountability. Agitation is invitational in character: the organizer seeks to stir the leader to action, but equally, the offer can be rejected. The invitation is weighty—it's an invitation to take action, to provoke a realization about one's social, economic, and political world. If a relationship is not there to hold the feelings of discomfort, to welcome the nerves and steady the conversation, what's happening is not agitation but something more akin to domination and mastery.[34] Agitation as a style of the practice of organizing helps organizers notice things, such as a capacity for leadership, a leader's sense of accountability—to whom they see themselves as primarily accountable—and how they understand leadership authority to be earned. Agitation is a way for organizers to expose the heart of what people care most deeply about and what they are most willing to fight for. When people get agitated about values they hold sacred, they often experience a sense of urgency. Words are not to be minced.

A good agitational question plays with the tempo of the conversation. In my organizing experience, I have been most agitated by a short and simple question: Why? For example, when I first started organizing in San Antonio, Texas, my lead organizer, Jorge, would often interrupt our conversations

---

[32] For more on the styles of organizing, see Braunstein, *Prophets and Patriots*.

[33] Agitation is not the only strategy, and at times not even the best one to use in the relational meeting. Other traditions of organizing use alternatives strategies that BBCO should learn from. Wood explores this at length in *Faith in Action*, ch. 3.

[34] On mastery, domination, and anti-Blackness in the United States, see Lloyd, "Human Dignity Is Black Dignity."

with "Why?" and wait for my response as to why I felt a certain way about a leader or why I had analyzed a campaign a certain way or understood my life experiences the way I had. Jorge would also take long pauses in our conversations. By his words and silences, Jorge would invite me to deeper reflection. Certainly, these relationships are power-laden, as I will explore below. But agitation is based on the reality that people live in urgent times. In the sense I am using it in connection to practice, *urgency* is related to a clarity of priority and sacred values. This is in contrast to hurried activity, in the way that hurriedness can convey confusion and a proneness to make mistakes.[35] That very use of time, however, forces a clarity of priority so that time is not wasted on unimportant items; a correct power analysis of an issue or "read" of a leader is crucial. This is why I was not interested in Tim's stories about other leaders' successes or trials. I wanted Tim to reflect on the motivating sacred value(s) for this work in his everyday life. Jorge's questioning or silence was attending to me and inviting me to deeper, more critical power analysis and reflection on the values that matter. Without trust and accountability, Jorge's silence would just have been bullying.

The reality that agitation happens only in relationship was forcefully brought forward to me after Tim read my account of our one-on-one. He felt I had drastically misunderstood him. He was "pissed." He had shared those stories about other leaders, he clarified to me on the phone later, because those are strategies and campaigns that he had helped develop. Those were pivotal stories in his own development as an organizer. For him, they exemplified the power of building and developing leaders who could make a difference in their community, and that sort of work is something Tim feels called to. Those stories of other leaders organizing in their community are very deeply connected to his sense of identity and what he held sacred. "Your account," he told me, "misses the 'point' of people acting on their values—one of which for me was that of building leaders for an organization." Tim and I shared an honest and frank conversation about how I presented the story. He didn't disagree with the "how" of the events. He agreed that that moment was apt in demonstrating the style of agitation. But he felt there was more to be said. He shared some choice words with me.

My experience of that phone conversation confirms for me the central place of agitation in BBCO, but it also raises another stylistic aspect of organizing: the role of anger. Organizers are trained and train leaders to

---

[35] For more on this sense of urgency in organizing, see Ganz, "Leading Change."

speak frankly—not offensively, but also not with a soft hand. Anger, not fury, is encouraged. Organizing is serious work and so demands the requisite emotional range to publicly express the private pain leaders often silently experience in their daily lives. And yet, if Tim and I had not known each other for years, if we had not become familiar with the role of anger and agitation, an exchange like that could have broken the relationship. Agitation and anger really work—in the sense of being efficacious in building democratic political power—only if there is a deep relational and value grounding of that emotion. Anger, in this sense, has a target. Fury, by contrast, is all over the place and misdirected. Tim was angry with me for a certain reason. That angry, frank conversation helped me understand him better. It returns us to the important point that BBCO exists in time and that relationships shift and deepen as people organize together.

Today there are plenty of examples of how agitation is used purposefully to provoke fury (not anger) and instill a politics of shame and disrespect. Consider how the political far right agitated its base under the Trump administration, where a constellation of abusive tactics, gaslighting, and conspiracy theories combined to amplify a politics of white domination. In this sense, agitation "works," but to antidemocratic, anti-working class, white supremacist ends. Such a crude sense of efficacy ultimately fails organizers seeking to build radically democratic cultures grounded in sacred values and democratic relationships. The work of building a democratic culture requires relational power sustained by relationships of trust and accountability. A politics of shame and domination put a rot in those relationships, breaking down the culture from within. Agitation that is done without tending to the dignity of the leader whom one is asking such probing questions tends toward domination: it ignores the voice and influence of the very person in front of you and attends only to the exercise of your will in the attempt to summon information rather than genuinely attending to their story from a place of curiosity, concern, and care.

In addition to power operating through deformed agitation, power also operates in the relational meeting in more implicit ways. The temptation to domination and mastery also come from the broader social world in which organizing takes place. Relationships of trust and accountability are under attack by a U.S. culture that constantly dismisses and undermines Black testimonies of anti-Black racism.[36] In a country that idolizes bootstrap

[36] Jordan, "Bearing Witness to Testimonies of Antiblackness."

individualism, workers collectively organizing out of their own agency are quickly demonized.[37] The power I have as a white, heterosexual, cisgender, Christian male permeates my style of organizing despite my best efforts to establish equal standing. But such power exists in fields and settings; it is possible that in other settings, where my race or gender is not normative—in counterpublics, say—my whiteness or maleness might not be dominating, but in fact hinders my ability to organize. Given the current reality of power dynamics in U.S. culture, oppressed communities and people are unlikely to enter easily into relationships of trust and accountability across racial, gender, or class lines where agitation can be successful. These conditions in which BBCO takes place raise the urgency behind the call to create a democratic culture. BBCO attempts to cultivate and establish spaces that decenter norms dominant in the broader U.S. heteropatriarchal racial capitalist culture. The art of forming and cultivating groups that foster democratic cultures requires centering norms other than those predominant in broader society: anti-Blackness, profit over people and planet, patriarchy, and heterosexism. It is not a guarantee that such spaces can survive or thrive, but the fact that our identities are socially constructed and driven by norms and exist in fields and settings that inform our action and stance-taking in relation to others raises the possibility of establishing counterpublics that challenge such dominant norms.[38]

This is where Winner's recent work about characteristic deformation of a practice is helpful. The deformation that occurs here is *about* the relational meeting, but the relations are unjust and dominating. The deformation is not with the relational meeting *itself*. It is crucial to acknowledge how the practice of organizing is pervaded by power and that democratic organizing is democratic only insofar as it is able to maintain radically democratic structures and relations within the constituency even as it seeks to establish deeper democratic conditions in the broader public.

Asking such probing questions with care and concern creates the space for Christians to listen to the movements of the Spirit in their everyday life and to then narrate that movement.[39] This expands our theological and political

---

[37] Cf. McAlevey, *No Shortcuts*.
[38] For more on this sense of counterpublics, see Fraser, "Rethinking the Public Sphere."
[39] Craig Dykstra and Christian Scharen are helpful here in teasing out the theological relevance of such practices of narrative work in the relational meeting. As Scharen writes, "Craig Dykstra has argued that such knowledge of grace and forgiveness, the core knowledge of faith, becomes embodied through practice.... Dykstra's larger point is that participation in the practices of faith (prayer, singing, hospitality, forgiveness, and so on) opens us to the work of the Holy Spirit and nurtures in

imaginations. The act of listening done in the one-on-one is religiously and politically powerful and generative. The act of narrating one's own story while feeling listened to and cared for creates space for critical theological and political reflection that can agitate and energize Christians toward political action.

Such narrative work is norm-guided and rational. The one-on-one creates space for expansion not only of theological imagination but also of political imagination in that it authorizes expressions often viewed as inappropriate by broader society. As I noted earlier, anger plays an important role in the relational meeting.[40] Leaders are looking for people who express anger at domination and injustice. The BBCO process hopes to develop anger away from fury—a passion that tends to overwhelm and isolate one from collective political work—and toward what is called "cold anger." Our broader racial capitalist culture disciplines us away from cold anger—and for women especially from expressing anger entirely. Cold anger is concentrated on its target; it does not consume those who feel it. Feminist Christian social ethicist Beverly Harrison captures this sense of the power of anger when it is rooted in the work of love: "To grasp this point—that anger signals something amiss in relationship—is a critical first step in understanding the power of anger in the work of love. Where anger rises, there the energy to act is present. In anger, one's body-self is engaged, and the signal comes that something is amiss in relation."[41] The relational meeting is not only focused on cold anger; it is also focused on identifying sacred values. The work of narrating challenges everyday Christians to connect that which they hold most dear to their religion as it is lived. This narrative work weaves together individual lived religious practice with the broader tradition. The crucial points of the narrative depend on those values that are normatively shaped by the Christian tradition and yet lived out in everyday Christian life.

An entire listening campaign and the relational meeting itself are Christian religious practices insofar as the church perceives the practice as fitting into the larger narrative of its life as the people of God. Again, practical theologians are helpful in drawing this out.[42] In her own study of a "worldly

---

us the sure knowledge of the grace of God in Christ Jesus" ("Learning Ministry over Time," Kindle locations 2952–53, 2954–55).

[40] Others have paid attention to the affective role of anger; see esp. Stout, *Blessed Are the Organized*, ch. 5; Rogers, *Cold Anger*.
[41] Harrison, "The Power of Anger in the Work of Love," 49.
[42] Mary McClintock Fulkerson's writing on the relations between church and organizing is helpful here: "Church, at its best, then, is about practices of community-in-process, offering opportunities

congregation" of Good Samaritan and its everyday theologizing, Mary McClintock Fulkerson writes:

> I contend that the theological challenge of Good Samaritan as [a] place is not to compel more control by doctrine, but to respect the way situations occur and to do so with particular attention to lived or everyday theologizing.... Theological reflection arises in an organic way out of Christian life in order to address real life problems.... Theological reflection is not a linear form of reflection that starts with a correct doctrine (or a "worldly" insight) and then proceeds to analyze a situation; rather it is a situational, ongoing, never-finished dialectical process where past and present ever converge in new ways.[43]

Each relational meeting is a moment of narrative work, where members of a church are asked to do this critical reflective theological and political work that centers on what they hold most dear, what they hold sacred. Everyday Christians are emotionally, theologically, and politically vulnerable in such meetings, opening themselves up to perceive the work of God in their own lives, their collective life as a church, and the BBCO constituency—in my example that started this chapter, NOAH. In chapter 7, I will develop this point more fully, defending the claim that the church cannot be understood apart from this communing, from this material embodied task of serving God and the world. The church's task of serving God and the world is to confront oppression and domination and co-labor with God in the liberation from domination.

Back in 2018, a few Sundays after Tim and I trained the group of Presbyterian listeners to hold their own relational meetings through the listening campaign, a commissioning service was held. The liturgy created for this service illustrates the interweaving of the theological and political elements of the listening campaign. The commissioning service took place after the sermon. In Reformed liturgy, the sermon follows the reading of the Scripture, and collectively the Scripture and the sermon comprise the liturgical moment where God's Word is proclaimed, and what follows is the congregation's response to this proclamation. Placing the commissioning directly after the proclamation of the Word is theologically significant: it enacts

---

for mutual honouring of one another as imago dei, of covenant, confession and forgiveness, and continued opportunities for change founded in ongoing hope" ("Receiving from the Other," 424).

[43] Fulkerson, *Places of Redemption*, 233–34.

the congregation's response to God's Word. The commissioning began with a Call to Discipleship read by the pastor to the ten leaders (listeners) gathered in the front of the sanctuary next to the baptismal font. The liturgical connection to baptism was intentional here, reaffirming that baptism is deeply tied to lifelong vocation and discipleship. After the Call to Discipleship was read, the pastor turned to the congregation and the listeners leading them in a litany.

Call to Discipleship

The call of Christ is to willing, dedicated discipleship.
Our discipleship is a manifestation of the new life we enter through baptism.
The ministry of listening is both a gift and a commitment,
an offering and a responsibility.
We are called by God to be the church of Jesus Christ,
a sign in the world today of what God intends for all humankind.

Commissioning Questions

To the listeners:

Do you welcome the responsibility of this service
because you seek to follow Jesus Christ, to love neighbors,
and to work for the reconciling of the world?
We do.

Will you serve the people with energy, intelligence, imagination, and love,
listening attentively for what lies in the hearts of God's people?
We will.

To the congregation:

Do you, members and friends of the Church,
welcome these listeners as people called by God for such a time as this?
We do.

Will you support and encourage them, and will you speak truthfully to them

as they seek to carry out their mission of listening?
We will.

Commissioning Prayer, concluding with . . .

**God of the still small voice,
Let your Spirit speak through your church,
so that we may be joined in love and service to Jesus Christ,
who comes to meet us in the promise of your reign. Amen.**

For this congregation, the act of listening to their members on what they hold most dear and what they perceive God has to say about those values and issues is part of what it means to be Christian. In this liturgy, the listening campaign is connected to the sacrament of baptism, to Christ's continuing work in their lives and the world, to their individual and collective discipleship, and to the collective task of living out the identity of the church. This liturgy is not exceptionally beautiful or theologically unique. It is apt because of its everydayness. The church is the people of God, who are formed around claims they make about God in Jesus Christ. The church's identity is a task, and listening to and crafting these stories are part of that identity. To live into this requires them to speak honestly about what lies in their heart. This liturgy demonstrates that something about the practice of the listening campaign itself, not merely the single act of the relational meeting, but the process of the congregation listening and speaking honestly to each other is a religious practice. It helps them discern how the Spirit is moving and calling them out into the public. As theologian Kathryn Tanner helps us to see, the listening campaign and the relational meeting exemplify what it means to be a Christian disciple in this church: "Called to the difficult work of being a disciple and witness of Christ in a way appropriate to one's own time and circumstance, one comes, by way of theological investigation into Christian practice, to understand more fully what one is doing and why, and to have a sense for how all that one believes and does as Christian holds together."[44] It is a concrete action that lives out the task of the Christian identity for this congregation. It demonstrates how listening to the church narrate its life is part of perceiving God's movement in the life of the church.

---

[44] Tanner, "Theological Reflection and Christian Practices," 234.

Organizing Lived Religious Practices for Power

Such a Christian practice is pervaded by power, and broad-based organizing is organizing for radically democratic power by working people for working people's communities. All that has been said above presumes this. Each action in the practice of organizing is geared toward developing stronger leaders for stronger institutions to ensure more powerful affiliates. Building power doesn't always take place in a straight line—you disorganize in order to reorganize; an apparent step back or recalculation and recalibration to changing political or economic circumstances is often taken with the long-term goal of building more democratic power. This is why negotiation and compromise have always been part of the organizing process. Developing stronger leaders is an experimental enterprise because humans bring complex and tightly knotted experiences to a politically pluralist and value-pluralist counterpublic that is the BBCO affiliate. But fundamental to the BBCO theory is the concept of power. Power is variously theorized in BBCO, but a key characteristic is that power is relational. Power exists in relationships.[45] When relationships become skewed and antidemocratic, domination and marginalization occur. The practice of organizing presumes political conditions of radically democratic publics.[46]

The argument of this chapter—that the relational meeting and the listening campaign are religious practices due to the political role of sacred value—requires centering the role of sacred values in the practice of organizing. To some, this might seem detrimental to any organizing strategy placing power at the center. How can such divisive valuations be capable of generating relational power? Such an argument goes to the heart of the longest running stock-reasoning behind avoiding sacred values in BBCO: they are divisive and they threaten the solidarity of the group. But we need not fear any supposed incommensurability of sacred values because, as I will show in the next chapter, social practical reasoning equips us with a variety of emotions that display how sacred values are woefully sacrificed, neglected, lost, grieved, or violated. The political role of sacred value raises the challenge of radical democracy in publics. In chapters 3 and 4 I will offer responses to the philosophical and political sides of this challenge.

---

[45] For a classic extrapolation of this point, see Loomer, "Two Conceptions of Power."
[46] My account of the relationship between radical democracy and broad-based organizing will receive a full treatment in chapter 4.

Centering sacred values in the practice of organizing expands our political theological imaginations. This is one upshot from the literature of lived religion that explores the generative political frames that emerge from lived religious practices. This literature also helps us recognize the manner in which such practices can go awry when the relations in which the practices subsist become dominating. This is Winner's point: that even practices held sacred to the Christian tradition like baptism, prayer, and communion can be characteristically deformed. Orsi is also particularly interested in the role of power in lived religious practices, especially in his own exploration of Catholic lived religious practices for the elderly, sexually abused, and mentally and physically disabled.[47] Orsi's point is that religion exists in relationships between heaven and earth, and such relationships are politically, socially, and theologically freighted.

Religious practices exist in power relationships, and the normative significance we ascribe to those relationships depends on our own narrations of our experiences in relation to the broader tradition. BBCO limits its theopolitical resources by excluding sacred values from its organizing process. By drilling deeper into the evaluative and normative nature of social practical reasoning, we get a sense of how religion and politics are deeply interwoven. Values and relationships sit at the heart of BBCO. What was previously seen as the limit of group solidarity and possibility in pluralist politics may turn out to be an expanding horizon.

My concern to center sacred values in the religious practice of organizing goes deeper than these conceptual points, however, to questions regarding the longevity and relational basis of the organizing itself. As one clergy organizer for Faith in Action said to me a few years ago, ignoring the theological differences may avoid initial conflict, but it in no way means that the theological work is over.[48] By focusing on how humans narrate their relationship to what they hold most dear and the broader fields that permeate human practice we can ask different questions that decenter the individual and instead focus on the relational fields and stances taken in those fields. This does not mean that we have to leave the theological (and questions of the church qua church) behind for the social scientific study of religious traditions or the power dynamics in the religious landscape. But it does mean that theology

---

[47] See Orsi, *Between Heaven and Earth* and *History and Presence*.
[48] Interview with author, February 21, 2018.

may need the social scientific study of religion in ways that the radical social gospelers understood.[49]

How does the organizing model shift when sacred values are taken out of their silos and put into play in the organizing process, in pluralistic settings that are not easily identified as religious or secular? One organizing network is asking questions like this. It is asking its Jewish clergy, for example, to construct a public action as if only rabbis were present. During a conversation several years ago, Megan, a national clergy organizer for Faith in Action, explained to me the theory behind this shift in organizing. Organizers are very good, Megan said, at articulating the pain and anger experienced in specific issues: criminal justice, immigration, or poverty. But we are not good enough at connecting those issues to the specific values and religious commitments that keep us in the struggle in the first place. Megan put it this way:

> You need people who have anger and you need people who have joy to get a sense of "This is where we're going." So there's a place where we start [anger] and a place where we end [joy], and if you don't have a sense of what that [joy] should look like, how do you get there? . . . We do a good job of telling these stories about [anger]. . . . What we don't always do is align them to very specific theological, scriptural, ethical commitments that aren't this kind of vague notion of "beloved community." . . . How are we holding [anger and joy] in concert so that we aren't telling the story without also making a theological declaration?[50]

Megan is driving at the relationship between issues and values in the work: our concern for concrete issues stems from values that we hold most dear and that are narrated in our social, political, and religious identities. Meir Lakein, director of the Jewish Organizing Institute and Network for Justice, has wonderfully deepened this point when he explores the Jewish religious and political roots of the act of gathering, a fundamental act in organizing.[51]

The point for Megan is to create religiously pluralistic *settings* that are not assimilationist to Christian liturgical styles or dominated by a Christian

---

[49] See, for example, "Norms and Valuations in Social Science," in Muelder, *The Ethical Edge of Christian Theology*, 135–66.
[50] Interview with author, February 13, 2018.
[51] Lakein, "On Gathering."

theological framework.⁵² The liturgy I shared above would not be appropriate for a NOAH gathering that is a religiously pluralist counterpublic. But it can serve as a map for how one tradition thinks about organizing as a religious practice. Individuals of different religious traditions might then be empowered to cultivate the values that ground and motivate their own concern for specific issues. What we end up with may be organizing settings that contain a mosaic of values and commitments and that effectively foster solidarity in a religiously diverse constituency. Because radically democratic counterpublics are discursive, and because practical reasoning is inferentially governed by normative commitments of responsibility and accountability, these values do not stay in silos but inform one another. I am arguing for a deeper entanglement between different religious values and organizing practices in a particular kind of organizing setting.

Such entanglement can create settings that are deeply tension-ridden. But tension is an important part of organizing; one cannot agitate except in relationships that are capacious enough to hold moments of deep discomfort. Such spaces are productively agitating to various members of the constituency who hold different values sacred. BBCO has gotten very good at building coalitions across lines of racial and economic difference where relationships are grounded in commonalities. Yet BBCO has continually stayed away from conflicts of sacred value. Such a turn away from sacred values is an ironic turn away from one of the core tenets of this model of organizing: that tension and agitation are crucial to the relational and value basis of such organizing. Spaces of conflicts of sacred value can be immensely agitational, causing leaders to do necessary self-reflection and narrative work that is so crucial to the formation of self-interest in organizing.

Conflicts of sacred value are a part of our everyday life, and politics is characterized by loss. But a conflict of sacred values is not rightly conceived as a war between locked, incommensurable positions. We are familiar with an emotional range of expressions to handle such conflicts, and it is part of social practical reasoning that we have a rationally grounded range of emotional expressions. This very practice inferentially commits us to being held accountable and responsible for our judgments. We enact these evaluative

---

[52] The relevant differences between "fields" and "settings" will be addressed in chapter 5, but for now, a quick way of understanding the difference might be to follow Paul Lichterman's definition of a setting as "the social and material coordinates of an interaction scene" ("Religion and Social Solidarity," 249). In this sense, settings can be pervaded by fields. The term "setting" is a sociological way to capture the political culture and grid and group aspect of social identity.

attitudes in practices in everyday life; some Christians are realizing that some organizing practices—namely the listening campaign and the relational meeting—are religious practices that help articulate what it means to be the church in the world in a way that fights for and protects those values. Such religious practices bring us into relationship with those who disagree with us. But disagreement—even a distinctly tension-ridden and agitational moment of disagreement—is a relationship that allows people to bring their whole self into the organizing space. When deep disagreement does occur regarding matters of sacred value, building value-based relationships and instilling an understanding with the constituency that these are matters of sacred value and therefore they play a crucial role in the organizing process—even if leading to different stances—can help build relationships of trust and accountability. Disagreement cannot and should not always be avoided, especially regarding matters that people hold most dear. In fact, sacred values can help deepen solidarity, even amid disagreement. The pragmatic process of political action will then take leave from that value and relational basis. Action is directed toward issues, but the range of actionable issues is now broader.

Organizers need to pay attention to how different religious narratives understand different values that are basic to the stories that guide this work. "We tend to only hear those in our own stories," a Faith in Action clergy organizer once told me. The work of organizing needs to be done in such a way that leaders "can understand how other leaders understand specific concepts in their own story." This is work that involves difficult conversations. Organizers need to ask, "How is it that you have come to understand these terms as your terms only?"[53] We need to create spaces that are emotionally, spiritually, and politically conducive to multiple values, each held as sacred in our organizing circles. We need to encourage the political reflection that affirms that some practices express and enact the lived religious aspect of organizing. Such creation of settings and enactment of practices need to be done in a way that centers traditionally marginalized voices and religions. Simply starting a public action with different faith leaders offering prayers in their own religious language is not enough—that merely places such traditions in their own neat silo without looking at the stances taken by various practitioners in a radically democratic public. We need to build relationships that ask leaders to do the necessary narrative work and self-reflection that challenge them to

[53] Interview with author, March 8, 2018.

consider their values that ground this work, how such values are in relationship with other sacred values, and how organizing enacts such values in lived religious practices.

It is as if BBCO organizers have not trusted their strategy of organizing enough; instead of doubling down on the value and relational basis of their strategy, they limit the sphere of organizing to common issues out of fear of splitting the coalition. But organizing will always deal in successes and failures, wins and losses, moments of relative strength and weakness. Those moments of loss are crucial moments in organizing and test the political and theological basis of organizing. A politics that seeks to avoid varied human expressions of sacred value turns out to be emotionally shallow and brittle; it cannot hold our whole narratives that seek to rationally express our relationship to values we hold sacred. We need a political theology of organizing that gives us our griefs and joys of sacred value. Organizers need to develop settings that allow for such expressions and enactments of sacred value. We need to explore the theological and political value of recognizing some organizing practices as religious practices. Allowing leaders to explore the discomfort of being agitated in relationship with others who hold different sacred values will deepen the relational bonds within the constituency, even if this means being uncomfortable. Such work is not only theologically and politically generative; it also allows our leaders to be honest and whole persons in the work of organizing.

It is hard to come up with examples that illustrate what I mean by calling for deeper tension and agitation in our organizing relationships that hold sacred values and enact these values through lived religious practices. Very few organizing networks are questioning this self-imposed limit in their strategy. One way to think concretely about this is to expand the sense of agitation beyond the relational meeting to the whole constituency. I am calling for collective efforts of holding discomfort and difference in relationship. Trust the process—value-based organizing does not leave us without resources to guide us through discomfort that arises when conflicts of sacred value arise. What keeps people involved in organizing for the long haul is not merely cold anger but a deep appreciation that BBCO constituencies are radically democratic counterpublics through which they can protect and fight for things and persons they and their fellow constituency members hold sacred. The sacred values keep us in the fight and get us through the tough times.

When constituencies create settings that hold tension in relationship across divides of sacred value, deep moral and political formation can take place. In those spaces of tension and agitation, deeper self-reflection can occur, leading to growth of self-interest in the constituency. Such moral and political growth takes place amid broader political conditions that center heteropatriarchal racial capitalism: the social norms and ideals that we trade in in social practical reasoning are given to us as much as we make them our own. This does not mean that revision of values and norms is not possible, but only that such revision is hard-won, driven by radically democratic processes that start with experiences of the marginalized, and takes place within certain limits.

Organizing is about values, relationships, and the stories we use to explain ourselves and the work. When these values or relationships are threatened or violated, we react in fear, anger, even horror—this is the basis on which specific issues are selected for political action. Social practical reasoning helps us navigate the political and religious waters of our life together. We hold each other accountable and responsible based on this social practice. Such narratives that we use to explain our past, present, and future actions help discern where we ought to start organizing and where we are going. Organizing in relationships grounded in sacred values includes agitating and tension-ridden moments. Organizing sacred values will include moments of discomfort, experiences of vast difference, expressions of personal and collective honesty, and enactments of practices that are cherished for religious and political reasons. By encouraging the connection between sacred values and organizing practices, we may come to see how organizing itself can be led by theology—led back to agitation and tension that are already at the heart of the model, yet refashioned in ways that go beyond self-imposed limitations.

The benefits of sacred values to BBCO are wasted if organizers and leaders do not do the basic work of the relational meeting and listening campaign. Organizers need to remind their leaders to really listen to their fellow constituency members. Such listening that takes place in the relational meeting requires a tempo different from politics as experienced in election cycles and ballot boxes. It is slow, patient work. It requires intuition and emotional intelligence. To hear the stories of another, to honor and respect them, requires creating emotional, spiritual space within our practice to reflect on how such listening and narrating builds relationships that enact sacred values amid vast differences. Such patient and slow work, however, builds relational power that is self-directing, and not at the whim of electoral campaigns—which never seem to end. Hearing how fellow leaders find theological and political meaning in organizing creates space for agitation and tension in relationship. Relational meetings have the power of literally *moving* leaders from one space to another, from one issue to another. It is politically and theologically agitating in a way that awakens us from our slumber of politics as usual.

For too long BBCO has illustrated its religious, racial, and gender diversity by opening public actions with various religious leaders offering prayers. This is exactly what I do not want to encourage. I am not against such public actions of prayer—they are fine and good as far as they go. What I am calling for instead is a deeper honesty about the role of theology and religious diversity within the practice of organizing itself, and I want organizers to help leaders articulate and enact that in all aspects of their organizing in a way that goes beyond recognition politics and such representationalist maneuvers. Lead with the values and relationships in a way that troubles neat, isolated distinctions of roles between religion (clergy) and politics (elected officials). Have leaders strategically confront politicians on moral and theological grounds without sacrificing attention to power politics. Center the organizing strategy around the relational meeting and values rather than the issue campaign, which only leads to electoralitis and voter fatigue. Hold public leaders accountable for their centering of white Christianity on theological and political grounds. Refuse to relegate religion and religious diversity to the opening three-minute prayer, and pay attention to how sacred values move your leaders in their religious and politics lives.

In the following chapters, I will explore two other examples where sacred values cause deep tensions in the organizing process and how the political role of sacred values opens the possibility of expanding our political theological imagination and developing more effective, relational, and value-based organizing strategies. Chapter 3 will address the philosophical theological grounding of my claims made in this chapter, turning to post-Hegelian thought. Chapter 4 will offer my own account of the sort of radical democracy in BBCO counterpublics that my account here presumes.

PART II
WHY SACRED VALUES MATTER

3
Our Political Relationship with Sacred Value

Several years ago I was organizing a public meeting in Nashville during Ramadan. Over the years, the Nashville Community Iftar grew from its first-year crowd of 75 people to selling out the 250 tickets over a weekend. City council members, the mayor, and powerful religious leaders were all regular attendees. The iftar's theme sought to make clear the deep connection between Islamic values and their public expression in the life of the Muslim community in Tennessee. We had two goals for the evening. First, that attendees would leave knowing a bit more about the beneficial contribution of the Muslim community to our common life in Nashville. Second, we hoped that attendees would be inspired by such knowledge and would sign up for future house meetings focusing on anti-Muslim bigotry in Tennessee. We had sign-up sheets and surveys to measure our success.

This event took place the day after the U.S. Supreme Court ruled on marriage equality. The main panel, featuring a rabbi, an imam, and an African American Baptist minister, addressed the challenges and opportunities of building relationships across religious divides. Going off script, the rabbi commented positively on the Court's ruling. He then turned to the imam and said that religious congregations have to be more welcoming to their gay and lesbian neighbors. This put the imam in a place where he felt obligated to, on the one hand, recognize (yet again) his minority status in relation to the larger community, and, on the other hand, to express an experience of loss of what his community holds sacred. He commented that while he recognized the legitimacy of the Court's rule, as a leader of a faith community he had to disagree with the rabbi's statement. For him as an imam and his community, it was a sad day.

This conflict exemplifies the untidy and contested status of sacred value in democratic politics. I want to postulate (not unduly, I think) that both the rabbi and the imam hold marriage sacred. If this is the case, how should organizers approach such conflicts of sacred value? Traditionally (and

Listening to the Spirit. Aaron Stauffer, Oxford University Press. © Oxford University Press 2024.
DOI: 10.1093/oso/9780197755525.003.0004

unfortunately) organizers have marginalized sacred values in their practice because they feared sacred values would splinter group solidarity. But that need not be the case. Conflicts of sacred value do not spell doom for our efforts to organize across differences of what we hold most dear. This chapter outlines the role sacred values play in our politics and in our social practical reasoning. In the following chapter, I will flesh out the sort of radical democracy that my account in this chapter presumes. Here, I seek to present an account of the political role of sacred value and a theory of social practical reasoning that can adequately explain to organizers the significance of the conflict between the rabbi and the imam.

My own account of the political role of sacred value brings insights from post-Hegelian social theory into conversation with political and theological insights from the radical social gospel. This is important because the most urgent matters of sacred value in our politics concern women and people of color. Social movements such as Black Lives Matter, the #MeToo movement, and the Women's March have shifted our political discourse, forcefully arguing that when it comes to those things the general public claims to hold most dear—life and liberty—people of color and women are systematically dominated, exploited, and expropriated by a heteropatriarchal, racist, capitalist society. The tragic causal origins of these movements lie primarily in the illusion that many tell themselves: that all lives are sacred and all bodies can move freely through the workplace and public space. Yet conflicts of sacred value like the one that starts this chapter are common in the workplace and public life, and so we need a political theory of the role of sacred value in our politics and of social practical reasoning that is attentive to these concerns, while not extirpating religion or talk of sacred value from our politics.

What we learn about our political and economic life will have important ramifications for religious identities themselves. Fallibility and corrigibility are crucial to our evaluative attitudes informed and shaped by broader social norms and ideals. What it means to be "Christian" needs to shift to incorporate such lessons. The political account of sacred value I offer here attempts to learn from radical social gospelers, feminists, and Black radical thought. Race, class, and gender are socially constructed and real, and the best thinking on the social and political implications of race, class, and gender reflect this reality. So we need to shift our understanding of "Christian" accordingly to think of religious identity as socially constructed. Our evaluative attitudes of sacred value turn out to be a vital element to such a conception of religious identity.

I should say at the start that I do not see any reason to curtail theological confidence by a constructivist account of Christian religious identity. Instead, such an approach better equips us to grasp the rich political theological meaning of sacred value in our political lives and what it means to take conflicts of sacred value seriously. Reckoning with the reality that conflicts of sacred value are not unique requires us to account for the role of sacred value in politics. But we cannot proffer any political *significance* for what we deem sacred if we don't first have clarity on the political *role* of evaluative attitudes like sacred values and how to make sense of the claim that such evaluations might be in incommensurable conflict with other values in our common life.

The chapter works dialectically, bringing philosophical theology into conversation with my own organizing experience. I begin with the anecdote of the imam and rabbi as a way to bring to the fore a common presupposition about the political role of sacred values: that sacred values are incommensurable (in a bad way) with other political values, and so they simply cannot be sources of group solidarity, especially when groups disagree on matters of sacred value. I call this the incommensurability argument. This approach presumes a monist theory of value conflicts: that all values in politics need to be able to be measured on a single scale. But this approach is wrong-headed in two ways. First, it adopts a mistake we found in chapter 1 in Ronald Dworkin's thought: that intrinsic values are only ends. But, I argue, our political life is better suited to a social practical account of evaluative attitudes like sacred values that adopts a pluralist theory of value. This line of thought is indebted to the philosophical theology of Hegel and his socializing and historicizing Kantian insights into the normative nature of reasoning.

In the first section I offer several challenges to monist theories of value and seek to correct a prominent way of understanding intrinsic value. This doesn't solve the question of whether sacred values are incommensurate values, nor does it answer the question as to whether incommensurability is even a problem. But the first problem—what I call the incommensurability problem—leads to another, what I call the problem of moral horror. The second section will raise the stakes of the unanswered questions of the first section. I approach the question of moral horror by working through the claims of Robert M. Adams. Adams's work is an alternative, negative way of approaching sacred values: we identify what we hold sacred by our responses of moral horror. In this section, I illustrate how Adams's approach fails to capture what is really going on for the imam in this scene.

The problem of this chapter is a big one, so Hegel's grand and expansive view of philosophy and historical, social, and normative nature of reasoning benefit my analysis, especially in the third and fourth sections. In the third section, I offer an account of social practical reasoning, sacred value, and the ethical life of Spirit, as I define it. The fourth section offers a political role of sacred values grounded in an account of social practical reasoning. Social practical reasoning requires practices of mutual recognition and determinate negation. Indeed, Spirit emerges as Absolute Spirit in Hegel's sense under conditions of reciprocal recognition. Tragic conflicts of value in social practical reasoning are cases of misrecognition. Organizing practices like the relational meeting and listening campaign, when done well, place individuality and reciprocal recognition at the core; they can be seen as religious practices that place evaluative attitudes like sacred value in the broader inferential scene of social practical reasoning. Reciprocal recognition is a potential outcome of a one-on-one.

By figuring scared values, mutual recognition, and the ethical life of Spirit in the relational meeting we gain epistemic, practical, and spiritual insight into the practice itself. We see just what is at stake in this organizing practice. Such practices provide us with a whole host of attitudes and inferential reasons to express our fraught experiences in political life with sacred values, including experiences of sacrifice, grief, loss, regret, and disappointment. Adams's work wonderfully highlights the urgency behind quandaries of moral horror in our world but fails to account for how choice situations are complex and value pluralist: sacred values are not always decisive of choice. Often, we sacrifice and grieve our sacred values in order to maintain group identities or other relationships we have reason to value. By adopting a post-Hegelian social practical account of reasoning—in comparison with Adams—we turn away from questions of resemblance and faithfulness to the Good, and instead take up questions of attending and listening to the Spirit as Christians experience it in their social practices of reciprocal recognition.

At this point in the chapter, the problem of incommensurability has been set within an account of social practical reasoning. The rabbi and imam problem is reframed as an opportunity for organizers to double down on the relational basis of their organizing practices, to build relational power with deep determinate difference, and to organize with sacred values because of the crucial role they have in our political life. The final section applies the lessons from my framework of social practical reasoning and teases out implications for questions of agency. The rabbi and imam as participants in the norm-governed practice of social practical reasoning are free to critically revise the norms that govern the practice, but only within limits. As I argue in this section, those who have argued that gender, race, and class are socially constructed categories and yet material and real can help us see how radical revision is possible. Our definition of "Christian" needs to adjust to this constructivist position. This has implications for conflicts of incommensurability like the rabbi and imam. Part of what I take it to mean to be a part of a tradition is to continue to trade in a discourse common to that community in a way that community recognizes. Yet, as this chapter shows, one can engage in an inferentialist, precedent-driven social practice of reasoning, without just using the old, tired language to talk about religion and politics, which in fact perpetuates ugly conventions or the status quo.[1]

The Incommensurability Argument: Pluralist, Not Monist, Conflicts

Return to the story of the rabbi and imam. The conflict is stark because of its publicity and its spontaneity: the imam was unprepared for the question (as was the entire room). It is perhaps not difficult to imagine the imam feeling caught between the value of his relationship with the rabbi and the value of his own theologically inspired understanding of marriage. Both are goods that the imam values in different ways. Yet in talking with other Muslim leaders about this exchange, they told me they felt he was backed into a corner without any way forward that would not leave someone hurt or offended. There is a sense of regret about his actions and disappointment regarding the fact that no best option was available. Later, I will turn to these sorts of considerations, which might be divided into our evaluative attitudes that are action-guiding or non-action-guiding.[2]

It is not hard to see that the imam feels the pull of two different values. He recognizes the good of the constituency that might result in political, economic, or social advantages for his community. At the same time, the imam is unwilling to publicly sacrifice the sacred value of marriage.[3] Monist theories

---

[1] I think Hegel, or certainly other readers of Hegel, would recognize this as a Hegelian account of tradition. See Brandom, *Tales of the Mighty Dead*, esp. chs. 6 and 7; Hector, *Theology without Metaphysics*.

[2] Stocker, *Plural and Conflicting Values*, ch. 4.

[3] This "caughtness" can also be found within a number of other religious traditions that do not grant the sacrament of marriage to gay, lesbian, and queer people. An Irish Catholic priest, for

of value claim that the imam's sense of "caughtness" stems from a mistake on his part. He fails to realize that all values can be weighed on a single scale. Formidable versions of monism have appeared in utilitarian and hedonistic kinds, where the good is viewed as overall happiness, pleasure, or utility. In monistic hedonisms, an agent may encounter different instances of happiness in choice situations, but entrenched conflict is deemed irrational. I don't mean to say that monisms do not allow for conflict in choice situations, but any sort of conflict is irrational because all goods present more or less of a single value.[4] The best action in utilitarian monisms is typically identified by some version of the following: the best action is that which accrues the most good for the most people. Conflicts of choosing between instances of the good are calculated away.[5] Anyone who doesn't agree, and who has a clear understanding of all the relevant information, hasn't done the math or is irrational.[6]

Monistic theories of value, if taken on fully, threaten to drastically alter our commonsense way of viewing the world. If followed with discipline, monisms threaten not only to change life as we fundamentally know it; they accomplish this by reducing the sphere of the moral to one value and by boiling ethics down to an undue emphasis on actions and therefore exclude evaluative attitudes other than the one defining their single concern.[7] Monisms tend to reject the idea that values can be incommensurable—that is, when two goods are neither equal to nor greater or lesser than the other. All values can be weighed in relation to a single overriding scale. As one feminist moral philosopher has put it, monisms tend to overlook nonrational motivations such as "moods, interests, whims, impulses, appetites, mere tastes, liking,"

example, would be in a similar situation as the imam, except in one important sense in this example: the priest would not be the leader of a religious and racial minority. The question of a minority group's sacrificing its values in democratic constituencies will be a large question of the next chapter. It is not lost on me that the imam represents an economic and racial minority, aspects of power relationships that need to be considered in counterpublics that proclaim to be democratic.

[4] In allowing for a certain sort of conflict in monism, I am following Stocker, *Plural and Conflicting Values*.

[5] As philosopher Elizabeth Anderson says of monistic theories of value, "they assume that value is normative for just one attitude or response, such as desire, mere liking, or being pleased" (*Value in Ethics and Economics*, 15).

[6] I avoid here the important issue of "weakness of will," or akrasia, because that would take me too far afield from the matter of sacred values. The literature addressing this topic is large, but I have found the following valuable: Davidson, "How Is Weakness of the Will Possible?"; Wiggins, "Weakness of Will, Commensurability, and the Objects of Deliberation and Desire"; and Nussbaum, "Plato on Commensurability and Desire."

[7] Cf. Taylor, "The Diversity of Goods"; Anderson, *Value in Ethics and Economics*; Nussbaum, "Plato on Commensurability and Desire"; Stocker, *Plural and Conflicting Values*.

while leaving "no room for the free play of these other motivations. This is a dull and rigid vision of human life."[8] Monisms, it would seem, tend to break up the richly experienced world into aggregative segments of value.[9]

In addition to these limitations of monisms, there tends to be a fundamental confusion and conflation of two distinctions in goodness at the heart of monistic thought.[10] We first encountered this confusion in chapter 1 with Ronald Dworkin. The confusion supposes anything that is valued intrinsically cannot be valued as a means, and anything that is an extrinsic value cannot be valued as an end. But there is a good argument as to why we should reject this.[11] The problem stems from a conceptual confusion (that intrinsic values are only ends and cannot be means). One reason for this confusion might be due to a vagueness attributed to the category of intrinsic value, which is often thought to mean "valuable for its own sake."[12] This is a mistake, because "intrinsic" specifies the location of the value (that it has goodness *in* itself) and suggests little about the conditions or the relations of the good.[13] The failure to properly recognize the distinction between intrinsic and extrinsic, means and ends has important implications for theories of value. One is that monisms that fail to make these distinctions tend to identify intrinsic value only with mental states or experiential concepts, such as pleasure or happiness. In the effort to isolate value from conditions, sources, or relations, monisms tend to internalize and cordon off value. Such a mistake reduces the experience of watching a beautiful sunset to the experience of pleasure in watching the sunset. But this doesn't make sense: the sunset is valued as an end, not a means to an experience of pleasure. We value the sunset as an end because we have the appropriate reason for valuing the sunset. It is extrinsically valuable, due to our reasons for valuing the sunset, yet it is an end, not merely a means to the experience of happiness. Monistic theories of value that fail to make the distinction between intrinsic and extrinsic, means and ends reduce all extrinsic values to instrumental goods. By making these two distinctions in goodness (intrinsic and extrinsic), we can also see how a case can be made that the sunset is intrinsically valuable but is instrumental to other goods. Defending this more difficult case will

---

[8] Anderson, "Practical Reason and Incommensurable Goods," 100.
[9] Taylor, "The Diversity of Goods," 230: "We cut and chop the reality of, in this case, ethical thought to fit the Procrustean bed of our model of valuation."
[10] Cf. Korsgaard, *Creating the Kingdom of Ends*, 249–75.
[11] This argument is first made by Christine Korsgaard in *Creating the Kingdom of Ends*.
[12] Ibid., 250.
[13] Ibid.

turn upon the reasons, the nonrational and non-action-guiding evaluative attitudes, and the conditions of our valuing and actions.

The imam in the example I am using in this chapter holds marriage as sacred and as intrinsically valuable, which is a means to maintaining his good relationship with his Muslim community that is racially, ethnically, and economically marginalized and exploited in the broader public. And yet he also values his relationship with the rabbi and the broader community—thus his caughtness between the sacred value of marriage, he and his community's marginalized position, and his standing in public. In this case, the sacred value was the decisive value, but it brought along with it the painful reminder that the Muslim community is once again in the minority. Choice situations are sometimes tragic. Tragic conflict, according to Molly Farneth's reading of Hegel's interpretation, is a "form of ethical conflict in which two goods or rights stand in opposition to one another, such that the pursuit of one entails the relinquishment or violation of the other."[14] I think this definition of tragic conflicts is apt, but I need to include the additional characteristic that tragic conflicts are often painful because of the reality that agents often experience non-action-guiding emotions like grief, loss, remorse, or disappointment. Choice situations are characterized by a plurality of values that play different roles. Some determine action; others do not. In this sense, the rabbi and imam example is a tragic conflict. The caughtness I spoke of earlier is one way of capturing the tone of tragedy that pervades this conflict. And yet the imam's response exemplifies the basic distinctions in goodness I outlined above. Here, a sacred value is intrinsically valued, is a means to maintaining the good of fidelity to his religious community, and yet is also a means to the experience of pain, perhaps even grief, of another value, which he relinquishes.

Intrinsic value, properly understood, is crucial to the theories of sacred value found in Dworkin, Adams, and Stout. This kind of value confounds aggregative frames. Not only do monisms threaten to drastically change life as we know it, but they also fail to reckon with common experiences of love, grief, regret, disappointment, admiration, reverence, and worship. We live lives full of plural values that refuse aggregation and a single scale.

The argument so far might seem to be making a case against commensuration of all values and, by implication, give ground to the claim that a pluralist theory of value opens the door for the incommensurability of

[14] Farneth, *Hegel's Social Ethics*, 32.

values. This line of argument might go as follows. A pluralist theory of value requires that different goods are the object of different evaluative attitudes that cannot be reduced to a single scale of value. So far, so good. A pluralist theory of value, it is then claimed, opens the door for two (or more) goods to be incommensurable because there exists no common measure. Incommensurability, here, entails incomparability, where goods are of neither lesser nor greater value, of different scales, and there is no way to compare them. How does one compare the value of friendship with the value of money or professional success? This latter step is a more complicated matter and opens a whole host of questions, one of which might be whether we can integrate incommensurate, sacred values into our deliberations at all. (Are sacred values—as incomparable, incommensurate values—always decisive in choice decisions?) I think monists are wrong to try to compare all values on a single scale. But I don't think incommensurability is the scary goblin some make it out to be. The problem of not being able to compare diverse values need not always be feared. We are equipped with a whole host of evaluative attitudes and expressive resources such as grief, regret, and loss in situations of incommensuration. There is good reason to refute the specter of incommensurability. Figuring the political role of sacred value in social practical reasoning helps bring incommensurability down to earth, so to speak, and helps us organize with it.

The Problem of Moral Horror

Robert Adams's theory of the morally horrendous argues that we find the Nazi practice of making lampshades out of human flesh morally horrendous because it violates an image of God, not because it breaks social boundaries.[15] Moral horror has to do with the ontology of a thing, not the blurring of socially established boundaries. For Adams, his metaphysical ethical theory picks out the *nature* of what we hold sacred by selecting the *role* of a finite instance's resemblance and faithfulness to the Good as God. The excellence of finite things is their resemblance to God, which is not entirely distinct from (but not reducible to) excellently sharing properties of God that give God reasons to love that excellence. Our sense of the meaning of excellence picks out a role for the nature of the Good. When Adams speaks of the sacred

---

[15] Adams, *Finite and Infinite Goods*, 126.

value of human persons as images of (and thus faithfully resembling) God and the morally horrendous act of violating human persons, his defense of such claims depends on what he means by the resemblance, nature, and meaning of the Good, a framework I outlined in chapter 1.

Adams's work on moral horror has been a rare resource in a dry land of writing on sacred values in politics, but I argue that his account captures our political relationship to sacred value in terms of resemblance and faithfulness to the Good—terms that connect with his metaphysical realism that I find ill-fitting to my organizing experience. Still, grasping Adams's account helps to make clear the importance of my own social practical one. Adams's metaphysical realism fails to capture the grief and sense of loss that is expressed when the imam responds to the rabbi. The imam is drawing on a range of action- and non-action-guiding evaluative attitudes, while continuing to recognize the authority of a tradition's precedent of reasoning for himself and his community.

Unsurprisingly, Adams is doubtful that we can provide an exact account of what the sacredness of a person consists in—say, in terms of only rationality or embodied consciousness.[16] Adams believes that our sense of sacred value is more successfully approached through the experiences of what he calls moral horror.[17] Our experiences of moral horror point us to a more objective sense of the "contours" of the image of God, that at least includes rationality, but Adams also thinks it has to do with our emotional, embodied lives. He "trusts" our experiences and concepts that provide us with a "grip" on our concept of sacred value, but our concepts fail us in identifying the nature of sacred value.

To experience moral horror is to suffer the violation of what we hold sacred. A violation is a serious and direct attack on the person.[18] What is needed is something about the nature of the bad, not the wrong. Now, Adams is quick to highlight that he does not favor a Manichaean division between the good and the bad. The bad is to be understood in terms of the good; it is to attack or be against the good. Something deeper takes place in a horrendous act of violation, however, than a simple infringement typically accounted for in our sense of a wrong. Adams thinks we are familiar with this distinction

---

[16] Ibid., 116.
[17] Ibid.
[18] See ibid., 107–12. Adams says that there are two conditions for violation: (1) an attack on the person, (2) which is serious and direct. See Decosimo, "Killing and the Wrongness of Torture" for a distinction between a violation and a destruction of a sacred value.

between the "bad" and the "wrong." We need to simply reflect on the different emotional responses to wrong actions as opposed to those that Adams is calling horrendous or bad. We are shocked and disgusted by horrendous acts; wrongness certainly provokes outrage, but not the sort of passion associated with an experience of violation.

That the horrendous is not captured in terms of "wrongness" becomes more obvious when we consider two further points. First, it is possible to consider something horrendous without thinking the action morally wrong. This is because, second, the horrendous "has what [Adams is] tempted to call a metaphysical depth."[19] The metaphysical depth arises from the violating of the nature of something that has sacred value. It is a direct and serious attack on the nature of the thing that resembles the good as God. Take the example of killing of a person, which is still a violation and thus a bad, but is not always a wrong.[20] The "metaphysical depth" is best explained by Adams's metaphysical claims to the nature of the finite things that resemble God. Wrong actions do not seem to merit the metaphysical depth and the distinct range of passion of the horrendous because they do not attack or stand against the nature of the Good in finite instances.

Adams is talking of horrendous actions, not horrendous people or the horrendous as a form of being. As such, these actions are primarily "signposts" to sacred value; they help pick out a role of the nature of what we hold sacred. The feeling of horror, Adams says, "is rather to be taken as a signpost to an objective fact that is independent of it."[21] This does not mean that our conceptions of the sacred and the horrendous are all the same across time and place. Our understandings of what we hold sacred are "culturally variable."[22] It follows, then, that the morally horrendous is better approached by paying attention to those specific passions provoked by the horrendous, that exceed our cultural conceptions of right and wrong.

By Adams's lights, sacred value gains a strong sense of objectivity due to the universal yet culturally variable expressions of moral horror. This is because we take the actions of horrendous evils to be objectively bad, aside from social standards. The morally horrendous is not a matter of blurring or breaking social boundaries and norms. The horrendous is a signpost of

---

[19] Adams, *Finite and Infinite Goods*, 107–12.
[20] Ibid., 105. "Even those who believe, as most people do," Adams says, "that there are at least a few circumstances in which it is right to kill another human being are apt to feel a metaphysical shudder, so to speak, at any prospect of doing it, and rightly so."
[21] Ibid., 106.
[22] Ibid., 116.

the sacred apart from what our current social boundaries deem to be wrong or right; it follows, then, that the nature of the resembling excellence can exceed our current conceptions of what is "right" while also being conceptually linked to its meaning. Rightness and the good have a complex and overlapping relationship.

Consider that the imam holds his concept of marriage as a sacred value, the violation of which he would deem morally horrendous. Adams's work here is crucial: we are not speaking of horrendous people, but horrendous acts. But Adams's approach to sacred value through moral horror quickly falls short. It fails to highlight the degree to which the imam's action is a *social* practice—that his reasoning takes place within the authority of other reasoners he recognizes and in which he wishes to continue to be recognized. Adams certainly recognizes that our concepts of moral horror are culturally variable, but a deeper account of how moral horror and sacred value are evaluative attitudes grounded in social practical reasoning helps make sense of the fuller range of emotions and reasons the imam voices in this exchange. To weigh the relevance of this point, consider how alternative figures from other religious traditions, like a Catholic priest, would be in similar positions as the imam. For leaders of other communities that are not as racially, economically, or ethnically marginalized as the Muslim community is in Nashville, the choice situation looks different.

But perhaps the conflict, continuing to follow Adams's thought in another direction, is merely a matter of right and wrong and not a horrendous violation of sacred value. One of the political fears of sacred values is that they tend to heighten and amplify emotions, therefore preventing people from reasoning and compromise.[23] Sacred values are flash points, so the objection goes; it is better to lower the heat and approach the conflict not as a matter of sacred value and moral horror but as an issue of right and wrong. Perhaps, to turn to Adams again, there is not a "shudder" of metaphysical depth in the imam's words. This might be a plausible response to our scene, but I think it gets things wrong not only for the imam but also for the rabbi. One persuasive reason why the rabbi put the imam in a difficult position in a public forum is because he felt this issue was not merely a matter of right and wrong but a matter of sacred value. Equally so, the imam did not give way to the rabbi's assertion of his value, when he (for that moment) chose to cherish

---

[23] This stance also implies that emotions are inherently unreasonable and ill-suited for politics. Besides the objections I give below, feminist philosopher Martha Nussbaum's *Upheavals of Thought* is a good example of why such an anti-emotional stances has its problems.

his community's theologically influenced conception of marriage over his relationship with the rabbi. As I have mentioned before, in this exchange the imam is reminded (once again) of his community's minority status. Framing this matter as an issue of sacred value helps to include in the picture these questions and to offer productive responses.

Adams is giving a Christian account, as I mentioned in chapter 1, but this need not be the only option for Christians engaged in interfaith organizing coalitions. In what follows, I offer my own social practical account of the political role of sacred value by outlining an account of social practical reasoning.

Social Practical Reasoning, Practices of Recognition, and the Ethical Life of Spirit

In social practical reasoning, our capacity for giving reasons turns on making inferential commitments when making judgments on and about objects in the world that stand in certain inferential relations.[24] This is just what self-conscious rationality consists in. The ability to make materially sound inferential commitments in our judgments entails agential responsibility and authority for other commitments about and of a world of objects and subjects that we take to be a certain way.[25] Such reasoning is normatively constrained so that we cannot, at the expense of being deemed irrational, take on materially incompatible commitments. Material compatibility refers to the ongoing inferential process and structure of social practical reasoning. It is another way of talking about what Hegel referred to as determinate negation. It helps explain how concept use brings along inferential relationships that include or exclude other concepts. In speaking of Nashville, my reasoning is constrained by the fact that the city is southwest of New York City. Everything else I say about Nashville should agree with that fact, or I need to correct a commitment or belief. Practical reasoning is mastering normative use of concepts and materially sound inferential commitments we are attributed and attribute to others by this practice. This understanding of concept use as entailing inferential commitments and responsibility means that

---

[24] Here, my reading of Hegel is influenced by Robert Brandom's reading of the idealism of Kant and Hegel in the first three chapters of *Reason in Philosophy*; as well as Dorrien, *Kantian Reason and Hegelian Spirit*, chs. 2 and 4 and *In a Post-Hegelian Spirit*, esp. chs. 2–4.
[25] Brandom, "Freedom and Constraint by Norms."

agents can be held accountable for concept use and the norms that guide discursive reasoning about the world. This is a social pragmatic approach to discursive reasoning, where meaning is defined through an ongoing inferential process and grounded in an inferential structure of relationships with others and the broader world.

Material incompatibility sits at the heart of Hegel's understanding of negation and mediation, and it is objective and subjective. Spirit moves by negation. As philosopher Robert Brandom persuasively argues, material incompatibility shapes up differently for objective and subjective poles: objective material incompatibility amounts to *relations* of inference; subjective material incompatibility amounts to inferential *process*.[26] This approach to the practice of reasoning stands in contrast with the traditional understanding of agents being directed by a superior to whom they are obedient, where sources or standards of normative authority are external to the community of individual reasoners.[27] Hegel teaches us that discursive reasoning depends on reciprocal recognition from other subjects and is expressed in history. Reasoning is diachronic, and previous concept use (and so previous meanings) constrain our own use.[28] His is a historical, social, and dynamic perspective. Hegel shows the openness of rationality. By grounding it in the ethical life of a community, practical reasoning is just as dependent upon an agent's taking up materially sound inferential commitments as it is on others attributing such inferential commitments to them. Practical reasoning is a social practice that is grounded in the ethical life of a community where normativity, responsibility, and authority all find their standards in the community's *social practice* of reasoning.

These points help reveal that the rabbi and imam are more than their individual selves as reasoners, and instead are participants in communities of reasoning to which they are accountable and for which they are responsible. For Hegel, the inferential social practice of practical reasoning doesn't get off the ground without recognition and determinate negation. Practices of recognition are crucial to social practical reasoning—Spirit moves through practices of recognition and determinate negation. But "Spirit" is a notoriously elusive

---

[26] Brandom, *Tales of the Mighty Dead*.

[27] As Brandom says, "The contrasting autonomy idea is that we, as subjects, are genuinely *normatively* constrained only by rules we constrain *ourselves* by, those that we adopt and acknowledge as binding on us" (*Reason in Philosophy*, 62, emphasis in original).

[28] "There is genuine room for choice on the part of the current judge or judger, depending on which prior commitments are taken as precedential and which respects of similarity and difference are emphasized" (ibid., 89).

term, and how an interpreter reads "Spirit" in Hegel tips readers off to larger interpretive stances. Thus, I need to make clear what I mean by my post-Hegelian account of Spirit and how practices of mutual recognition and determinate negation are opportunities for Christians to listen to the Spirit.

Listening to the Spirit is a Christian social practice. Thus it is a normative and ethical affair. For my purposes, "Spirit" in Hegel is ethical, social pragmatic, idealist, political, and theological. "Spirit" refers to the normative structure of reciprocal relations and the individual and collective inferential practice of reasoning. Reciprocal recognition gets Hegel's conception of individual and collective identity off the ground, but mutual recognition is a *social practice*: the human practice of determining conceptual content is a social, historical one, in which conceptual content is worked out through relationships of authority and accountability.[29] Unless we *count* as a fellow practitioner and mutually recognize others to count as such, the ethical shapes of Spirit are incomplete.

Spirit develops through mutual recognition and determinate negation. When Spirit's development is frustrated or incomplete, as imaged in Hegel's *Phenomenology of Spirit* by the figures of the lord and bondsman or in the wicked and judging consciousness (before their reconciling mutual recognition), our practice of determining conceptual content itself goes off the tracks, and—at least in Hegel's story—we remain in a lower shape of Spirit.[30] For Hegel, recognition is both an epistemic and a practical matter. As Farneth explains, "To recognize something is both to identify it (in an epistemic sense) and to bestow a status on it (in a practical sense)."[31] Recognition involves treating something as a "locus of authority and accountability," as a mediating self-conscious subject of intersubjective meaning—not as a mere object.[32] Evaluative attitudes like sacred values are a crucial part of this story of recognition because values are normative attitudes we take up and enact and others recognize (or do not). This is, in part, what makes the conflict with the rabbi and imam so relatable: the case puts forward the question of how and under what conditions certain members of our political

---

[29] Cf. Brandom, "Freedom and Constraint by Norms"; Brandom, *Tales of the Mighty Dead*, chs. 6 and 7.

[30] Cf. Dorrien, *In a Post-Hegelian Spirit*, 125: "Hegel argued that single individuals are incomplete Spirits. Even a robustly autonomous rational will is no substitute for social subjectivity. Genuine knowledge is earned only at higher stages of the coming-to-be of Spirit, which are social and spiritual." See Lewis, *Religion, Modernity, and Politics in Hegel*, 122–32; Lewis, *Freedom and Tradition in Hegel*, 34–39.

[31] Farneth, *Hegel's Social Ethics*, 57.

[32] Ibid., 58, 70.

groups *matter* in the relevant sense as authoritative bearers of values that are mutually recognized in the group. Deformed recognition of the imam is misrecognition of the imam himself as a bearer of such values. Reciprocal recognition is crucial for individual *and* social formation.

Some religious practices can be crucial human practices of mutual recognition in the story of Spirit.[33] In this book, I have made the case that the listening campaign and the relational meeting are religious practices due to the role of sacred values in those practices. In key moments of Hegel's story, as Farneth has highlighted, confession and forgiveness are sacramental practices that we individually and collectively take up and through which a new shape of Spirit emerges.[34] The role that practices of confession and forgiveness play in recognition's development will be instructive for us in gaining insight into how reciprocal recognition comes about in the relational meeting.

When I speak of listening to the Spirit, then, I mean to call attention to the way that our social practical reasoning is grounded in mutual recognition and determinate negation. Spirit in this sense refers to normative structure and the inferential practice of determining the meaning of our concepts. But I also mean more than this: mutual recognition can also be an experience of love, of grace, of God's Spirit transforming how it is we are with each other and how we are in the world. A spiritual, ethical bond is formed between those who mutually recognize one another. Spirit moves through and in between us, turning us inward and outward to encounter the other, beckoning us toward social practices of recognition. "The road to interiority passes through the other," one philosopher says of his Hegelian point.[35] This is often how people experience the organizing practices of the listening campaign and the relational meeting. They are surprised by how spiritual it is. When we engage in practices of mutual recognition like the relational meeting and the listening campaign we engage in forms of reasoning that connect us to others in moral, ethical, and theological ways. These bonds of love transform our own sense of self and our community. By framing organizing practices like the relational meeting and the listening campaign

---

[33] Cf. Peter Hodgson, "Editorial Introduction," 39: "When purity of heart is properly 'cultivated,' it issues in *ethical life*, which is 'the most genuine cultus,' but only to the extent that consciousness of God remains bound up with it. Thus social and political ethics represent an extension and 'realization' of the religious cults—a point that Hegel elaborates only at the very end of the lectures, in his treatment of the Christian cultus."

[34] Farneth, *Hegel's Social Ethics*, ch. 5; Farneth, "'The Power to Empty Oneself.'"

[35] Williams, *Hegel's Ethics of Recognition*, 49.

as religious practices because of the role of sacred values in the practices, we can see that broad-based organizing is fundamentally about building a democratic culture, of reweaving relationships of liberation grounded in practices of recognition.[36]

When the rabbi says to the imam, "Our religious leaders need to do a better job of welcoming our gay and lesbian neighbors," and the imam responds to the rabbi by saying, "For me and my community, it was a sad day," they are engaging in their own social practical reasoning of sacred value. The imam is recognizing certain evaluative values as having authority over his own life and practices; he is claiming that such precedents also hold authority over the community he recognizes and which recognizes him. But he is also recognizing that other communities value things differently. Social practical reasoning takes place in relationships of power, and my account of the political role of sacred value presumes radically democratic political conditions that I will outline in the next chapter. But figuring the political significance of sacred value first requires that we understand the role of sacred value in our political discourse, as it plays out, for example, in quotidian scenes like the imam and rabbi exchange that started this chapter.

Spirit is driven by mutual recognition and determinate negation. For philosopher Robert Williams, "recognition is a mediated self-coincidence made possible by and conditioned on allowing the other to be what it is, a letting the other go free.... The recognition that is needed and really counts is one that is not at the disposal of the self. The self depends on and is bound up with an other that cannot be cognitively or emotionally mastered."[37] Social practices of mutual recognition and determinate negation (material incompatibility) actualize and concretize Spirit. Ethical life depends upon social practices of recognition.[38] Seeing practices of reciprocal recognition as constitutive of Spirit's emergence through determinate negation staves off any putative claims of Spirit as a transcendental unity that swallows up individuality.[39] Spirit needs to be actual in the life of people for it to continue its development. Individuality is only a social ethical possibility.[40]

---

[36] As I noted, my account of how mutual recognition and determinate negation are crucial aspects of the relational meeting depends on a particular reading of the role of religious practices of confession and forgiveness in chapters 6 and 7 of Hegel's *Phenomenology*. This reading is largely indebted to Molly Farneth's analysis in *Hegel's Social Ethics*, chs. 4 and 5.
[37] Williams, *Hegel's Ethics of Recognition*, 57
[38] "Recognition is the medium in which and through which ethical life is constituted" (ibid., 77).
[39] Ibid., 80.
[40] Ibid., 80–81.

When people engage in the relational meeting, they create the possibility of mutual recognition. In what follows, I briefly outline, with help from Williams and Farneth, how mutual recognition and determinate negation play out in the relational meeting. By showing how reciprocal recognition is a potential outcome of a one-on-one, we gain epistemic, practical, and spiritual insight into the practice of the relational meeting. We see just what is at stake in this organizing practice. We also concretize the conversation around practices of recognition in social practical reasoning and can therefore more easily apply this post-Hegelian frame of social practical reasoning to the conversation on broad-based organizing and the rabbi and imam example.

As I argued in the previous chapter, the organizing practice of the relational meeting and the listening campaign are lived religious practices because of the role of sacred value in these practices. They are social practices that communities take up to listen to what they hold most dear and to identify what they are willing to do to fight for and protect them. They are human practices through which social practical reasoning takes place and in which reciprocal recognition can be accomplished. But reciprocal recognition cannot occur in conditions of domination, where either party is one of two positions in a relation of domination. When an arbitrary power is able to exercise its will over another, domination exists; the prototypical relationship here is master and slave. Even with a benevolent master, the slave is still dominated. For reciprocal recognition to occur, participants cannot assume either the position of the "slave" or of the "master." One cannot assume that they are the self-sufficient authority of moral and ethical reasoning without accountability ("master"); nor can they assume they are the sole accountable party without authority ("slave").[41] Being neither "slave" nor "master," one is invited into a different sort of ethical form of intersubjectivity, a different shape of Spirit.[42]

Consider what happens in a relational meeting when someone is asked to tell a story about why they hold something sacred. In these exchanges, people are invited into the actualization of their individuality, which is possible only by referencing their formation in and through communities.[43] It should be obvious that this form of individuality is not *individualism* but a

---

[41] Cf. Farneth, "'The Power to Empty Oneself.'"
[42] Pinkard, "What Is a 'Shape of Spirit'?"
[43] Williams, *Hegel's Ethics of Recognition*, 80. Williams's account outlines four features of recognition, but I do not claim that all features are necessary or sufficient for reciprocal recognition to play out in the relational meeting. Instead, my account depends more on the role of confession and forgiveness as Farneth argues in "'The Power to Empty Oneself'" and *Hegel's Social Ethics*.

social view of the self. Through this story work people can craft a narrative identity of how they came to be who they are, what they care most about, and why they hold certain things or people sacred. But reciprocal recognition is not guaranteed. People could easily assume one of the one-sided characters of the master or slave (all authority and no accountability; all accountability and no authority). Practically, if someone does not assume any accountability, they could reject the invitation. I have seen this happen in relational meetings: people demur, avoid, ignore, or outright refuse the invitation to share in this vulnerable way. Or, if someone does not assume any authority, their story lacks individuality; I have witnessed this too, when people in the meeting will not offer any reflection on the sources of their beliefs or values, or appear uninterested in such reflection. In this case, it appears as if the individual has not done the necessary reflective work to consider themselves a source of authority and accountability. In both cases, recognition is deformed, and the relationship breaks down. The meeting tends to lead nowhere.

When individuals are asked to craft a narrative of self in a relational meeting, the organizer or leader listening to the stories needs to take these accounts *seriously*. This means that I see the other as an authority of moral and ethical standards. Practically, this does not mean that I take as "Gospel truth" everything that someone tells me, but it does mean that I take them to believe what they say and I pursue their reasons why. The person listening probes deeper into these stories, asks *why* they value certain things in the way they do. Taking someone seriously means that I recognize you as an ethical authority for certain norms, that I hold you responsible to and accountable for those norms, and I see myself as an adequate judge and fellow reasoner.

Let me give a small example to illustrate. In a recent relational meeting an organizer challenged me to give an account of why I believed that as a Christian I am called to work for relationships of liberation and love. After explaining that I believed the Christian community is called to transgress unjust social, economic, and political boundaries that exploit and dominate the love and justice humans are due as children of God, he asked me, gently but with force, "So, what boundaries have your transgressed?" I paused; it took a moment for me to find my feet, so to speak. Then I offered a reply that recounted the relationships I formed in organizing. In this particular case, I told stories about my experience organizing with Muslim communities in the South. Building economic and political power in exploited and marginalized communities, grounded in relationships of solidarity, I argued, involves transgressing racial, religious, economic, and political boundaries. By asking this question, my counterpart was asking me to give an account, to hold myself responsible to others, and to release any sense of ethical or moral self-sufficiency. The form of his question communicated that he took my original claim seriously. In my response, I opened myself to criticism, became vulnerable to his judgment. His question is an invitation—an invitation to build relational power by opening oneself to another and to be transformed by mutual recognition.

This story work is vulnerable, hard work. It is an act that bares aspects of one's story to the listener that are seldom told in public. And such a gift creates the possibility for a powerful relationship, grounded in reciprocal recognition. When someone asks why I care about my sacred values, they are asking for reasons and narratives that authorize and give an account of such values. Such a request can be rejected as I outlined in the paragraph above; these are the most tender moments of the relational meeting because these stories can also stir up trauma and hurt, so recognition is not guaranteed. But Hegel sees a power in the vulnerability of mutual recognition, a power that is relational power, not unilateral or dominating power.[44] This is the sort of power that grounds the practice of broad-based community organizing.

Williams argues that mutual recognition requires ethical love; I agree. There is a deep relationship between Hegel's conceptions of love and the ongoing practices of Spirit.[45] In the relational meeting, such stories need to be held with a sense of ethical love—that is, a love that empathetically honors and values the individuality of the person testifying.[46]

Exchanges like the one I just recounted occur often in relational meetings; they are the crux of the matter, where people are invited to testify to the values they hold most dear and to give an account as to why they care so much about what they do. In so doing they establish a relationship with their counterpart because both parties can mutually recognize the other as a locus of authority and accountability. Through this recognition, Spirit emerges into a new shape. The logic of this exchange mirrors that of the sacramental practices of confession and forgiveness that Farneth claims are crucial to the emergence of absolute Spirit in Hegel's *Phenomenology*. For her, confession

---

[44] Farneth, "'The Power to Empty Oneself,'" 169.
[45] Henrich, "Hegel and Hoelderlin," 151.
[46] "Love does not produce a fusion with or absorption of the other. As we shall see, love overcomes not otherness per se but enmity, conflict, and estrangement" (Williams, *Hegel's Ethics of Recognition*, 81).

and forgiveness are sacramental practices that Hegel uses to illustrate how two shapes of consciousness (what Hegel comes to call the wicked and the judging consciousness) mutually recognize each other and how absolute Spirit emerges out of this reciprocal recognition.[47]

The religious and theo-logic at work in practices of recognition is crucial. Confession and forgiveness exemplify a form of *kenosis,* or self-emptying, that allows for mutual recognition. Confession, here, does not mean a humiliation but a release from any pretense to epistemic or subjective self-sufficiency.[48] By confessing, one acknowledges "[one's] particularity, recognizes the legitimacy of the other's judgment, and gives up [one's] false claim to self-sufficiency. [One's wicked consciousness's] confession sets the stage for the reconciliation of the two consciousnesses and the appearance of absolute spirit."[49] In other words, when I take someone seriously, I take them as a locus of authority and accountability and I release any pretense of my own epistemic or practical self-sufficiency. We are both in positions to testify and judge, mutually held together in a relationship of reciprocal recognition that builds relational power. Spirit's movement builds relational power.

One of the points of the relational meeting (and the listening campaign, for that matter) is to weave a relational fabric out of which political and economic power can be built. Relational meetings mean to break people out of their isolation and connect people to take powerful public action. By telling our stories we move private pain into the sphere of public action. We realize that our stories are not ours alone but are shared, and a collective emerges out of which action can be taken. The listening campaign seeks to reweave the relationships within and between our institutions of a broad-based organizing coalition in order to win political and economic freedoms. Wins are gained, in part, by building relational power. In philosophical terms, relationships of reciprocal recognition build relational power. They are nondominating, built on "humility without humiliation," as Farneth puts it.[50] But such storytelling requires determinate negation—individuality, not individualism. As we engage in the process of telling our stories, of determining our identity as distinct from others—as not *mere* difference but *actual* difference grounded in determinate negation—we create the ethical conditions

---

[47] Farneth, *Hegel's Social Ethics*, 72–90.
[48] Williams sees a similar aspect of reciprocal recognition but names it "release" (*Hegel's Ethics of Recognition*, 82).
[49] Farneth, "'The Power to Empty Oneself,'" 166.
[50] Ibid., 158.

for social freedom. As Williams says, "What is *lost* in mutual recognition is egoism and the desire for domination; what is gained through mutual recognition is substantive ethical freedom and community with other[s]."[51]

Reciprocal recognition requires individuals to trust their own and others' authority as bearers of ethical and epistemic standards and to hold themselves accountable to the relevant communities of practice that constitute the relational fabric making such inferential practices possible. Confession and forgiveness are actual human practices that Hegel found best exemplified in the Christian community.[52] Ethical life is achieved when a community fosters ongoing social practices of mutual recognition that allow absolute Spirit to emerge. This step of recognition is Spirit's recognition that it is an I that is a We and a We that is an I. Freedom here is social and intersubjective from the beginning. The sort of ethical community that fosters such freedom does "not absorb or reduce individuals to some homogeneity but rather presupposes, requires, and accepts individuals in their differences."[53] Unity is established in and through difference.

Recognition that is established through the relational meeting forms an ethical community that can foster relationships of liberation and love—love that is grounded in individuality, in the worth of one's story, experience, and values, which is possible only because individuals come from communities that form and shape them. The process of recognition itself is built into social practical reasoning because such a community mediates our selfhood and provides us with a language to tell our stories in the first place. As we tell these stories we depend upon inferential practices of reasoning insofar as we recognize others as bearers of the community out of and through which we identify ourselves. The relationships of love and liberation that are established through the practices of mutual recognition are mediated through relations of inference and inferential practices of social practical reasoning.

For Christians engaging in this work, the relationships of love and liberation that grant mutual recognition can also been seen as gifts of the Spirit. Spirit is self-moving. Recognition is not guaranteed. But the spiritual bond that can be established through the one-on-one can be experienced as Divine gift and the storytelling work can be captured in terms of testimony. Spirit graces the participants, ethically transforming their relationship in and

---

[51] Farneth, *Hegel's Social Ethics*, 82.
[52] This leads Farneth to see confession and forgiveness as sacramental practices grounded in Lutheran theology.
[53] Farneth, *Hegel's Social Ethics*, 84.

through their actions, connecting them together, helping them to co-create a vision of social freedom possible only because they build relational power grounded in sacred values.

The reason the relational meeting is the bread and butter of BBCO is because it is meant to be a daily practice, something done over and over and over again. It is a practice, not a science. Hegel's social practical account of reasoning is grounded in communities of reason, and the Christian tradition provides practitioners with language to which we are held accountable and for which we are responsible; it helps us make sense of the pursuit of goods and values Christians hold sacred. Innovation and revision of this language is possible, but only within limits, and such revision is always laid within relations of power. When the relations become skewed and recognition is not achieved, domination raises its ugly head. My account of recognition in the relational meeting presumes radically democratic political conditions within the BBCO counterpublic, and I outline those conditions in the next chapter.

Hegel's socializing and historicizing of practical reasoning opens the possibility for conceptual improvisation because agents mutually recognize one another and hold each other accountable to social, historical, and normative constraints. Humans often make mistakes in their practical reasoning, in their application of concepts. Failure and fallibilism are basic to the ethical life of a community. This is not a view that baptizes the status quo or cements conventionalism, as some have thought.[54] Sometimes we fail to recognize how one concept commits us to others or how one concept precludes previously accepted attitudes.

Conflicts of incommensurability like the one between the rabbi and imam are not isolated incidents, but such conceptual conflicts (between diverging interpretations of the meaning of marriage, say) are entangled with a whole host of inferential relations and processes. Incommensurability is a fact about our world: humans are lovers who cherish different goods differently, and some of these goods they hold sacred. But these sacred values are connected to a web of other values and goods and experiences that help us figure their proper role in our political life.

An age-old organizing adage is relevant here: when in doubt, do a one-on-one. We need to understand the accompanying emotions and inferences concomitant with sacred values. The rabbi and imam example puts deformed

---

[54] For an account of these critiques of Brandom and Hegel see, Springs, "Dismantling the Master's House"; Farneth, *Hegel's Social Ethics*.

recognition on display. To repair the relationship, to organize with sacred value, a relational meeting could be held between the rabbi and imam to build a deeper relationship between them to hold the difference that exists. This is a very Hegelian point: determinate difference is a relationship—a very deep one, that should not be ignored.[55] The more we ignore such conflicts, the more they will bubble up in unfriendly places. We did not anticipate the rabbi's statement, but organizing takes place in time, by which I mean that the deformed recognition that occurred here will reverberate throughout their relationship and even impact others. The relational ripple effects of the deformed recognition need to be dealt with. Organizers should not ignore the source of incommensurability. To repair the relationship and reestablish recognition organizers need to organize with sacred values. As I've tried to show, the relational meeting opens the possibility of recognition in deep difference. BBCO itself has the tools that can hold such tension and determinate difference. Conflicts of sacred value *are* relationships. More than this, offering recognition in determinate difference is key to building relational power, which is necessary for diverse constituencies to achieve political and economic wins. We are better off if we understand the broader social practical picture of these conflicts and organize with them.

Our Political Relationship with Sacred Values

We are now at a place to proffer a political role of sacred values grounded in an account of social practical reasoning. By outlining the political role of sacred values in social practical reasoning, we can gain a firmer grip on how evaluative attitudes like sacred values impact our political and economic life in a way that will shine light on the conflict between the imam and rabbi. To do that I need to state what I mean by calling sacred values evaluative attitudes and how they are situated in social practical reasoning.

To start, I need to clarify that implicit in this account of social practical reasoning and mutual recognition is that *experiences of value* and *evaluative attitudes* are different in important ways. I can at first value something in a certain way and then later judge it differently. Suppose I was completely

---

[55] As Farneth says, "Absolute spirit does not eliminate conflict; rather, it is characterized by agonism, ongoing difference, disagreement, and struggle in the context of reciprocal recognition, punctuated by moments of reconciliation" (*Hegel's Social Ethics*, 99).

unfamiliar with jazz. At first, I find the music confusing, unpleasant, or haphazard. Later, after being educated in the social practice of jazz, the necessary virtues and skills needed to perform a good jazz solo, I then judge the music beautiful and pleasing. Or say that I laugh at a tasteless joke and later, after consideration and reflection, realize my error in embarrassment. Our experiences of value express first-order attitudes, experiences, and emotions. But this is not the same thing as valuing something. To express an evaluative judgment directs my care and concern about the action, object, or person. Our evaluative attitudes are "second order attitudes, or attitudes about other attitudes."[56] Judging jazz music as beautiful or a tasteless joke as not genuinely funny helps to illustrate the difference between experiences of value and our evaluative attitudes. Practical reasoning guides our aims and considerations in the world. Evaluative attitudes are attitudes we take up toward objects, persons, and states of affairs in the world.

Not all judgments of evaluative attitude need be action-guiding. Judgments of value such as regret or luck need not guide action, but can instead guide the expression of that value and still be justified.[57] The agent's valuations are justified insofar as the agent's expressions are in accord with their rationally established social norms. Consider situations where we take an action out of our control or we wish was not the case, and rightly feel a sense of regret. Cases of regret help illustrate the importance of non-action-guiding evaluative attitudes.

There is a sense, here, of the objectivity of value, but without requiring the existence of a structure of value that is *completely independent* of our social practices. I want to emphasize the *interdependence* of our evaluative attitudes, the normative nature of social practical reasoning, and the conditions in the world.[58] Value in my account of social practical reasoning allows for a qualified realism. Because our social practical reasoning depends on a set of inferential relations and through an ongoing process of inferential giving and asking for reasons by which we are held accountable and responsible, we can say that value exists in the world regardless of whether we accurately recognize it. Other views—either monist or pluralist—that may run the gamut from irrealism to metaphysical realism miss the social pragmatic nature of

---

[56] Anderson, *Value in Ethics and Economics*, 3.
[57] Cf. Williams, "Moral Luck."
[58] Cf. Johnston, "Objectivity Refigured"; Smith, Lewis, and Johnston, "Dispositional Theories of Value," esp. 170–73. But note that my theory of value does not need to follow Johnston's "response-dependent" account outlined in these articles.

reason-giving.[59] A person has a valid reason to value something if certain standards of reason and conditions in the world are met and they rationally express such an evaluative attitude.[60]

Criticism about the establishment and upkeep of such norms and reasons are a welcome enterprise, as the following section will show. Indeed, this is the value of critiquing the social construction of class, race, and gender categories: if our social practice of reasoning itself becomes dominating or exploitative, we have good reason for radical revision. We have norms that guide our evaluative attitudes in a similar way as norms guide our behaviors and emotions. Social practices and the sustaining institutions serve to establish social norms that guide our sense of practical appropriateness or inappropriateness. Think of the various social norms for women. An additional group of social norms can be listed based on racial and class classifications; another list of norms can be given as intersectional analysis unveils continuing and ever shifting degrees of exploitation, expropriation, and domination. There are good reasons to criticize these institutions and their pedagogy of appropriate womanly behavior, attitudes, and concerns, say. But a thing's goodness does not depend on our ability to perceive its goodness. Nor are our evaluative attitudes infallible. Fallibility and a sense of qualified realism are important to my account. When we talk about the nature or meaning of value in our evaluative attitudes we are interested in what they mean to us.

The plurality of goods in the world means people will care about things in different ways and for different reasons; the rationality of our evaluative attitudes depends on the socially established norms for rational expression. Social norms and ideals are normative for how we engage in social practical reasoning.[61] Without social norms, our deliberation about the appropriate reasons to justify our concerns and attitudes would be adrift, moved only

---

[59] I agree with Anderson when she claims goodness as a "function of an object's relation to rational principles," principles which meet certain social norms and conditions in the world that support our endorsement of our evaluative attitude (*Value in Ethics and Economics*, 94).

[60] "Express" here returns us to points regarding the inferential process of social practical reasoning. Even if someone has a valid reason for acting, but they communicate such a reason in a way that doesn't align with the objective inferential structure or subjective inferential process, we would deem that person's expression as going against rationally established social norms that guide our actions.

[61] Anderson, *Value in Ethics and Economics*, 24: "Recall that the plurality of goods arises from the fact that people care about different goods in different ways, care about the ways they care about goods, and institutionalize different ways of caring about goods by embedding them in distinct social practices of production, distribution and enjoyment. These social practices are governed by norms that highlight some features of the goods in question as important for action concerning them and subordinate others."

by individualist nonrational moods, motivations, desires, wishes, and so on. The normative practice of rationally valuing different goods differently is a social process: such reasons, attitudes, and concerns have little meaning outside of social deliberation.

Social practices are social because they are based in shared assumptions, norms, patterns of behavior, and goods internal and external to the practice itself.[62] Often, social practices become part of broader cultural institutions, which can work to cultivate the goods internal to a practice, thereby fostering and cultivating virtues that serve to realize the internal goods. Here, social structures are collections of social practices. Habit and intentionality can and do go together in this account, where reasoning takes place in time and makes possible the critique of our social practices based on normative analysis of that very practice. Our social practices, the institutions that hold them, and social practical reasoning itself are not naturally immune from criticism. A Christian practice may be racist, misogynistic, or dominating of the vulnerable, and so we can critique such a practice on its own Christian terms and norms of justice and love. The claim that theology is socially constructed is a welcome one in this account. Theology is fundamentally about human responses to God's action and so liable to the sin of being twisted and deformed into dominating practices. Yet, as human responses they are also open to virtuous and right worship and praxis.

Social practices are not hermetically sealed off from the broader context, setting, other practices, or evaluative attitudes.[63] We hold each other accountable and responsible for our actions and evaluative attitudes. If someone fails to value something appropriately, a recriminating behavior follows. As writers on feminism, race, and class have shown, there are resources in social practical reasoning for radical criticism and revision.

Ethicists who are concerned to illustrate the social nature of reasoning can turn to immanent criticism, adjacent social practices, or other social norms to radically criticize examples of injustice and domination. Theories of value that emphasize similar points emphasize that "individuals are not self-sufficient bearers of practical reason: they require a context of social norms to express their attitudes adequately and intelligibly in action, to express them in ways others can grasp."[64] This *interdependence* explains the role

---

[62] For works in religious ethics that have influenced my own take, see Stout, *Ethics after Babel*; Stout, *Democracy and Tradition*; Bush, *Visions of Religion*, esp. part 2; Farneth, *Hegel's Social Ethics*.
[63] The implications of this point for religious ethics is addressed by Bush, *Visions of Religion*, ch. 7.
[64] Stout, *Democracy and Tradition*, 18.

of norms in social practical reasoning while illustrating that this theory does not need to cede ground to conventionalism. Social practical reasoning is constantly open to criticism and revision. In a world of plural goods, an account of social practical reasoning and evaluative attitudes like sacred value aptly explain and justify why one option is higher than or preferred over another. Such an explanation is interdependent with social practical reasoning, the norms guiding the reasoning, and the conditions in the world constitutive of available options.

Our political relationship with evaluative attitudes like sacred value is thus deeply set within the broader inferential structure and ongoing inferential process of social practical reasoning. We seek to protect and fight for what we hold sacred because we have good reason to value those goods and people in the way we do. They are relationships we have reason to hold dear in a world of plural goods, and we cherish them in the way we do for good reason. This goes to the heart of this book's argument: to exclude sacred value from politics asks people to lop off part of their individual and collective life; it limits the frame of politics and ignores the reality that people are formed in and through communities and construct their identity through a range of social practices, some of which circulate around, trade in, and depend on sacred values. We have to see people as whole people: participants in historical communities, which are bearers of social practical reasoning. Traditions and norms that have been built up around such evaluations guide people's daily action. Conflicts of sacred value (and by extension incommensurability) are common to our world. But social practical reasoning is equipped with resources and practices to help situate such conflicts in a broader narrative. Specifically, for our case of the rabbi and imam, BBCO itself cultivates certain practices of reasoning and recognition—religious practices like the relational meeting—that open up the possibility for recognition in (and *not* in spite of) deep, determinate difference.

What's left for organizers to do when faced with conflicts of sacred value? Even when conflicts like the rabbi and imam are reframed and reestablished within their social, historical relationships, are they bound to their polarized positions? I think not. Incommensurability may be a common fact of our political life, but it need not haunt our politics, for two reasons. First, social practical reasoning, especially in practices like the relational meeting, allows for mutual recognition under conditions of deep difference. Second, and this goes to the core of my project, revision of positions is possible. Social change is possible. It does not come quickly, but this means that we have a different understanding of the conflict of the rabbi and imam. No longer are we stuck with the sense that they might be cultural warriors locked in their positions. Instead, we see them engaged in a long conversation within their own community about what they value and why, and what they are willing to do with others to protect and fight for all the many goods they value differently. The relationship that can be established here, when recognition grounded in difference of sacred value is achieved, is stronger because of the differences.[65] What is more, such relationships build relational power, which lies at the heart of BBCO. In the final section of this chapter I explore how radical criticism of our traditions can and does take place, by learning from similar work on race, gender, and class. I then follow through the implications from this account to our conception of religious identity.

Radical Criticism of Social Norms, Christian Religious Identity, and Sacred Value

In recent decades, philosophers of race and gender have powerfully and convincingly demonstrated the way socially constructed gender and race ideals and norms form and shape our world.[66] Some scholars, inspired by more postmodern arguments, have also claimed that race and gender are socially constructed. Yet in academic and popular discourse to say that something is socially constructed does not immediately or necessarily provide insight into *how* or *what* is socially constructed. Moreover, too often constructivist arguments fail to illustrate the *realness* of these constructs or the *purpose* of constructivist arguments.[67] Constructivist arguments contest a kind's inevitability and naturalness. The world is not (and need not be) the way it appears.

When I claim that gender is socially constructed I do not mean merely to say that the concept of gender is socially informed, that it is not natural or inevitable. I mean at least two more things. First, in some cases, like gender, race, and class, it is to say that our world as built around these concepts and in reference to them is bad as it is. Second, in those cases of domination and

---

[65] What the BBCO counterpublic decides to take public action on is a subject of my next chapter, but my account of social practical reasoning presumes radically democratic political conditions between members of the group. If the group consistently dominates one faction of its constituency, then it no longer remains democratic.

[66] This section is largely built off of the insights of Sally Haslanger's work. Especially *Resisting Reality* and "What Is a Social Practice?"

[67] Cf. Hacking, *The Social Construction of What?*, esp. ch. 1.

exploitation, it is to say that we would be better off if gender, race, and class were not the way they are now.[68] Agency is navigated through our social practice of reasoning and a matrix of relationships that is pervaded by power. Individuals change their behavior to incorporate and embody socially established norms and ideals (individual women acting *womanly*; individual men acting *manly*). Feminist critiques, for example, can thus be leveraged at the ideals themselves that authorize the normative behavior instilled in individuals. When counterpublics develop new ways of talking about their ideals and norms that they hold themselves accountable to and authoritative for, they can begin the process of building relational power to shift the broader social, political, and economic power relations that uphold unjust norms and ideals embodied in social structures and institutions.

Talk of social construction like this often trades in social kinds. Race, class, and gender are socially constructed yet real by claiming that class, gender, and racial identities are *social kinds*, in the relevant sense that a grouping or type shares a unity of some sort. In this way the members of a group all share an *objective reality*. Such a unity of the objective type holds independently of me. This way I can distinguish objective types that share a common unity apart from other objective types in the world. Things can be more or less strongly unified in such a way to constitute a type. Talk of social kinds is based on a notion of realist social constructivism, where realism refers to reality in the relevant sense of independence.

Gender, race, and class are social kinds. The racial type "white" is a social kind in that whites share a certain unity with others that objectively sets white people apart from others. To be white is to occupy a certain racial, social, political, and economic position in U.S. society, but it is also to embody certain norms and expectations about what are appropriate attitudes, actions, and concerns for white people.[69] Whiteness as an objective social kind also involves being physically marked by a society denoting superiority. Social kinds are not mutually exclusive, where racial, gender, and class social kinds can work intersectionally to expropriate, dominate, or exploit people. Multiple subordinate social kinds can reinforce and implicate each other to further subordinate and dominate certain positions in society. A number

---

[68] These qualities are built off Hacking's first chapter in *The Social Construction of What?*, where they are mentioned explicitly. See esp. 5–14. But such points are evident in Haslanger and the work of many other feminists.

[69] Haslanger, *Resisting Reality*, 227–39. For a good example of this, see how the legal construction of whiteness becomes a form of political and economic expectation in Harris, "Whiteness as Property."

of recent theorists have followed this intersectional line of thought, either by defining "class" as a relational category, by analyzing race and gender together, or by examining how race and capitalism are interwoven.[70] Thinkers in the Black radical tradition and the radical social gospel continually saw (and still see) how categories of difference and value develop together, so that to speak of capitalism today is to speak of a racialized economic order built on economies of desire concretized in heterosexist patriarchy.[71]

Norms guide behavior, but they are not inevitable or natural. Social kinds may serve to select out shared unity, but they are revisable and negotiable. The social kinds of racial, gender, and class types are not fixed. For example, consider the varying and contested meanings of "class" as primarily referring to either income, social status, or power.[72] This is the point of speaking of broad-based organizing constituencies as counterpublics that are discursive arenas that contest domination or exploitation, by inventing new discourses or building economic and political power to change the social conditions. This approach to social constructivism and social kinds allows us to illustrate the way that this constructivist viewpoint still seeks to track properties in the (social) world.[73]

But this is not a theory that proves how our concepts track the "joints" of *nature*, so to speak. Social constructivists help us to see the social forces that act as intermediaries with a world independent of us. Such constructivist arguments help us see how our social practices are "world-involving."[74] This means at times our social practices create situations of injustice and domination in our material world. Allowing that there might be an independent reality does not mean that we can access it without intermediaries such as language. Such a move places the debate of the status of such a reality on a political plane where dialogue and contest take place between *norms*, and not direct, certain, and definitive epistemological claims to the way the world really is.[75] The status of norms is contested in our social practices,

---

[70] Good examples of defining class as a relational category are Gerteis, *Class and the Color Line*; Rieger, *Theology in the Capitalocene*. Of those who analyze race and gender together, see Alcoff, *Visible Identities*; on race and capitalism, see Du Bois, *Black Reconstruction in America*.

[71] Crenshaw, "Mapping the Margins."

[72] For an account that advances a relational understanding of class as power, see Rieger, *Theology in the Capitalocene*.

[73] Cf. Kukla and Lance, "Intersubjectivity and Receptive Experience." See also Haslanger, "What Is a Social Practice?"

[74] Haslanger, *Resisting Reality*, 25.

[75] Ibid., 155.

the values we accord to our practices, and the world in which they are interdependent.[76]

Our evaluative attitudes are guided by ideals and norms that train and shape our behavior; social practical reasoning is pervaded with personal and social power, meaning, and experience. Our evaluative attitudes are not natural or inevitable. And some of our evaluative attitudes, namely those at which feminist, racial, and economic justice concerns take aim, are unjust and dominating when they arbitrarily interfere by disciplining, shaping, or denying the agent's own social practical reasoning. Our sense of how individual women and the ideal of woman are socially constructed provides important leverage points. We can now grab hold of and pull down these dominant and hegemonic ideals that normatively govern our sense of appropriate and inappropriate valuations. Such a move is crucial to contest their inevitability or naturalness. We can tell different, emancipatory stories of self and community, and we can build the sort of power needed to materialize such stories.

This approach breaks open the potential evaluative range of gender, racial, and class identities. Gender, race, and class identities still exist in socially, politically, and economically established institutions and relationships that make progress slow, and materially significant when it does occur. But the relations of power, semantic meaning, and the material world that limit our future improvisations are basic to reinterpretations of social ontologies—and the evaluative range therein—of gender, race, and class identities. Liberation is not easy to come by because domination is very real and powerful. We cannot proffer new understandings of gender identity, say, that completely transcend our historical and normative context, so as to be wholly unaffected by our social positionality. It requires great collective effort and the building of social and political power to shift the scales in the directions of justice.

I want to end this chapter by returning to the conflict between the rabbi and the imam to draw a few final lessons for the relationship between sacred value, community organizing, and Christian social ethics. This social practical account avoids a debate on whether sacred values are secular or religious. Such distinctions, as I outlined in chapter 1, fail to appreciate how such categories are themselves socially constructed, how such social kinds

---

[76] As Sally Haslanger writes, "Practices shape us as we shape them. This provides resources for understanding why social practices tend to be stable, but also reveals sites and opportunities for change. (Challenge social meanings! Intervene in the material conditions!)" ("What Is a Social Practice?," 231).

are in relation to other social constructs like race, gender, and class, and the power relations that undergird such constructions. By focusing on certain evaluative attitudes like sacred values, we can bring our attention to religious identities and religion as it is lived on the ground, and inductively draw inferences from such examples. This is why the case of the imam and rabbi is so valuable: it helps us see how religion and politics are already deeply interwoven in supposedly secular spaces. Sacred values play a large role in our sense of religious identity because sacred values are crucial plot points in constructing a narrative of our religious identity.

Let us say that "Christian" is an objective type. There is enough unity in the variety of application and use to provide for objectivity in the relevant sense. One factor of unity is the obvious point that a Christian is a member of the religious tradition, whether Catholic, Protestant, or Orthodox. But there are further inferential commitments that can be attributed to someone who claims to be a Christian: certain beliefs about Jesus, God, the Christian Bible, the Christian church. There need not be complete consensus about the status of each of these claims; in fact, controversy and conflict are common, but there is little disagreement on what things are of significance, regardless of the status of the significance. Christians tend to argue about the meaning of Jesus's life, not the life of Diana, Princess of Wales. For some, this disagreement and argumentation is part of what makes Christianity a tradition.[77] I take it that claiming the objective type Christian involves internalizing certain normative standards. There is such a thing as Christian valuation insofar as Christian is an objective type with normative attitudes and behavior and concerns. Recently, Jonathan Tran has illustrated the power of Christian critique of racial capitalism and the potential of thinking theologically about racialisms in late modern capitalism.[78] This turn in theology finds its origins in Black radical thought and thinking theologically about *Christian* identity.[79] Christian critique as I mean it here is itself a vibrant voice in the debate on what it means to be Christian.

That someone identifies as Christian gives them a reason to value certain things as sacred. Christian sacred values are held to certain rational

---

[77] Alasdair MacIntyre's work is exemplary here in defining a tradition as an argument in and throughout time. See his *After Virtue* and *Whose Justice?*
[78] Tran, *Asian Americans and the Spirit of Racial Capitalism*.
[79] See Political Theology Network, "Perspectives on Asian Americans and the Spirit of Racial Capitalism" on the book. For more on what I mean specifically by Christian identity for Tran and his metanarrative, see Stauffer, "Attuning the Church, Debating What Lies beyond Racial Capitalism."

standards normatively established in the tradition.[80] But the tradition, and such rationally and normatively established evaluative attitudes, are always open to contestation and transgression. I want to be clear, however, that saying someone holds something as sacred is not an endorsement of that evaluative attitude. This is where the example of the rabbi and imam is again helpful: the imam and rabbi hold differing conceptions of marriage, and both of them hold their conception as sacred. I do not endorse the imam's conception of marriage, but still claim he has reasons within his tradition to value marriage as he conceives it as sacred. Claiming that someone holds something as sacred and endorsing that evaluative attitude are two different things. I can recognize that someone holds a certain evaluative attitude, that someone holds something as sacred, and recognize the reasons why they do so, without agreeing with such an evaluative attitude. This is what mutual recognition (if such recognition is reciprocated) in deep difference is all about.

What is more, my social practical account places fallibility and corrigibility at the center of our practices of valuing something as sacred. Even if we hold something as sacred, we can still be mistaken. This is why my account prizes criticism of norms and ideals that guide social practical reasoning. Both the rabbi and the imam, as participants and authorities of traditions of social practical reasoning, can be invited to revise their position (no easy task). But we cannot expect the imam to adapt to the rabbi's "liberal" view so quickly. The norms that guide his community are different and powerful. But this does not mean that there are not alternative standpoints within his own tradition. Social practical reasoning is a contestable process all the way down. This does not mean we cannot judge his position, but it does mean that true recognition requires we see him as an authority of epistemic standards and accountable to that ongoing social process.

The evaluative attitudes of sacred value are part of being accountable and responsible for the Christian tradition in social practical reasoning. Christians make sense of such evaluations by narratively positioning such evaluative attitudes and their own valuing self in such a way as to cohere with the broader tradition (or in critical relation to it). What is unique about my contribution to this conversation on social practical reasoning and the social construction of religious identities is the crucial role of sacred value.

---

[80] In *Theology without Metaphysics*, Kevin Hector gives a similar, social practical account of the Christian tradition and Christian theology, one that takes inspiration from Friedrich Schleiermacher's theology.

The religious identity of Christian is socially constructed. Such evaluative attitudes of sacred value are germane to this ideal, whose rational expression is normatively guided. My emphasis on social construction and the interdependence of our social practices and the material world allows for a qualified realism of value, as I've spoken of it in this chapter.

Not all our evaluative attitudes need to guide action: situations can be unfortunate, tragic, or horrific precisely because we are prevented from protecting or revering things we hold sacred. Situations of regret are aptly described as regretful because we have not revered such values appropriately. We rightly feel a sense of failure when we fail to value what we hold sacred and instead devalue those things or persons. We grieve when we face situations where we are forced to sacrifice what we hold sacred. Crises of identity occur when we inappropriately sacrifice values held sacred. Regret, failure, grief, and identity crises can all be non-action-guiding evaluative attitudes. Yet even in these instances of non-action-guiding values, sacred values are still crucial to our sense of self and our judgments in the world. At other times our valuations do guide our action in influential ways. We need to pay attention to the myriad ways plural values conflict and how our evaluative attitudes guide action or characterize the particular choice situation.

The world does not conform to our ideals, and so abiding by normative attitudes, actions, and concerns is not always easily accomplished. Practices, norms, and values that are unjust and dominating ought to be challenged by other Christian norms of social justice. The plural theory of values helps us see that the specter of incommensurability need not haunt our choice situations. Furthermore, the practice of the relational meeting uniquely equips organizers with a practice of mutual recognition in deep difference that is crucial to the ethical life of a community and social practical reasoning. What is more, my post-Hegelian account of social practical reasoning deepens my account of how such practices of recognition like the relational meeting are religious practices, because of the role of sacred values. When Christian congregations engage in relational meetings, they are listening to the Spirit. When diverse constituencies engage in this work, they open up the possibility for mutual recognition and thus deeper relational power building in deep, determinate difference.

What the ideal of Christian normatively judges as sacred guides our evaluative attitudes of sacred value. Critical revision is possible and at times required by other Christian norms of justice, love, and equality. The contestation and debate that characterize the social and historical process of social practical reasoning mean such evaluative attitudes are not inevitable or natural. In the next chapter I will explore how it is that democratic constituencies can navigate these tragic conflicts. But organizers do themselves no favors to ignore these deeply held values, and their role in religious identities, or in our collective political life.

4
Radical Democracy and Sacred Value

Democratic politics is typically captured in campaigns focused on single issues. BBCO, however, is more closely aligned with radical democracy as an ethical way of life. This kind of organizing is "relational organizing" that, as sociologist Mark Warren says, brings people "together first to discuss the needs of their community and to find a common ground for action."[1] BBCO is first and foremost about organizing the relationships and values of working people for greater democratic power in their communities. The value-laden relationships are enacted through a political culture consisting of radically democratic social practices.[2]

This chapter elaborates the political conditions that are implicit within my social practical account of the political role of sacred value and social practical reasoning. To do that, I will turn to how counterpublics like BBCO affiliates habituate individuals in radically democratic social practices and what political conditions are required for individuals and groups to engage in an ethical way of life free of domination, exploitation, expropriation.[3] I have a particular interest in showing how the political culture of radical democracy is lived out in BBCO and that it not be prejudiced against sacred values commonly held dear by religious political participants. Sacred values are an important part of the political cultures of counterpublics embattled in some of the most urgent political fights of our day. To make this case I turn first to John Dewey's thought on democracy. But there are particular problematics that exist in Dewey's thinking of the political, namely with stark challenges in our time regarding the role of power in democracy and the dangers racial capitalism poses for radical democracy. Sheldon Wolin's democratic theory might be one source to address these problematics, but his notions of "democratic fugitivity" and his "politics of tending"—two key concepts

[1] Warren, *Dry Bones Rattling*, 31.
[2] Portions of this chapter appear in print as "Radical Democracy and Sacred Values: John Dewey's Ethical Democracy, Sheldon Wolin's Fugitive Democracy and Politics of Tending, and Cornel West's Revolutionary Christianity," *American Journal of Theology and Philosophy* 42.2 (2021).
[3] In chapter 1 I offer some commentary on the significance of counterpublics in BBCO.

in Wolin's democratic thought that are basic to my own concept of radical democracy—ultimately fall short, too, if such concepts are not made to address the deep levels of domination, exploitation, and expropriation caused by racial capitalism. My reading of Cornel West's work helps to address these shortcomings in Dewey and Wolin and in so doing come to terms with the way the everyday patient work of BBCO recasts Dewey's and Wolin's theories of radical democracy. Bringing BBCO together with Dewey, Wolin, and West generates a unique theory of radical democracy that is capacious enough for political struggles involving sacred values and honest enough about racial capitalism and power in democratic life.

Democratic Individuality, Sacred Value, and Political Culture

To be radical, democracy must start at the root of our associational life, asking questions about the kind of persons and power formed within groups. This ethical conception of democracy places a premium on democratic individuality and each individual's potential for political participation.[4] Democracy as merely about institutional arrangements or states of affairs is too "external" for Dewey. Democratic societies arise from personal "ways of life" and "habits."[5] To say that democracy is "social" and "ethical" means that democracy exists as a form of government and in its institutions only insofar as it exists in the "dispositions and habits" of its groups and individual members.[6]

Democratic individuality requires individuals take responsibility for freely made choices that are possible only in association with others.[7] Dewey is concerned about cultivating a democratic society grounded in self-reliant individuality.[8] The heart of the ethics of democracy is democratic individuality, a form of association that Dewey defined as "having a responsible share according to capacity in forming and directing the activity of the group to which one belongs and in participating according to need in the values

---

[4] Rogers, "Democracy, Elites and Power," 86.
[5] Dewey, "Creative Democracy," 226.
[6] Ibid.
[7] Ibid., 244.
[8] The reference here to self-reliance hints at the influence of Ralph Waldo Emerson on Dewey, as pointed out in a number of Dewey's best interpreters, including Cornel West, Jeffrey Stout, Melvin L. Johnson. Cf. Dewey, "Emerson."

which the groups sustain."[9] My sense of democratic individuality is built on work done by Dewey, Wolin, and West, and my own contribution to this conversation will develop slowly throughout this chapter as I correct and affirm aspects of radical democracy in those three thinkers.

Democratic individuality depends on a certain definition of freedom as a nondomination, which draws from a civic republican understanding of freedom.[10] It is contrasted with alternative definitions of negative or positive freedom. Negative freedom posits an arena of personal freedom that is free from interference. Coercion, then, involves an infringement upon an individual's arena of agency. Negative freedom is most often found in "freedom from" discourse. Positive freedom, by contrast, is most often found in "freedom to" discourse and is conceived primarily as self-development, as autonomy, as being one's own master in pursuing one's goals. Positive and negative versions of freedom imagine the unfree individual as bound and gagged. In both of these versions of freedom it is possible to conceive of a free person as having a benevolent master. By contrast, the democratic individual is free in the sense of nondomination. Domination exists when someone is in a position to *arbitrarily* exercise their own will over someone else. Masters dominate and the dominated individual is prototypically imagined as the slave. Democratic individuality cannot exist even with benevolent masters.

Democratic individuality is required of individuals who engage in social practical reasoning that depends on mutual recognition and determinate negation.[11] Reciprocal recognition requires individuals to trust their own and others' authority as bearers of ethical and epistemic standards and who hold themselves accountable to the relevant communities of practice that constitute the relational fabric making such inferential practices possible. Recognition that is established through the relational meeting forms an ethical community which can foster relationships of liberation and love. By "individuality," I mean to call attention to habitual character formation and formation of selfhood that is possible only in certain kinds of associational life.[12] Individuality, here, is contrasted on the one hand with individualism,

---

[9] Dewey, *The Public and Its Problems*, 175.

[10] Cf. Berlin, *Liberty*; Pettit, *Republicanism*. See also Rogers, *The Undiscovered Dewey*, esp. ch. 5.

[11] I define "determinate negation" in terms of material compatibility. An inference is materially sound when the contents of the concepts are not excluded by the inferential process of social practical reasoning. Social practical reasoning is normatively constrained; material compatibility has to do with the content of the concepts, not with the form of, say, a sound syllogism. Determinate negation helps explain how concept use brings along inferential relationships that include or exclude other concepts.

[12] See also Bush, *William James on Democratic Individuality*.

which assumes that the self is an atom isolatable from its surrounding material reality and the relationships that support its life and, on the other hand, with forms of group life that dominate the individual person (groups that can have individuals who are "free" either in the negative or the positive sense).

Democratic individuality not only emphasizes responsibility for freely taken choices in society but also raises the challenge of self-reliance over against a culture of conformity. Social practical reasoning gets off the ground when subjects take themselves and others as loci of authority and accountability. This social view of the self raises the possibility that one's values and interests cannot be realized or accurately recognized until one cultivates and establishes relations that are free in the sense of lacking domination in arbitrary influence over one's life. One way of putting this kind of responsibility in a democratic community is BBCO's term "self-interest."

Democratic politics, as I define it, is fundamentally about the collective pursuit of the common good. One's self-interest is a crucial part of democratic politics because self-interest, as Jeffrey Stout writes, "is the interest that everyone who wishes to avoid domination has in the common good."[13] Self-interest is a crucial part of democratic individuality as it requires recognizing one's responsibility for, accountability to, and participation in the broader democratic community. Democratic individuality is crucial to overcoming certain political deformations in our collective life, but such overcoming is possible only by reflecting on the values and relationships that make such a politics possible in the first place.[14] Self-interest properly understood (not either selfishness or altruistic do-gooderism) has a "real depth" and is most accurately pinpointed when the individual's good is identified with the community's good.[15]

Democratic individuality requires individuals take responsibility for freely taken choices that are possible only in association with others.[16] Ethical and social democracy is primarily concerned with the kinds of individuality habituated in associational life. Radical democracy needs to be grounded in what Dewey's forerunner, the proto-pragmatist and philosopher of democracy Ralph Waldo Emerson, called "self-reliance."[17] Dewey's

---

[13] Stout, *Blessed Are the Organized*, 41.

[14] Romand Coles looks to the Latin to highlight the relational root of self-interest (*inter esse*, meaning "between-being"): "[A]t the same time that a focus on self-interest propels the cultivation of self-recognition, respect, and determination, this focus on self-interest also propels us into receptive political relationships with others" (Coles and Hauerwas, "Of Tensions and Tricksters," 288).

[15] See Wood, *Faith in Action*, 189–91.

[16] Dewey, *The Public and Its Problems*, 244

[17] Dewey, "Emerson."

attention is attuned to the democratic ways of life that are habituated in groups, but also with the quality of communication present in associational life between publics. Ethical and social democracy "is not an alternative to other principles of associated life. It is the idea of community life itself."[18] To think of the ethics of democracy is to turn, first, to the conditions of self-actualization and social practical reasoning present in our society and, second, to the quality of the social practices and the values attended to in each group. Some of these values present in BBCO counterpublics are sacred values and play an especially important role in the radically democratic social practices of BBCO.

To accord something sacred value is different from claiming it is "the sacred." Such values are evaluative attitudes grounded in the broader practice of social practical reasoning. Social practices are social because they are based in shared assumptions, norms, practices, and goods internal and external to the practice itself. A social practical account of evaluative attitudes claims that reasoners are held inferentially accountable to fellow reasoners and responsible for their concept use. The ethical life of Spirit—a post-Hegelian term I use to refer to the ongoing inferential process and structure of relations of social practical reasoning—moves through mutual recognition and determinate negation. Reciprocal recognition, as it occurs in the life of Spirit, is an experience of love that transforms our sense of self and builds relational power. But recognition is possible only if reasoners trust one another, take each other as sources of authority and accountability for Spirit's development. When Christians engage in the listening campaign or the relational meeting, they are listening to what they hold sacred and attending to how Spirit is moving them to act in public life. Such a norm-driven account need not baptize the status quo or tend toward conventionalism, nor is it inherently conservative. Critical revision of such norms and ideals that guide our concept-use can be radically revised only within certain limits. To be a participant in a larger tradition you need to become familiar enough in the social practice of practical reasoning so that others can recognize your concept-use as following along in the same way as the relevant precedents.[19] A social practical account of evaluative attitudes like sacred value grounds the practice of valuation in time and space; it allows for fallibilism and

---

[18] Dewey. *The Public and Its Problems*, 175.
[19] Cf. Brandom, *Tales of the Mighty Dead*, esp. chs. 6 and 7. See also Hector, *Theology without Metaphysics*.

constructivism of our norms and ideals, thereby also allowing for the possibility of radical revision of norms and ideals.

What is unique about my contribution to this conversation on social practical reasoning is the explicit connection between BBCO, sacred value, and radical democracy that extends and refines Dewey's and Wolin's theories of radical democracy through conversation with West. For my part, that someone identifies as Christian gives them a reason to value certain things as sacred. Christian sacred values are held to certain rational standards normatively established in the tradition. Individual Christians, as Christian, stand in certain relations of judgment as to appropriate action, attitude, and concern between other Christians and to others outside their religious and ethical community. As the tradition has developed throughout time, normative standards of Christian sacred value have developed and individual Christians have taken these norms as authoritative, incorporating and embodying these standards of value in their everyday lives. But contestation and revision go all the way down in this view; radical revision within certain limits is possible. Social practical reasoning is set within power relationships, which can be transformed. Counterpublics, as dialogical arenas that can invent discourses to redefine social meanings and material conditions, exert new meanings in conditions in the world that uphold social structures and institutions that are collections of social practices.

A social practical account of sacred values requires certain political conditions to avoid domination as arbitrary influence. Domination occurs when someone has the power to arbitrarily influence another. In my account we owe one another justifiable reasons for our actions and concept-use, and others hold us accountable and responsible for those reasons. Reason giving acts as a constraint against domination. BBCO builds political and economic power to add further constraints.

One way that Deweyan radical democracy trains our attention to the quality of the social practices and values is by asking us to think about *political culture*. Democratic political cultures consist in and foster relationships grounded in habits and social practices that were first born in the life of local groups and associations.[20] It is crucial to see that the political culture (the habits and social practices of a public) of radical democracy is value-based.

Democratic habits are instilled in the members of a democratic community, but they are not merely rote activity. Individuals are habituated into

[20] Dewey, *The Public and Its Problems*, 209–11.

the customs, mores, and norms of groups. Habits establish the "objective conditions which provide the resources and tools of action, together with its limitations, obstructions and traps."[21] Habits of thought and action, like social norms, discipline and shape individuals, but they are equally sites of critical revision and targets by movements for social change: "Emotional habituations and intellectual habitudes on the part of the mass of men create the conditions of which the exploiters of sentiment and opinion only take advantage."[22] Democracy as a habitual way of life has to do with what democracy looks like—the "emotional habituations and intellectual habitudes"— that each public instills in its members.

The political culture of BBCO counterpublics consists of democratic individuals, each a part of a larger relational fabric, enacting this ethical way of life in habits of thought and action. To speak of the political culture of these counterpublics is to say certain actions and values are permissible while others are not. This is why, as sociologist of religion Richard Wood writes, value-language is the "first-language" of organizers, and this language is carried in "specific symbols, stories, songs and institutions of the divine."[23] Those values and their "carriers" are not disconnected from democratic habits that make up the basic work of organizing accountability sessions and listening campaigns, collecting voter data, mobilizing neighbors around a specific platform during a neighborhood walk, or engaging in issue-related research.[24] The habitual life of a constituency reveals the deep connection between collective values and self-interest, political culture and democratic individuality.

The political culture holds the broader narrative of who we are, what we care most for, and what we are willing to sacrifice for those sacred values or do in public to protect them. Paying attention to political culture helps us see how value-work pervades democratic habits and practices. Too often we fail to notice the role values play in BBCO and instead focus only on political issues. This leads to a vision of democracy as merely a state of affairs or institutional arrangement and not as an ethical way of life.

Take the example of how the Gamaliel affiliate Nashville Organized for Action and Hope (NOAH) organized a collective response to the police shooting of a young unarmed Black man in the summer of 2018. On July

[21] Ibid., 186.
[22] Ibid., 192.
[23] Wood, *Faith in Action*, 179.
[24] Ibid.

26 a police officer fatally shot Daniel Hambrick in the back as he was fleeing for his life after the police illegitimately stopped him to supposedly investigate a stolen vehicle charge. At the time of Hambrick's murder, NOAH was already engaged in a number of research actions on police activity and practices in Nashville, but they had not taken public, confrontational action. Tim, the white middle-aged organizer for NOAH, recounts how NOAH's tactics shifted after a video was released detailing Hambrick's brutal murder. "We had to do something," he explained. "This was here, this was our city."[25] Angela, a Black organizer for NOAH, agreed: "With this particular situation it was a case where 'enough is enough' and it was time to make a response."[26] Soon after the video was released NOAH held a press conference issuing a public statement with three primary demands: (1) the immediate dismissal of the chief of police; (2) mayoral endorsement of the Community Oversight Board, a citizen-led effort to establish a police oversight board; and (3) expedited deployment of body and dash cameras throughout the Metropolitan Nashville Police Department.

In order for NOAH to issue the public statement a quorum of its sixty-three member institutions had to adopt the statement. A board meeting was called to discuss the demands. For Tim, this sort of discussion was truly unique after a horrendous shooting: "Where else in the city was that discussion going on—particularly with white and Black groups in the same meeting? Where was this kind of representation?"[27] That meeting, for Tim, was NOAH living out a democratic political culture, expressing its values in dialogue, discussion, negotiation, and contestation. The cultivating of this political culture is hard won. In the face of death-dealing racial capitalism, solidarity is not easily gained, but when it is, when people build relational power grounded in sacred values, it is to be cherished. Angela recalled a particularly important moment: "In the past NOAH has always done a good job of responding strategically. But I remember one point brought up during that meeting was that we can't keep making strategic plans while people lay dead in the street."[28]

NOAH's statement was not successful in removing the chief of police, but perhaps it is best to see this action's purpose as that of ratcheting up the political pressure on the police chief, while leveraging the group's values and

---

[25] Interview with author, October 11, 2018.
[26] Interview with author, March 4, 2019. Name changed to ensure anonymity.
[27] Interview with author, October 11, 2018.
[28] Interview with author, March 4, 2019.

self-interest in the public arena. NOAH as a group decided that the shooting of Hambrick violated a value they held sacred, that of Black life, and as Angela said, "Enough is enough." The violation of their sacred value clarified their self-interest. The political culture of NOAH—enacted in this example through habits and practices like debate, discussion, disagreement, and negotiation—allowed the group to act in a publicly powerful way. They acted because a sacred value within their political culture had been violated.

Examples like NOAH illustrate that the ethical life of radical democracy inside counterpublics is just as important as the quality of democracy in the broader political context. In *The Public and Its Problems*, Dewey argues that ethical and social democracy is grounded in a theory of publics making judgments about and taking action on interests that concern them. Publics are groups formed around "the perception of consequences which are projected in important ways beyond the persons and associations directly concerned in them."[29] Two crucial points follow from Dewey's concept of "public" that are relevant for our conversation on radical democracy and BBCO. The paragraphs that follow offer a different—although related—account of radical democracy in BBCO than the consociationalism that Luke Bretherton has recently offered. Although I am broadly in sympathy with his consociationalism, in *Resurrecting Democracy* Bretherton builds his account off a rendition of Carl Schmidt's "friend-enemy" distinction and in conversation with Jeffrey Alexander's work on the civil sphere, whereas mine is built off a social practical account of sacred value, democratic individuality, counterpublics, and political culture.[30]

First, radical democracy as I envision it claims that there is something fundamental to the Spirit of radical democracy in face-to-face encounters. Dewey was certainly clear that publics consist not only in "face-to-face relationships" and "immediate contiguity." There are ethical lessons for democracy that cannot be captured except in the kinds of community found most prototypically in groups like BBCO counterpublics. "There is no substitute for the vitality and depth of close and direct intercourse and attachment," Dewey teaches us.[31] The local community is the "home" of ethical and social democracy.[32]

---

[29] Dewey, *The Public and Its Problems*, 87.
[30] An additional issue has to do with Bretherton's ecclesiology (Stauffer, "How Do Christians Practice Democracy?"). See, Bretherton, *Resurrecting Democracy*; see also Bretherton, *Christ and the Common Life*.
[31] Dewey, *The Public and Its Problems*, 229.
[32] Ibid.

This is clearly borne out in the fact that BBCO starts with local institutions and the practice of relational meetings—one-on-one meetings that establish a public relationship and provide clarity on mutual self-interest and the values that might ground and sustain participation in the BBCO affiliate. The first step in organizing is to engage in relational meetings. After enough relational meetings have been held, a connection can be formed between individuals and their institutions based on values and issues (indirectly or directly experienced), thus laying the groundwork for a new counterpublic to emerge.[33] The political culture of BBCO counterpublics is pervaded by its members' faith and values. Publics, as Dewey helps us see, are groups formed around concern for and interest in "extensive" and "enduring" consequences by people directly and indirectly impacted by them.[34] BBCO constituencies are a specific sort of counterpublic insofar as they cannot be accurately classified separately as either a "secular" or a "religious" public.

By calling BBCO constituencies "counterpublics" I mean to complicate how we talk about religion and politics and thereby heighten the utility of a term like "sacred value" and its political role in our social practical reasoning in and between groups. But I also mean to call attention to the material, social, and political conditions that constitute the relationship between the counterpublic and that larger social arena. Counterpublics contest domination, exploitation, and expropriation of a group and those in solidarity with that group. Broad-based constituencies are counterpublics that attend to the dynamics of how power shapes up in our society: it builds relational power to counter the hegemony of heteropatriarchal racial capitalism. In racial capitalism, difference yields differential value.[35] BBCO builds relational power through democratic social practices like the relational meeting and the listening campaign, grounded in sacred values. BBCO builds solidarity through determinate difference in democratic individuality, a form of association possible only in certain ethical forms of community life. Social practical reasoning, as it moves through practices of mutual recognition like the relational meeting and the listening campaign, allows democratic individuals to

---

[33] What I mean by "enough" here varies by context and is a judgment of the organizer and leaders. Organizing is a practice, not a science.

[34] Dewey, *The Public and Its Problems*, 69, 87.

[35] Take, for example, the work of Lisa Lowe, herself deeply influenced by the Black radical tradition: "Elaboration[s] of racial difference were not universal or transhistorical; they did not occur all at once but were local, regional, and differential, articulated in dynamic interlocking ways with other attributions of social difference within various spaces in an emerging world system.... To investigate modern race is to consider how racial differences articulate complex intersections of social difference within specific conditions" (*The Intimacies of Four Continents*, 7).

attend to our varied subject positions in social, political, and economic life. Our unique circumstances, our determinate differences, enhance the Spirit of radical democracy. Determinate differences enrich the ethical life of radical democracy. BBCO builds relational power by engaging in practices of mutual recognition made possible by determinate differences. For Christians in this work, such practices can be seen as religious practices. The Spirit of radical democracy circulates through social practical reasoning and practices of mutual recognition of the relational meeting and the listening campaign. The solidarity of counterpublics constitutes relational power.

It is often said that BBCO has difficulty scaling up and cannot match modern state politics. The critique seems to be that BBCO is too local and cannot address political problems at the regional, national, or global level. There is some merit to this claim: some BBCO national networks seem allergic to sharing power; some BBCO networks have vested too much in the veritable claim that all politics is local. But BBCO has seen its organizing strategy win at the state level in harsh political conditions.[36] Doubling down on the lesson that relational meetings drive organizing, other BBCO networks are building national strategies and taking the social practice of radical democracy as an ethical way of life to federal levels.[37] More needs to be written on the theory of subsidiarity and BBCO organizing, but if such a subsidiary model is further incorporated, the BBCO networks will remain democratic only insofar as they habituate members into the social practice of radical democracy within and between its various publics.[38]

Second, publics are more than local relationships; they include those who are indirectly concerned with the "extensive and enduring" consequences and outcomes of certain actions.[39] A democratic public consists of responsible, free, and accountable individuals who engage in democratic habits and practices grounded in values and interests affected by the outcomes of "public" actions. Public actions—as opposed to private actions that concern only those directly involved—include those who are affected by "extensive and enduring" consequences of "transactions between persons in the *Populus.*"[40] People organize themselves into publics insofar as they seek to

---

[36] Warren, *Dry Bones Rattling* examines the success of the IAF-Texas network. In 2017–18 Gamaliel established two new affiliates in Tennessee, crucial steps to building a statewide network.
[37] Wood and Fulton, *A Shared Future* examines the national organizing strategy of Faith in Action.
[38] For a recent account of subsidiarity and broad-based organizing, see Hinze, *Prophetic Obedience*.
[39] Dewey, *The Public and Its Problems*, 69.
[40] Ibid.

care for and protect their interests and values that are indirectly affected by enduring and extensive consequences.

Dewey made much of the distinction between private and public. A democratic public could never renounce face-to-face relationships, but Dewey was wary of publics that remained too narrow in their relations or strict in their internal roles.[41] Take the patriarchal family, with its clear system of role classification based on gender, age, seniority; or take Dewey's example of a small village with intimate ties throughout where "the temper, the mood, the outlook of the individual and the village would be the same."[42] Dewey notes that in some associations "personal loyalties to elders take the place of political obedience."[43] Equally so, publics can be plagued by too strong a sense of group identity such that a public "has no appreciable consequences for an-other."[44]

Anthropologist of religion Mary Douglas would later elaborate and bring theoretical clarity to Dewey's inchoate intuition on these matters by identifying "grid" and "group" aspects of social identity.[45] "Grid" aspect refers to the internal order and the shared understanding that helps to order one's experience as a member of the group.[46] Social identities, however, are also informed by what Douglas came to call "group" aspect, which captures degrees of inclusion and exclusion in the boundaries of the group.

Publics vary in the strength and weakness of grid and group aspects. Attention to these two variables in our accounts of democratic publics, as one political theorist comments, "can help us to get an analytical grip on the salient identity-categories, their resilience and stability, and the social pressures associated with them, from one public to another."[47] It is true that grid and group help us think about social identities in a unique and apt way. More important, however, such a focus on grid and group also helps leverage normative critiques on the types of publics cultivated in a broader political culture.

---

[41] "There are those which are too narrow and restricted in scope to give rise to a public, just as there are associations too isolated from one another to fall within the same public" (ibid., 88). "Is it possible for local communities to be stable without being static, progressive without being merely mobile?" (228).

[42] William Henry Hudson cited in ibid., 89.

[43] Dewey, *The Public and Its Problems*, 89.

[44] Ibid., 90.

[45] Douglas, *Natural Symbols*, esp. ch. 4. My account of Douglas's formulation of grid and group and its relation to Dewey's account of democratic publics is informed by Isenberg and Owen, "Bodies, Natural and Contrived," esp. 3–8. See also Ward, "Public Reasoning and Religious Difference," esp. ch. 5.

[46] Isenberg and Owen, "Bodies, Natural and Contrived," 6.

[47] Ward, "Public Reasoning and Religious Difference," 214.

Douglas aptly captures my interest in applying grid and group to radical democracy and BBCO counterpublics when she says, "What it feels like to have other people controlling one's behaviour varies with the quality of restraints and freedoms they can use. Each social environment sets limits to the possibilities of remoteness or nearness of other humans, and limits the costs and rewards of group allegiance and conformity to social categories."[48] At a minimum, a focus on grid and group brings to the fore questions for BBCO counterpublics such as how affiliates decide (1) which issues are actionable, (2) which are winnable, (3) what values are sacred, and (4) what political conditions necessitate sacrificing certain group values and issues in the pursuit or protection of other values. In the NOAH example above we saw (1) the murder of an unarmed Black person, (3) Black life, and (4) though the chief of police was not dismissed, NOAH achieved its goal of ratcheting up political pressure.

This analysis of Dewey's influence on radical democracy introduces a number of crucial concepts and terms in thinking about radical democracy: political culture, democratic individuality, self-interest, democratic habits within and between publics, and democracy as an ethical way of life. As I will attempt to show in the conclusion, this focus on the *quality* and *character* of relationships that pertain to BBCO counterpublics helps to leverage the relevance of Christian critique in spite of a broader political culture dominated by heteropatriarchal racial capitalism.

Dewey's conception of democracy has drawbacks that need to be addressed, and in the following sections I do just that. For example, Wolin claims that Dewey's ethical democracy, for all of its moral and ethical power, depoliticizes democracy. Dewey is rather weak on ethical democracy's grasp of modern power, and his focus on inquiry and experimentalism reduces democracy to a "method of discussion." "The result," Wolin argues, "is to homogenize democratic action while stripping it of dissonance so that it merges with the ideal form embodied in the actual behavior of scientists. In the end Dewey's most crucial concepts—experimentation, method and culture—were ways of evading questions about power."[49] To Wolin, Deweyan radical democracy reeks of "methodism" that trivializes the drama and demands of theorizing that cannot be boiled down to methods of data

---

[48] Douglas, *Natural Symbols*, 63.
[49] Wolin, *Politics and Vision*, 517.

collection or communication.[50] Radical democracy needs to be freed of its naive assumptions that a correct method of inquiry will yield a political culture ethically and morally consonant with democracy. Instead of a toothless account of radically democratic political culture, Wolin turns to deeper criticisms of modern and postmodern power while offering his version of fugitive democracy as an ephemeral experience of commonality on the plane of the political. This attention to power is crucial for any theory of radical democracy—especially any theory that claims to wrestle with capitalism's late modern and neoliberal forms. But Wolin's thinking is not enough, either. His conception of fugitive democracy ends up being ephemeral and momentary. Still, a notion of fugitive democracy and a politics of tending are important additions to my conception of radical democracy. In the next section, I explore those concepts and recast them in my own theory of radical democracy. The penultimate section will turn to West's sense of prophetic Christianity and radical democracy, providing for me the final aspects of radical democracy I need to adequately address the domination, exploitation, and expropriation of racial capitalism.

Democratic Fugitivity and the Politics of Tending

Broad-based organizing is about building power for working people and their communities. As such, power sits at the center of my account of BBCO, but much depends on the sort of power I find praiseworthy (relational power, rather than unilateral, dominating power) and what communities hold the power (working people and those in solidarity with them). This sort of relational power is built in BBCO's Spirit through an ethical way of life that is radically democratic and found in the practices of mutual recognition like the relational meeting and listening campaign. Radical democracy's Spirit energizes, rejuvenates, and restores the ethical life of democratic politics of BBCO. Wolin, as a theorist of radical democracy, put power and pluralism at the center of his thinking, and he theorized them primarily through notions of economic polity, fugitive democracy, and a politics of tending.

Wolin's fugitive democracy, however, as it is experienced on the plane of the political, is different from democratic politics. The political is the plane of generality, the space where, Wolin claims, commonality is generated despite

---

[50] Cf. "Political Theory as a Vocation," in Wolin, *Fugitive Democracy*.

relevant differences and where the demos achieves a unity capable of powerful political action.[51] Here we have a contrasting account of the power of the demos: power is not built through solidarity within the demos grounded in mutual recognition of determinate differences. Much turns for Wolin on the difference between the political and politics. Politics is the activity of legitimate contestation between organized and unequal parties vying for access to the public resources available to political authorities. "Politics is continuous, ceaseless, and endless," Wolin writes. "In contrast, the political is episodic, rare."[52] In Wolin's larger project, it is the political as experienced by the fugitive demos that he is really after.[53] Fugitive democracy recalls and renews what it means to be the demos. As I will show, radical democracy as it is practiced in BBCO presents particular challenges for Wolin's account of fugitivity and his politics of tending. These challenges go to the very heart of his conception of radical democracy: the moments of solidarity established on the plane of the political and the temporality of what Wolin calls a politics of tending. And yet democratic fugitivity and a politics of tending are aspects of radical democracy that I want to embrace, but not without adjustment.

Recently Juliet Hooker has worked to "extend and sharpen" Wolin's conception of fugitivity by exploring Frederick Douglass's own wrestling with democratic and Black fugitivity.[54] Black fugitivity is a recurring theme within Black political thought, Hooker tells us, and Douglass squarely belongs in the tradition. This is because of Douglass's intimate understanding of the "necessarily different and fraught relationship of the enslaved to the rule of law" and the "fundamental" and "permanent" way that slavery has shaped "political subjectivity" for Douglass, thereby transforming the temporality and the actual practices of democratic politics. The tensions between democratic and Black fugitivity can be stark, but elements of both can be found in Douglass's life and work, which makes him a better partner than Wolin to today's democratic fugitives, "the DREAMers or Black Lives Matter protesters who enact exemplary democratic practices even as their status as citizens is precarious, and as their political activism renders them vulnerable to increased state reprisal."[55] Similarly, I work to recast Wolin's sense of fugitivity and a politics of tending in order to come to terms with radical democracy as it is practiced in

[51] Wolin, *Fugitive Democracy*, 100.
[52] Ibid.
[53] Ibid., 96.
[54] Hooker, *Theorizing Race in the Americas*, 29. See especially, ch. 1, "A Black Sister to Massachusetts."
[55] Hooker, *Theorizing Race in the Americas*, 32.

BBCO. Wolin and Dewey both provide crucial insights into radical democracy, but we'll need to turn to West's work to grasp the depth of structural white supremacy and power in racial capitalism. First, it helps to get Wolin's view out in front of us.

According to Wolin, a narrow focus on politics without the political has prevented political theorists from adequately assessing modern and postmodern forms of power. Modern power as it is embodied in the nation-state is primarily centripetal. The modern nation-state dominates political life, so that politics is merely electoral politics and opinion polls and is experienced through mass communication like TV and the internet. Citizens are more like subjects (not political agents) at the mercy of a virtual reality built on an inauthentic politics by lying politicians.[56] What was previously the public is now dominated by private interests and the free market, and so society is effectively depoliticized. All other aspects of life are to be placed under the logic of bureaucratization and rationalization of modern science.[57] But modern power has been eclipsed by a centrifugal manifestation of postmodern power that decenters state power without decentralizing it.[58] Postmodern power is both centrifugal and centripetal and thus totalizing. "What might be emerging in the United States," Wolin wrote in 1989, "is a new form of totalizing power that blurs the domination of the state by contracting its functions to the representation of civil society while at the same time the disciplinary procedures of society are being tightened."[59] Wolin would come to call this death-hold on political life "economic Polity," and later "inverted totalitarianism."[60]

The true loss at the advent of economic polity is the receding of a truly democratic political culture.[61] In economic polity all other social and political

---

[56] These themes of authenticity, truthfulness, trust, and virtual reality are large themes in Wolin, *Democracy Incorporated*, esp. chs. 10–13.

[57] Wolin, *Fugitive Democracy*, 318. In another essay in the same volume, Wolin names these three elements of modern power as the New Trinitarianism of modern power: "capital (the father), state bureaucracy (the son), and science (the holy ghost)" (354). See also Wolin, *Tocqueville between Two Worlds*, 17.

[58] Wolin, *The Presence of the Past*, 27.

[59] Ibid., 29.

[60] Wolin does not explicitly connect his earlier work on economic polity with his later work on inverted totalitarianism, but the two concepts share much: a focus on privatization of public goods, domination of politics by economics, an apathetic and naive citizenry. I stay with economic polity because it more accurately captures the core problem: the culture and politics of late modern capitalism.

[61] "The persisting conflict between democratic egalitarianism and an economic system that has rapidly evolved into another inegalitarian regime is a reminder that capitalism is not solely a matter of production, exchange, and reward. It is a regime in which culture, politics and economy tend toward a seamless whole, a totality" (Wolin, *Democracy Incorporated*, 269).

relationships are subverted and dominated by economic relationships that are shorn of their material and human roots. The economy is a form of political power that is completely autonomous, that simultaneously totalizes its power while running straight through limits of community, government, or territory previously thought to be secure. Economic polity is politics without the polis and is dominated by a corrupt political culture. Wolin's perspicuity into the nature of postmodern power forces radical democrats to contend with how late modern neoliberal capitalism exerts and sustains itself. Mere class analysis will not suffice to capture the intersectional and overlapping nature of power today, but too often, as Wolin helps us see, political analysis lacks any class analysis. Economic polity conceptually illustrates how economic and political power interact today. To counter postmodern forms of power, movements of radical democracy need to build political *and* economic power. And yet, as I will show, we need an intersectional analysis of power, one that Wolin's economic polity does not provide. We need to analyze how power shapes up in its myriad forms and articulations today. More than this, this power building needs to be set within a relational fabric and way of life that never loses sight of the humanity of the demos, of the democratic individuals who are the people.

Yet the archaic specter of a politics of countermemory, of fugitive democracy, haunts our reality.[62] The power of fugitive democracy is the genuinely alternative political vision imaged in the historical countermemory of the demos. By turning to the countermemory of the demos, theories of radical democracy ground their ethical life in the social practices of grassroots movements. This memory appears out of time and out of synch with postmodern power. It is a "new interpretative mode of understanding that is able to connect past and present experience."[63] Fugitive democracy seeks to play a whole new political game. It is "attuned to slower rhythms" than economic polity, Wolin tells us; fugitive democracy takes time. Political judgments and democratic deliberation that lead to "the likelihood of durability" emerge in their own time.[64]

---

[62] Interestingly, Wolin writes in a much less rosy manner about the "archaic" in *Democracy Incorporated* (see ch. 7) But my understanding of his turning away from the archaic is that in *Democracy Incorporated* the archaic has more to do with the specter of nostalgia deployed by political figures he deems to be players and architects in what he calls "inverted totalitarianism." The power of the archaic is still present in *Democracy Incorporated*; it is just that he sees it as dominated by religious conservatives and the radical political right.
[63] Wolin, *The Presence of the Past*, 141.
[64] Wolin, *Democracy Incorporated*, 267.

The metaphor of "players in a game" helps redirect my vision of radical democracy. The "rules" of our current political "game" are set by economic polity and rigged for corporate elites and increasingly deregulated financial capital flows. In this political landscape, citizens are more like "players" gambling not only their labor but their moral, ethical, human, and spiritual health.[65] Wolin's fugitive democracy changes the game by archaic moves, recalling democracy as grounded in a demos and a democratic political culture.

The Spirit of radical democracy arises through and in practices of mutual recognition within and between the demos. The time of radical democracy, when it is grounded in the experience of actual democratic fugitives, breaks with the logic and efficiency of postmodern power. When NOAH engaged in its internal debate as to what the proper response to the murder of Hambrick should be and then called for the firing of the chief of police, they were engaging in a form of radical democracy grounded in the memory of fugitivity. Democratic fugitivity keeps radical democracy radically democratic. As people who are dominated, exploited, and expropriated by racial capitalism build relational power, it is fugitivity that grounds the political culture in a subversive force, upending economic polity's hold on our political culture. As counterpublics build relational power through BBCO, they cultivate a political culture infused with a Spirit of radical democracy.

A politics of tending is crucial to the democratic political culture at the heart of Wolin's fugitive democracy and it is equally important for my account of radical democracy in BBCO. Fugitivity needs to be attended to, as our theories of democracy should never lose sight of those who are demoralized, crushed, ground up, and tossed aside by the wheels of economic polity. As I will show, however, Wolin's politics of tending and his fugitive democracy fail to adequately attend to late modern capitalism's racial order. In short, it is because Wolin is inadequately intersectional in his power analysis that I join others in describing our current form of late modern capitalism as racial capitalism rather than economic polity. To sustain a political culture that prizes and cares for democratic fugitives, counterpublics need to cultivate a Spirit of radical democracy that prioritizes democratic individuality and democratic fugitivity; it does this through a politics of tending.

---

[65] There is a particular postmodern subjectivity that Wolin investigates in nearly all of his writings on postmodern power. Take, for example, this description of the good citizen for economic polity: "[H]e or she is one who is mobile, who is willing to tear up all roots and follow the promptings of the job market" (Wolin, *Presence of the Past*, 45).

Pluralism and determinate difference are basic to a politics of tending. Tending implies attention to and care for "historical and biographical beings," Wolin writes, and so "proper attendance requires attentiveness to differences between beings within the same general class."[66] Tending to differences is inherent to radical democracy because it implies discussion and dialogue, contestation and negotiation. Here is where Wolin's concept of a politics of tending and mine part. For Wolin, differences do not remain on the plane of the political because fugitive democracy is "a recurrent aspiration."[67] Constitutionalism, which codifies and institutionalizes democracy, is the limit of and brake against fugitive democracy because founding moments of democracy are akin to revolutionary moments that give birth to the demos. Differences are politically relevant but only for politics, not the political, where differences are bracketed and a fugitive impermanent commonality lives.[68] For my part, fugitivity is a human experience of racial capitalism, which subsumes humanity and nature in its ever increasing desire for capitalist power and domination. Wolin's concept of the political silences actual experience of fugitivity that are given voice in democratic politics. I prize the messy, historical work of democratic politics and a politics of tending. Counterpublics like BBCO can foster and build the necessary relational power to counter racial capitalism by attending to democratic fugitivity in social practices of mutuality like the relational meeting and listening campaign. Radical democracy is Spirit-driven, as our social practical reasoning is grounded in relational power.

Wolin infuses Dewey's concepts of public and political culture with power and difference. He does this because he thinks that democratic politics is not enough. In his later writings Wolin is pessimistic about the possibility of democratic politics, dropping the term in *Democracy Incorporated* and adopting instead "demotic politics." The future of the demos and fugitive politics lies in demotic politics. What is needed is the ephemeral and fugitive experience of the demos on the plane of the political that overcomes a democratic politics of publics. "Publics do not, unfortunately, a collectivity make," Wolin writes; "they do, however, point in the right direction, that of the need to subordinate economy to polity."[69] Insofar as radical democracy

---

[66] Ibid., 89.
[67] Cf. Hooker, *Theorizing Race in the Americas*, 29.
[68] Wolin, *Fugitive Democracy*, 412ff.
[69] Wolin, *Presence of the Past*, 46.

starts with publics and political culture, it should not stay there.[70] Demotic politics is a politics of tending to difference in search of a fugitive commonality. Democratic individuality and actual individual human experiences of fugitivity are lost here as Wolin moves to center the demos.

Attending to experiences of fugitivity and creating a political culture of democratic individuals who build relational power in counterpublics takes time and requires us to listen to the Spirit of our practices of mutual recognition. Democratic politics is slow, timely, and patient work and requires authentic democratic deliberation, trust, expression of determinate difference, judgment, and reflection. Citizens as political agents and members of the fugitive demos need to be tended to as they are in their whole selves, and yet I cannot see how a politics of tending is granted the necessary time in Wolin's sense of the political or fugitive democracy. Tending to actual experiences of fugitivity that cause the very differences that Wolin wishes to bracket on the plane of the political makes solidarity hard won, if possible at all in Wolin's fugitive democracy. I doubt such solidarity can be achieved by excluding experiences of fugitivity from the political. Wolin speaks about democracy in terms of people coming together as political agents, but he does not elaborate on how such a politics is possible under conditions of fugitivity. He speaks of the local, of a slower rhythm of democracy, but his concept of the political is only ever momentarily realized.

For all of the attention Wolin's fugitive democracy gives to power, he never seriously considered the corrupting and co-opting forces of white supremacy and racial capitalism. And that is why I leave behind his concept of economic polity and instead adopt racial capitalist analysis, taking in tow his keen insights into postmodern power. His conceptions of fugitivity and a politics of tending are ill-equipped to come to terms with radical democracy as I've encountered it in BBCO. At points it seems Wolin has stripped radical democracy down to the fleeting experience of the political, giving us little motivation to engage in the patient, slow-going work of democratic politics. For as much attention that Wolin gives to the importance of democratic political culture, he fails to take seriously how racial capitalism corrupts values, distorts and disciplines political habits, and constricts human strivings toward self-realization. I know from my organizing experience how powerful

---

[70] But the importance of political culture is a lasting theme in Wolin's writing. For example, "If democracy is about participating in self-government, its first requirement is a supportive culture, a complex of beliefs, values, and practices that nurture equality, cooperation and freedom" (Wolin, *Democracy Incorporated*, 261).

the political culture of a BBCO affiliate can be: certain norms and patterns of behavior are dominant; certain expressions of religion are appropriate at certain times. Much goes into the cultivation and maintenance of the *style* of organizing. In recent years, I have witnessed efforts by Faith in Action and the Gamaliel Foundation that have started the difficult work of creating styles of organizing that do not center the white, cisgender, heteronormative, Christian male.[71] To imagine the aspiration of democratic politics as a bracketing of differences tells the lie that politics can be practiced without attending to our determinate differences, to the varying experiences that arise from our racial, class, gender, sex, and religious identities and how they are caught up in the game played by postmodern power in racial capitalism. It is to image a pure form of whiteness as constitutive of the solidarity achieved on the plane of the political.

Recall Angela's comment that NOAH's internal dialogue about a response to Hambrick's murder was uniquely characterized by an urgency grounded in the sacred value of Black life: "We can't keep making strategic plans while people lay dead in the street." NOAH's political action was grounded in a distinct experience of fugitivity by some of its members. NOAH's own history finds its roots in the Black Nashville community, as it started due to the leadership of several Black congregations. Here, the experiences of fugitivity are not bracketed in moments of solidarity, but instead certain values and experiences are the basis for solidarity and the ethics of democracy in a diverse group, each joining together with their own reasons (or, as one member of a NOAH congregation did, leaving a member institution due to this action). Tending to these differences refines what a politics of tending consists in and the temporality of fugitivity. Radical democracy as it is experienced in BBCO is slow and patient work.

Radical democracy as it is practiced in BBCO recasts Wolin's sense of fugitivity and a politics of tending in way that expresses harmony with West's sense of the tragicomic. If radical democracy is to offer a robust account of political culture, democratic individuality, a politics of tending, and fugitivity, it needs more than Dewey and Wolin have provided us. It needs a thoroughgoing critique of racial capitalism. For these reasons, the version of radical democracy offered here cannot end with Wolin.

---

[71] Mark Warren, in *Dry Bones Rattling*, ch. 5 first documented how the IAF wrestled with this reality by inviting the late Rev. Dr. James Cone to an organizing seminar with the Southwest IAF. In *A Shared Future*, Richard Wood and Brad Fulton write about Faith in Action's efforts.

Prophetic Christianity and Radical Democracy

Few thinkers have grasped the spiritual depth and political possibility of democratic individuality as West has. From his earliest work he was clear that individuality is the moral core of African American prophetic Christianity.[72] The struggle for self-realization in community—the struggle to achieve democratic individuality—is a distinctly *tragicomic* dialectic for West, as individuals experience the limits and possibilities of both human nature and human history. This dialectic is driven by the struggle for existential and social freedom. Democratic individuality is about character and political and economic conditions. But West's work chastens our sensibility of what democratic individuality can amount to in light of the postmodern power of racial capitalism. Inevitably the historical limits of the possibilities of freedom circumscribe our herculean efforts toward freedom and individuality. And yet such struggles are communal because self-realization cannot happen except in community.

West situates the trials and tribulations of Black people in the United States in a history weighted with despair and hope, and so his sense of the tragicomic is familiar with catastrophe and compassion. The catastrophic in the tragicomic points to the history of struggle for freedom in the face of oppression, "the piling of wreckage, generation after generation, all of those precious lives lost, wasted potential, witnessed generation after generation."[73] West's religious sensibility operates with a deep sense of urgency. The problems the poor and marginalized face are not mere misfortunes, but are existential, social, and political catastrophes. Radical democrats need to always keep these struggles in front of us and hold our power-building accountable to these experiences of fugitivity. Those Black thinkers, writers, and artists saw slavery and Jim Crow as the catastrophe that they were and understood them as emergency situations.[74]

And yet "despair and hope are inseparable," West writes. "One can never understand what hope is really about unless one wrestles with despair."[75] For West, as a Christian, Anton Chekhov's Russian Christian Orthodoxy

---

[72] "A transcendent God before whom all persons are equal," West teaches, "thus endows the well-being and ultimate salvation of each with equal value and significance. I shall call this radical egalitarian idea *the Christian principle of self-realization of individuality within community*" (*Prophesy Deliverance!*, 16, emphasis in original).

[73] West, *Cornel West on Black Prophetic Fire*, 45.

[74] Ibid.

[75] West, *The Cornel West Reader*, 554.

communicates fundamental principles such as "absolute condemnation of no one, forgiveness for all, compassion to all." In an 1998 interview, West reflects personally on the value of Chekhov's compassionate insights: "For me those principles cut very deep."[76] His religious sensibility is tragicomic because it emphasizes "the cross more than the crown, Good Friday more than Easter, love through the darkness of life more than triumphant bliss at the end of the life. Ours is in the trying—the rest is not our business."[77] The depth of individuality—its trials and triumphs—needs both the tragic and the comic, the blues and Chekhov. The tragicomic sustains West's unwavering inquiry into this historical struggle for freedom of the oppressed. Though I would not dub my account of radical democracy tragicomic in West's sense, I am indebted to his keen insights into the dialectic between hope and despair in our racial capitalist times. Radical democracy in BBCO cannot survive on political attitudes of despair that often show up under the pretense that every issue is the absolute or ultimate fight. Such attitudes fail to recognize that loss is a reality of political life, as the NOAH campaign to remove the chief of police reminds us. And so radical democracy as an ethical way of life must include more than single-issue campaigns. The Spirit of radical democracy—its ethical life—needs to attend to individuals as whole, time-bound beings. West's comments here return us to the challenges faced by Wolin's *demotic* politics and fugitive democracy: democratic movements need to be sustainable for the long haul. The Spirit of radical democracy is strengthened by a religious hope that focuses on the "cross more than the crown." The deep connection between despair and hope is grounded in a prophetic form of Christianity that calls out concrete evils while affirming democracy as a lived reality in practices of mutual recognition that foster dialogue, negotiation, trust, and compromise.

This historical struggle for freedom(s) makes democracy all the more crucial to the possibility of democratic individuality and social freedom. Undemocratic individuality misshapes and corrupts the self and leads to social relations of deformed recognition. Racist norms and cultural practices operate independently of (but are not separate from) our economic and political life, and so the Spirit of radical democracy needs to fundamentally oppose such normatively established cultural practices.[78] Democratic

---

[76] Ibid., 555.
[77] West, "Afterword," 353.
[78] Cf. West, "Toward a Socialist Theory of Racism": "[W]hite supremacist logics are embedded in philosophies of identity that suppress difference, diversity and heterogeneity. Since such discourses

individuality relies on accountability and participation. Democratic individuality and social freedom require that institutions are accountable to their members and make freely accessible the participation necessary to sustain such democratic institutions. "Democratic participation of people in the decision making processes of institutions that regulate and govern their lives," West writes, "is a precondition for actualizing the Christian principle of self-realization of human individuality in community."[79] The concept of individuality at the heart of African American prophetic Christianity could not be realized without a dialogue with democracy. Even West's understanding of prophecy is connected to radical democracy. To prophesy is to call out concrete evils: to "negate what is and transform prevailing realities against the backdrop of the present historical limits."[80] The concrete evils of white supremacy occupy a central concern for West, and rightly so—any conception of radical democracy needs to wrestle with the depth to which white supremacy pervades our discursive and nondiscursive realities.

West's work brings together attention to white supremacy with concerns about capitalist exploitation and expropriation. His attention to the psychosocial, cultural dimensions of white supremacy give us a broader sense of how postmodern power shapes up today. For these reasons, my account of radical democracy follows his analysis. For West, white supremacy is intractable in modern society, more than contingent or absolutely necessary.[81] White supremacy exists not only in the modes of production, the legal system, or the political interests of a white ruling class. White supremacy also goes to the "inception" of modern discourse and corrupts its "metaphors, notions, and categories" which "produce and prohibit, develop and delimit, specific conceptions of truth and knowledge, beauty and character, so that certain ideas are rendered incomprehensible and unintelligible."[82] West's genealogy of modern racism emphasizes how the everyday life of Black people "is shaped not simply by the exploitative (oligopolistic) capitalist system of production but also by cultural attitudes and sensibilities."[83] A "normative gaze"

impede the realization of the democratic socialist ideals of genuine individuality and radical democracy, they must be criticized and opposed" (103).

[79] West, *Prophesy Deliverance!*, 18–19.
[80] Ibid., 19.
[81] As West says, "The specific forms that racism takes depend on choices people make within these structural constraints. In this regard, history is neither deterministic nor arbitrary; rather it is an open-ended sequence of (progressive or regressive) structured social practices over time and space" ("Toward a Socialist Theory of Racism," 104).
[82] West, *Prophesy Deliverance!*, 47.
[83] Ibid., 65.

emerges in our modern discourse and is further entrenched by our capitalist system of production that disposes of and subjugates Black people. West's socialist theory of racism illustrates how his notion of power differs from purely discursive or material analyses.[84] For radical democrats like West and my own account here, power exists when people can exercise control over the forces that govern their own lives, whether the power is political economy, discursive capillary power, psychosocial, or social practical.[85] This account of power as exercising control over the forces that govern their lives aligns with my account of freedom as nondomination.

The role of prophetic Christianity is crucial in contributing to the Spirit of radical democracy as an ethical way of life. Any social vision of individual and collective freedom for the oppressed cultivated within prophetic Christianity must connect discursive practices "to the role they play in buttressing the current mode of production concealing the unequal distribution of wealth, and portraying the lethargy of the political system."[86] Prophetic Christianity is revolutionary, in the sense that it turns our world upside down. For West, revolutionary Christianity is anticapitalist, antiracist, and anti-imperialist, nurtured by those who are dominated, exploited, and expropriated by racial capitalism.

What becomes clear throughout West's work is his primary concern with the power prophetic Christianity gives to radical democracy, and it is a power that my account of radical democracy equally cherishes. West notes, "The legacies of prophetic Christianity put a premium on the kind of human being one chooses to be rather than the amount of commodities one possess[es]. . . . They marshal religious energies for democratic aims, yet are suspicious of all forms of idolatry, including democracy itself as an idol."[87] Radical democracy is a way of life, a cultural way of being. "Democracy is more of a verb than a noun," West writes; "it is more a dynamic striving and collective movement than a static order or stationary status quo."[88] The Spirit of radical democracy has to do with what sort of individuals we can be together and what kind of communities we collectively construct. This form of prophetic Christianity

---

[84] "To put it somewhat crudely, the capitalist mode of production constitutes just one of the significant structural constraints determining what forms racism takes in a particular historical period. Other key structural constraints include the state, bureaucratic modes of control, and the cultural practices of ordinary people" (West, "Toward a Socialist Theory of Racism," 103).
[85] West, *Prophesy Deliverance!*, 50.
[86] Ibid., 114.
[87] Ibid., 163.
[88] West, *Democracy Matters*, 69.

provides insights into a deeper sort of freedom that cultivates democratic individuality and radical democracy.

What do secular democrats lose by not taking up this mantle of prophetic Christianity? Prophetic Christianity contributes to radical democracy in unique ways, in ways other traditions cannot. It provides moral fervor, vision, and courage and helps us claim our political birthright. But does my account (and West's, by implication) peg secular democrats as weaker in the face of racial capitalism because they lack prophetic Christianity?

For West's part, he has always been clear about his own unique voice and vocation as a Chekhovian Christian and a radical democrat. As he says, "Since radical democracy for me is not simply an institutional arrangement or form of governance but also a way of life and struggle, the world-denying love of Jesus and the world-transforming love of the radical democracy are closely related (though not identical)."[89] Radical democracy for West has always been a big tent, and his individual identity as a Chekhovian prophetic Christian ought to be seen in light of his emphasis on democratic individuality rather than as a requirement for radical democrats everywhere. For my own account, radical democrats need to pay better attention to the role of sacred value in the Spirit of radical democracy. In the big tent of radical democracy, we need deep coalitions of secular and all kinds of faith-rooted radical democrats. Prophetic Christianity does not have a monopoly on radical democracy's Spirit. But it is a crucial voice. The two-story house analysis, with its economic base and cultural superstructure, does not adequately capture postmodern power in racial capitalism, but more important, it cannot offer a complete vision of what democratic individuality and radical democracy amount to for individuals and communities struggling to build relational power in their everyday lives and social practices.

A Vision of Radical Democracy

Radical democracy would be weaker without its religious participants. As we saw in the example of NOAH, some of the most urgent fights in holding police violence accountable are grounded in values that democratic publics hold sacred. The dialogical process of NOAH members agreeing to the public statement and list of demands included *parrhesia* and self-interest. Such a process

---

[89] West, "Afterword," 353.

includes a politics of tending, of attending to experiences of fugitivity, rooted in sacred values. By issuing demands, NOAH is saying: In light of the horrendous violation of Black life that has taken place, *these* are NOAH's demands; *we* stand here. Crucially, this democratic dialogical process depends on clarity of self-interest within NOAH's membership. Individual members have to come up with their own reasons for supporting these demands. Self-interest is an important part of the shared understanding of NOAH's internal order. Building relational power requires that democratic individuals trust one another as loci of authority and accountability. Differences have to be tended to and the group has to build relational solidarity around values and issues that arise from concrete experiences of democratic life together.

Radical democracy in BBCO is slow, patient work, and it is hard won, but it is not done by attempting to rise above the messy historical reality of radical democracy and sacred values to an imagined, fleeting space of white solidarity. Organizing has always been about a political culture and the values therein. Those committed to radical democracy need to pay attention to the role of values, especially sacred values in organizing, and double down on the self-reliant, relational, value-based political culture that Dewey, Wolin, and West rightly worked to help us see.

This vision of radical democracy argues that BBCO counterpublics build relational power: radically democratic power grounded in the ethical life of the community's social practice of reasoning. Social practices of reasoning, like the relational meeting, open the possibility for mutual recognition. And as democratic individuals weave deeper relationships through the listening campaign or the one-on-one that ground such relationships in sacred values, they collectively give shape to a new collective ethical life, one that my post-Hegelian framework captures in terms of Spirit's development. Through such practices, the Spirit moves us together, in powerful, practical ways, inviting us to be more than we have been before. Organizing practices in BBCO like the relational meeting can be seen as religious practices because of the role of sacred value. Sacred values go to the heart of the ethical life of radical democracy; they are essential to the social practice of building relational power. Our political and theological imaginaries can now contend with the political and theological possibilities in radical democracy, which everyday people organizing in BBCO counterpublics often experience. This is what organizing sacred value is about: building relational power by doubling down on the social practices of BBCO in a way that adequately pushes back against the bulwarks of racial capitalism.

Radical democracy places a certain account of selfhood at the center, but democratic individuality emerges only in certain kinds of associational life. Counterpublics that foster such forms of selfhood are not naive to broader power relationships. Power shapes up in broader society in a deeply intersectional way, and power analysis needs to attend to how difference and value develop conterminously within our political life. Class, race, and gender power relationships are mutually implicating. Building power in a way that transforms the structures of society—and the social practices that make up such structures and institutions—in the direction of justice requires a deeply contextual sense of power and a commitment to radical democracy as an ethical way of life.

PART III

NOW WHAT?

*How Organizing and Theology Can
Change Going Forward*

5
On Organizing as Practice

Broad-based community organizing is a practice more than it is a craft or art. Most accounts of broad-based organizing tend to frame it as an activity by single individuals. The lone professional organizer has become the emblem of BBCO, a single stand-in for a collective practice.[1] Now, some sociologists have rightly focused on the role of political and religious culture, and some theologians and theological ethicists have paid attention to the wealth that BBCO provides for theological reflection.[2] There is, however, little work done on organizing from the field of practice theory, which emphasizes the setting and scene styles of collective action. What results is a tendency within the scholarship to privilege the "entrepreneurial actor" or the "unitary actor model" as the primary frame to understand BBCO.[3] This chapter argues that BBCO is a *practice*. The activity of organizing can be best understood by following the action itself rather than focusing on individual actors or actor organizations. One consequence of this account is a richer description of the role of sacred values in the life of BBCO counterpublics and a truer account of the feel of the practice of BBCO. By figuring BBCO as a practice, we can gain greater insight into how sacred values fit into the life of the BBCO constituency and how the organizing involves individual and collective agents taking positions in fields of power where sacred values play important roles.

The chapter moves through five sections. I begin with an example from my own experience with the Gamaliel Foundation affiliate NOAH. The second section argues that framing organizing as a practice—rather than a craft or art—matters for organizers, scholars who study organizing, and for my broader Christian social ethical argument. In the third section I introduce some of the key concepts and terms that are basic to the theoretical frame: settings, scenes, and styles of the practice of organizing. The fourth

---

[1] My overview of the literature on BBCO is given in the book's introduction.
[2] Cf. Wood, *Faith in Action*; Wood and Fulton, *A Shared Future*.
[3] Paul Lichterman outlines the entrepreneurial actor and his counterapproach "civic action" in *How Civic Action Works*, ch. 1. Lichterman first made this argument in earlier essays, where he dubs the problem, the "unitary actor model" ("Religion and Social Solidarity").

Listening to the Spirit. Aaron Stauffer, Oxford University Press. © Oxford University Press 2024.
DOI: 10.1093/oso/9780197755525.003.0006

section returns to the NOAH example and brings to bear the insights of the theoretical frame. Finally, the fifth section ties the resolutions of this chapter into my broader Christian social ethical concern about the ways racial capitalism haunts the practice of BBCO itself. Organizers need to double down on the relational and value basis of organizing, to build relational power that can counter the exploitation and expropriation of racial capitalism, a theme that is central to the next chapter.

An Example: NOAH's Clergy Caucus

At a NOAH board meeting in January, in a small Methodist church in North Nashville, about fifty people have gathered in the sanctuary. They sit in brown wooden pews all facing the pulpit, with its humble wooden cross hanging overhead. Bright white banners adorn the sanctuary, marking the liturgical season of Epiphany. This church has its own history, being where Rev. James Lawson trained young Black students in nonviolent civil disobedience that led to the Nashville sit-ins. People chat and mill around a few minutes before the meeting starts; the majority of the crowd have broken up into institutional membership, with small collections of three to four people scattered throughout the sanctuary. As the more long-standing active members find their seats, however, they blur such institutional lines and instead sit mixed in with friends. Eventually the sanctuary fills so that people cannot sit isolated. Promptly at 6:30 p.m. we are welcomed by the pastor, who mentions this congregation's history with the civil rights movement and Rev. Lawson, and the meeting begins.

Halfway through the meeting, Rev. James, an African Methodist Episcopal minister, stands before the group to introduce the topic of discussion: forming a NOAH clergy caucus.[4] Rev. James has long been the chair of the executive committee; he was one of the founders and is respected for his leadership. He brings earned authority not only from his work in NOAH but also from his own work on racial justice within the African Methodist Episcopal conference in Tennessee. He tells the group that the executive committee is recommending the formation of a clergy caucus and he is bringing it to the floor for a vote by the whole body. Clergy caucuses are common in many other BBCO affiliates, he explains. Pastors and preachers, he continues, are

---

[4] I have changed names in this example to ensure anonymity.

important to the work of organizing, and the clergy caucus is a way NOAH can organize them. Talking slowly and with intention without searching for words, he tells NOAH that the clergy caucus is meant to bring together clergy of all faiths (he mentions explicitly Christians, Jews, Muslims, and Unitarian Universalists) to develop their own theological resources to help their congregation in organizing.

As soon as he finishes his pitch, a few hands are raised and he points to a white middle-aged man, John, who is a lawyer and a member of the Unitarian Universalist Church. John leads NOAH's criminal justice task force, which recently celebrated a big win. The task force played an important role, along with several other powerful groups in Nashville, that mobilized voters, generated press, and pressured the metro council to establish a community oversight board.[5] John has some questions about the purpose of the clergy caucus: Will this body have voting powers in deciding what issues we get to work on? What will this mean for the nonreligious institutions, like unions? He compares the idea of the clergy caucus to a special interest group and worries that the clergy will lobby their members, much like he sees in city politics. Rev. James responds to these concerns, saying that the clergy caucus will not have voting power but is instead meant to help clergy organize their own churches. John is unconvinced. This doesn't prevent the clergy from attempting to hold NOAH hostage if the organization moves in a way the clergy caucus doesn't like. Rev. James looks a bit despondent at this point and the conversation continues.

Another powerful leader, Shannon, a Black woman who leads the economic equity and jobs task force, echoes John's concerns. Shannon's respect and authority as a local activist have recently been recognized by a Nashville magazine, which profiled her as the "Best Activist." More pertinent to NOAH, however, is Shannon's commitment to NOAH: she has been a long-standing leader helping her task force pass the first community benefits agreement in the construction of a new soccer stadium.[6] We already have lots of clergy represented here, Shannon says. Why do we need another group to organize just them? Rev. James attempts to respond to her questions, but

---

[5] Several other crucial organizations are worthy of note here: Community Oversight Now is especially important as that organization led the effort: https://communityoversightnashville.wordpress.com/.

[6] NOAH's work on these issues, like the issue, is hardly ever done alone. On the community benefits agreement with the Major League Soccer stadium, a broad coalition supported this issue, successfully pressuring the metropolitan council to yield to their demands. See Garrison, "Nashville MLS Ownership Reaches Terms on Community Benefits Agreement for Stadium Project."

admittedly fumbles his words and repeats what he has already said about the value of clergy to NOAH and that clergy caucuses are common across BBCO networks. After all, he says, NOAH will soon form a union caucus too, so this is not to play favorites to clergy. Rising to the defense of the clergy caucus is Rev. Mary, a Black clergywoman who is also a member of the executive committee. Rev. Mary has recently finished campaigning for metropolitan council in North Nashville. She explains that clergy are the foundation of NOAH: clergy members across Nashville coming together saying we need to organize and fight for our city. The conversation ends after this exchange, and NOAH votes to form a clergy caucus, but not without some visible discomfort from those who voiced objections.

Why Practice Matters

Calling organizing a practice turns our attention to the flow of the action, the collective action that happens in a setting and scene. But by calling organizing a practice, I also mean to call attention to *how* the action happens—its style. Practice theory today is a broad and multidisciplinary field.[7] According to feminist philosopher Sherry Ortner, theories of practice typically trade in a constellation of terms: "practice, praxis, action, interaction, activity, experience, performance. A second, and closely related, bundle of terms focuses on the doer of all of the doing: agent, actor, person, self, individual subject."[8] Across the wide literature in sociology, politics, religious studies, theology, and Christian ethics that addresses community organizing there is an equally diverse collection of terms to describe BBCO. There is a danger, however, in speaking of BBCO without attending to relationships of power within the organizing constituencies themselves and attending to how those relationships of power have a bearing on the collective action of organizing itself. Ortner is keen to stave off theories of practice that fail to account for "slippages in reproduction, the erosions of long-standing patterns, the moments of disorder and of outright 'resistance.'"[9] Ortner argues that theories of practice that do not account for mistakes and slippages tend to see practice and social reproduction in a "loop."[10] The problem with a "loop"

---

[7] Ted Smith gives a good overview of the field in religious studies, theology, and social ethics in "Theories of Practice."
[8] Ortner, "Theory in Anthropology since the Sixties," 662, 660.
[9] Ortner, *Making Gender*, 17.
[10] Ibid.

theory of practice is that it maintains troublesome dichotomies like structure versus agency, objectivism versus subjectivism, or individual versus community. Organizing does not just happen; it is a group process that occurs within and is possible only in relational fields in material settings and with particular styles. For this reason and others, I seek to critically engage the work of Pierre Bourdieu in explicating what I mean by calling organizing a practice. Bourdieu's work helps us bypass the seemingly intractable choice between structuralist or existentialist theories of practice or the entrenched antinomy between objectivism and subjectivism.[11]

Theories of practice need to pay attention to systems and structures as much as individual action. In keeping both of these arenas within our purview, we must also allow for mistakes and slippages, for breaks in the relationships of domination and power, for innovation in the structures and traditions of practice. Such theories of practice help account for the richness of what Ortner calls a "serious game." Ortner allows for the influence of social constructions such as race and gender—with their correlate material norms and practices embedded in cultures and institutions—on the context and the discourse of the rules of the game, so to speak. Each player's role or position in the serious game is caught up in "webs of relationship and interaction," and these positions shift. Agents are playing multiple games at a time, since the webs of relationship and interaction are not occurring on only one plane of economic, social, and political life. Consider how race and class and gender (among others) are all games that complicate one another and are interlocking; players navigate these games in real time in different settings and in different ways. In calling organizing a practice, I mean to attend to how organizing happens and is influenced by these games. Racial capitalism haunts the practice of organizing itself in a way that characterizes its style and logic of power, a point I will address further at the end of this chapter and in chapter 6.

My attention throughout this chapter will be focused on the practice of organizing in BBCO, but I will attempt to honor Ortner's insights by continually reflecting on the normative and institutionalized social, economic, political, and religious constructs that form and shape BBCO itself. We have to consider how BBCO as it is lived out in counterpublics is shaped by larger systems and structures like white supremacy, heteropatriarchy, and racial capitalism. Such social practices like gender have become institutionalized

---

[11] "Objectivism and subjectivism, mechanicalism and finalism, structural necessity and individual agency are false antinomies" (Bourdieu and Wacquant, *An Invitation to Reflexive Sociology*, 10).

and calcified as dominating and oppressive structures in our society.[12] As such they are inherently antidemocratic; such institutions perpetuate norms that are taken up and lived out, causing real harm to people who do not abide by or represent dominant categories or norms.

In Christian social ethics, however, Bourdieu is not the main figure of inspiration on the topic of practice. Instead, Alasdair MacIntyre is typically followed. MacIntyre's influential definition of practice in *After Virtue* is often cited in the field.[13] His work on virtue, practical reasoning, narrative, and neo-Thomist Aristotelian concepts of politics and ethics might seem to be well-suited for BBCO. It is certainly true that one can make a case for the role of virtues in organizing, though I have not done that here. I have developed my own post-Hegelian account of social practical reasoning and narrative in the radically democratic life of BBCO that differs in important ways from MacIntyre's neo-Thomist Aristotelianism. Moreover, MacIntyre's most recent work has seemed to correct his concern with modernity: he is not opposed to modernity as such, but instead certain forms of selfhood and community that emerge from it. And he has returned to his long-established interest in Marxism and Marx's keen insight into how capitalism deforms our basic social relations.[14] Still, what I find missing in MacIntyre is an attention to institutions (where institutions are collections of social practices, like class, race, and gender) and power relationships within local group life, of which he is so fond.[15] Moreover, his attention to local cooperative movements fails to attend to the critical and fraught role of counterpublics like economic cooperatives in the history of racial capitalism.[16] MacIntyre's turn to the cooperative economy is a selective one, meaning he holds up specific examples of local cooperative economics without attending to their own power struggles in racial capitalism, or even the broader economic challenges that cooperatives face in market socialism.[17] My account attends

---

[12] Sally Haslanger offers a similar understanding of how practices are related to institutions and social structures: "On my view, social structures consist of interconnected practices. Structures are of different sizes and can be found at different levels" ("What Is a Social Practice?," 232).

[13] MacIntyre, *After Virtue*, 187: "By a 'practice' I am going to mean any coherent and complex form of socially established cooperative human activity through which good[s] internal to that form of activity are realized in the course of trying to achieve those standards of excellence which are appropriate to, and partially definitive of, that form of activity, with the result that human powers to achieve excellence, and human conceptions of the ends and goods involved, are systematically extended."

[14] MacIntyre, *Ethics in the Conflicts of Modernity*, 183–84.

[15] See Rhodes, "Virtue and Power."

[16] Cf. Gordon Nembhard, *Collective Courage*.

[17] For MacIntyre on cooperatives, see *Ethics in the Conflicts of Modernity*, 176–83. On cooperatives in market socialism, see Dorrien, *American Democratic Socialism*, 508–17.

to the temporal and collective reality of the group activity of broad-based organizing. I strive to illustrate how organizing is only collectively possible—happening in relational fields, material settings, and strips of action (scenes) that are characterized by styles. The political role of sacred values in our social practical reasoning is an active one: values matter, because relationships matter. Humans form relationships to protect and fight for what they hold sacred. When organizing is in motion, a lot is at stake for the people and collective. As people take positions in relationship to one another, where they are, who they are with, how the moment is framed are all relevant to the practice.

If we tune out these sorts of questions about agents and groups in relationships of power, we miss much of the feel of organizing. And instead we seek to impose a foreign frame on what is actually happening. We need to follow the action of organizing, not just the actors (individual or collective agents). Following the action helps us to see that we need to also attend to the Spirit of organizing itself, the ethical life—the relationships and values of organizing. By "Spirit" I mean the ethical life of a BBCO constituency, the quality of its social practical reasoning and practices of mutual recognition, like the relational meeting and listening campaign. But I also mean attending to how participants of BBCO themselves see certain practices as religious practices because of the role of sacred value in the practice of organizing. Organizing is Spirit-filled, theologically rich and ethically deep, and it is enacted in fields of power, in specific settings, and defined by scene styles.

Framing the Action

Examples like the exchange that starts this chapter illustrate several important points about the practice of organizing. First, the activity of organizing takes place in a larger *setting* and in *scenes*: a historic Black church or a metropolitan council meeting hall or the mayor's office. A setting carries with it a group's normative sense of *style*: what is appropriate or inappropriate action and valuation is collectively and dialogically established. Settings and style matter, as I will show, because the material and group identity that organizing takes place in is incorporated into the practice itself. But style takes place in *scenes*, "strips of action" that are set off by physical or temporal boundaries.[18] As we will see, the setting and scene styles of organizing forms and influences,

---

[18] Lichterman, *How Civic Action Works*, 26.

constricts and expands the possibility for action. This point extends to the basic fact that organizing is an embodied activity, and human action has an important spatial reality that communicates emotions and passions. Social practices are social because they are based in shared assumptions, norms, patterns of behavior, and goods internal and external to the practice itself. My social practical account of sacred value is grounded in an account of social practical reasoning, which is enacted, embodied, expressed materially and spatially. The practice of organizing is inherently relational and takes place in a setting.

Important to note in Bourdieu's field theory is the broader material, embodied, structural environment of organizing. Earlier, I addressed how norms influence our ideals. But social practical, norm-driven, and habit-grounded accounts of human action tend to be misconstrued as focusing primarily on social reproduction. Often it is claimed that such accounts cannot explain social transformation. This is a common critique of Bourdieu's concept of *habitus*—that his thought does not allow for the transformation of habitus, just its reproduction. On my account of social practical reasoning, critical revision of social norms and social practices can take place, but only within certain limits. My account emphasizes the fallible and constructivist aspect of norms and social practices. Such limits are important, however, because they help us get a grip on what we are speaking of when we speak of the practice of organizing. I mean to point to certain human activities and not others. Organizing cannot include all (or even any given) human action. To gain such specificity, I need more examples, but I also need to point to certain transposable dispositions and actions, combined with distinct uses of time that are characterized by an actor's own style in a specific scene. As I will outline in the next section, Bourdieu's habitus helps me to specify my account of organizing itself in relation to its settings and scenes.

Attention to an agent's style and use of time might suggest that my account of organizing follows what Paul Lichterman has identified as the entrepreneurial actor model and thus is in tension with my articulated desire to situate the practice of organizing in its setting and in the broader group political culture.[19] By drawing critically and creatively from Bourdieu's thought I mean to surpass such dichotomies like that of the individual and community. Similarly, by focusing on democratic individuality, I am arguing for a social view of the self, where development of the self is possible only in certain

---

[19] See ibid.; Lichterman, "Religion and Social Solidarity."

sorts of associational life, and insofar as qualities of character are misshapen, so are the self's relations. Self-interest, that is, the value-laden and relational stake a person has in the common good, is a crucial part of democratic individuality. One's self-interest is grounded in one's values and the relationships that enact and sustain these values.[20] More than this, to figure organizing as a "practice" is to focus on the *action*, not the actor—to see how organizing takes places in scene styles and is made possible only by the form of culture of the group. Such a focus on action does not lose the actor. My theory of organizing situates the actor in networks of value-laden relationships, settings, and scene styles. Focusing only on the actor and their activity or only the setting is insufficient because it gives ground to dichotomies that pervade our political and social imaginations like individual versus community, structure versus agency; these are dichotomies that Bourdieu consistently sought to overcome. Here I will argue that the practice of organizing itself is a shared activity.

The practice of organizing does not exist in a vacuum: setting, scene style, and habitus all help us get a deeper sense of the relational, temporal, and value-laden reality of the practice of organizing. This frame provides a more holistic understanding of the practice of organizing. The next section will examine two concepts of Bourdieu's thought—namely, field and habits—while freely critiquing and adjusting where necessary. Like the role of Dewey in chapter 4, Bourdieu gives us a useful place to start, but I do not end with him and the corrections are crucial to my overall argument.[21]

The Practice of Organizing

In my account of organizing as a practice, the basic elements of analysis are seen in terms of relationships to others, to power, to discourse, and to context. The concepts of self-interest and democratic individuality in BBCO capture the radically democratic life of BBCO because they illustrate how

---

[20] Hart, *Cultural Dilemmas of Progressive Politics*, 76–77.
[21] As Rogers Brubaker says, "Just as Bourdieu is fond of describing his relation with 'canonical' theorists in terms of 'thinking with a thinker against that thinker,' so too we can and should think with Bourdieu against Bourdieu. But we can do this only by appropriating his sociological dispositions, his thinking tools, making them ours and making our own use of them, testing in practice their practical productivity along with dispositions and thinking tools appropriated from other sources" ("Social Theory as Habitus," 219).

certain forms of selfhood are possible only in particular forms of value-laden associational life.

Bourdieu's concept of the field opens new doors and raises new questions that allows us to see how BBCO is a dynamic and relational practice. To think in terms of the field is "to think relationally."[22] The field is a network or configuration of positions and is characterized by power relations, by unsettled relations of domination.[23] In field theory, what deserves attention is not individual actors separable from structure, nor only the structure in which such agents exist. Surpassing antinomies like structure versus agent and subjectivism versus objectivism: here, "the real is the relational."[24] This approach allows us to dislodge the supposed transcendental status of the norms of a field and instead to historicize and place such norms in power relations.

A field is a semi-autonomous "network, or a configuration, of objective relations between positions," governed by regularities that are established through structurally organized competition, in a way similar to a game.[25] No field is completely isolated from effects outside the field; thus fields are semi-autonomous. Agents are only incompletely aware of the fields that they take positions in; the field appears external to us and similar to the image of a player standing in a soccer field, only partially visible to us. The various stances that players take in a field are made possible by what feels "natural" to the game and what is possible by their currently held position.[26] But contrary to the image of a soccer field, the social space that Bourdieu speaks of in using "field" is not an equal playing field. Fields are hierarchically structured.[27] Fields overlap, with different relationships influencing various positions in multiple fields. Individual and collective agents take various stances and positions in relation to one another, but their stances are made possible or prevented by relations of power, and we should not mistake single moves for the entire action as it happens by particular players in

---

[22] Bourdieu and Wacquant, *An Invitation to Reflexive Sociology*, 96–97.

[23] Cf. Bourdieu, "The Force of Law, " 817: "For example, as their power increased, the legal status of American labor unions has evolved: although at the beginning of the nineteenth century the collective action of workers was condemned as 'criminal conspiracy' in the name of protecting the free market, little by little unions achieved the full recognition of the law."

[24] Bourdieu, "What Makes a Social Class?," 3.

[25] Ibid., 98.

[26] Thompson, "Field," 38.

[27] Thompson, "Field." Bourdieu did posit, however, a larger social field called the "field of power" that is interdependent on other, more restricted fields: the economic field, the fields of literature, art, science, and so on. The field of power itself is hierarchically structured, so that not all fields within it are on equal footing. A field is a network of objective relations, influenced by other relations in broader fields.

a game. Field theory conceptualizes social space in terms of historicity (how such relational networks came to be, how various players continue to "play the game"), relationship (what various position-takings or stances are possible in relationship to others), and power (how the social space is internally hierarchically structured and how the field itself is set in a hierarchy in relation to other fields).

Struggle and historicity are crucial to understanding how players gain a sense of the "feel of the game" in a particular field. In chapter 3, I argued for a social practical account of evaluative attitudes of sacred value. This social practical account turned my attention to the role of social norms in social practical reasoning. That account helps illustrate the contingency, fallibilism, and constructivism of social norms and sacred values, while recognizing the power of sacred values in our choice situations. Field theory complements my earlier comments on practical reasoning, illustrating that such social practices are embodied and material and governed by *regularities* instead of *rules*. We take our fellow reasoners to be (and are taken to be) inferentially responsible and accountable for their (and our) concept use. Mistakes and incorrect judgments are issues collectively established and authorized, but not because societies have been able to articulate completely the rules that govern them.[28] Nor is any society at one point in history infallible. As feminist theorists have helped us see, social norms are socially constructed and thus open to radical revision within certain limits.

The assertion that fields are governed by regularities returns us to the role social norms play in our social practices, while emphasizing the importance of history and power within our practices.[29] Accounts like my post-Hegelian one of social practical reasoning do not commit me to the kind of specificity of social norms and social practices found in rational actor theory or deterministic accounts of structuralism, vulgar orthodox Marxism, or legalism. Such accounts depend on self-clairvoyant subjects or economisms or attribute intentionality without self-reflexivity of the theorist.[30] The social practical account of evaluative attitudes outlined in chapter 3 allows for

[28] For more on the distinction between regulism (as rule-governed) and regularism in social practice of reasoning, see Brandom, *Making It Explicit*, esp. 20–21, 26–29, 36–42.
[29] Patricia Thompson notes how Bourdieu uses *le champ* in French "to describe, inter alia, an area of land, a battle field, and a field of knowledge" ("Field," 66).
[30] As Bourdieu says, "To slip from regularity, i.e., from what recurs with a certain statistically measurable frequency and from the formula which describes it, to a consciously laid down and consciously respected *ruling (réglement)*, or to unconscious *regulating* by a mysterious cerebral or social mechanism, are the two commonest ways of sliding from the model of reality to the reality of the model" (*The Logic of Practice*, 39, emphasis in original).

such vagueness of regularities (rather than explicit rules) in normative social practices.[31] The basic lessons from pragmatic theories of social practice and social norms do not require that we set out the rules that govern our social practices. Claiming that sacred values are grounded in social practical reasoning does not commit me to comprehensively articulating the rules that govern their practice (as if that were possible). Christian social ethics as I practice it looks inductively to human action as it is lived and seeks to illustrate the know-how rather than the know-what.[32]

Comparing fields to games is a helpful way of taking what is relevant and useful from field theory to our interest in BBCO. Games are played by mastering the regularities pertinent to the task at hand, which involves having a sense of style and an apt use of time. But BBCO is not its own field, as soccer is its own game. Here, I am speaking of broad-based community organizing generally—as a practice employed across contexts and time, found in national and international networks of organizing like the Industrial Areas Foundation, Faith in Action, and the Gamaliel Foundation. This is because, first, BBCO is more accurately described as a practice that occurs in settings and scene styles where multiple fields (politics, religion, economy, etc.) converge.[33] The dominant fields in BBCO are politics, economics, and religion. I do not claim that BBCO is generative of its own values, but rather that such values as sacred values, which stem from larger traditions and narratives, are at play in the practice of BBCO. But such narratives are political, economic, and religious. To try to separate these fields in BBCO returns us to previously explored problematics encountered in attempting to separate the category of

---

[31] Although he is speaking in terms of his own deontic scorekeeping, Robert Brandom's comments are relevant here: "In games such as baseball, which are not purely formal games (by contrast to chess or tic-tac-toe), the manner in which the score is changed cannot itself be specified entirely in terms of the concepts by means of which the score itself is specified. The complex manner in which a concrete performance qualifies as having the status of a strike or an out invokes such further concepts as the swinging of a bat, the passage of the baseball through a certain region of space specified relative to the position of the batter's body, catching the baseball on the fly, and so on. These further concepts give a material content to the scorekeeping concepts, beyond the formal content they have in virtue of their lore in scorekeeping" (*Making It Explicit*, 183).

[32] The larger point of Bourdieu's field theory as the "model of reality" has relevance for theorists of practice inspired by Wittgenstein, who perhaps would agree with Bourdieu on the relational and social practical nature of norms, but who might lack the attention to the effects external to a specific field and division of labor within each field: "Those who refuse to accept (as do Wittgenstein and Bachelard) that the establishment of 'the authorities,' which is the historical structure of the scientific field, constitutes the only possible foundation of scientific reason condemn themselves either to self founding strategies or to nihilist challenges to science inspired by a persistent, distinctly metaphysical nostalgia for a 'foundation,' which is the nondeconstructed principle of so-called deconstruction" ("The Force of Law," 819).

[33] As Loïc Wacquant tells us, "[E]ach field prescribes its particular values and possesses its own regulative principles" (Bourdieu and Wacquant, *An Invitation to Reflexive Sociology*, 17).

the secular from the religious. BBCO is certainly a form of radically democratic politics, as I sought to show in chapter 4. But the political culture of radical democracy is infused with many values, some of them being held sacred. I have not attempted to separate the field of religion or other fields in BBCO because I think such an analysis mishandles the lived and practical reality of BBCO.[34] Such a mishandling is often accompanied by the "entrepreneurial actor" or the "unitary actor model" that fails to reckon with the variety of expressions of religion in many different environments. As Lichterman says, "Invoking the unitary actor model, research ends up assuming that the actors we researchers have designated as 'religious' are acting on religious beliefs continuously. Yet everyday life offers many examples of people—clergy as well as laity—who express religious sentiments in different ways in different social circles, and who express it in some settings but not others."

A second, more concrete reason for not claiming that BBCO is its own field has to do with the organizational structure of BBCO affiliates. The home of BBCO is the local affiliate organization, which is a counterpublic organization consisting of many other organizations. The affiliate consists of member institutions.[35] As some theorists have argued, the fluid and amorphous nature of organizations today makes separating out an organization as its own field extremely difficult and problematic.[36] Difficult, because as we see in the example of the clergy caucus, each stance taken by Rev. James or Shannon is enabled by not only their participation in NOAH but also their leadership and earned authority in their church or other organizations. This makes analysis of the organization of NOAH as a field extremely complicated, requiring attention to potentially any individual from any one of the sixty-three member organizations of NOAH.

The fluid and amorphous nature of organizations makes it problematic to conceive of organizations-as-fields because drawing rigid field boundaries around organizations fails to explain the influence of strategic alliances formed with other organizations on critical issues. An analysis that would posit BBCO affiliates—like NOAH—as their own semi-autonomous field needs to account for local contingencies and idiosyncrasies generated and

---

[34] Cf. Lichterman, "Religion and Social Solidarity."

[35] Here I am speaking contextually and organizationally: even NOAH is not its own field.

[36] Emirbayer and Johnson, "Bourdieu and Organizational Analysis," 24: "From a relational perspective, then, there can be no *a priori* answer to the question of boundaries, and the issue can be decided by imposition on the part of the researcher no more than it can be decided by decree on the part of the (dominants within) the organization or law."

accumulated synchronically and spatially.[37] But this is a different claim than saying BBCO, broadly speaking across contexts, is its own semi-autonomous field in a manner similar to the field of politics or economics. Field theory helps us see the relational, dynamic, power-laden structure of relations captured in the lived social practice of BBCO.

In order to make their case, Rev. James and Rev. Mary take particular stances (position-taking, in Bourdieu's terms). Rev. James introduces the idea of a clergy caucus by highlighting the recommendation from NOAH's executive committee, implying that this issue has already been thoroughly vetted and received the approval of the elected leaders of NOAH. Rather than taking the position of a religious leader, Rev. James presents the issue as NOAH's executive chair. His position is endowed with political and religious authority. Rev. Mary takes a distinct position as a member of the executive committee, but rises to support the clergy caucus only after it has been challenged by the floor. Her stance is as a founding member of NOAH. Clergy have a crucial role to play in NOAH's organizational life, she tells us. Her stance is that of the well-respected and long-standing leader in NOAH; the strength of her claims is generated from years of laboring to build and sustain relationships in NOAH.

Field theory turns our attention to the stances taken in relation to each other within a specific network. It asks questions about the struggle and historicity of conflicts between relationships of domination. But sociologists like Lichterman and Nina Eliasoph have helpfully drawn our attention to the role of settings.[38] To a large degree, according to Lichterman and Eliasoph, we act due to our position in webs of relationships. Stances individuals take are always in relation to other stances, and such position-taking is made possible by those relations. This network and configuration of relationships, Lichterman's work suggests, exists in particular *settings*. Lichterman's term "setting" is a sociological way to capture the political culture and grid and group aspect of social identity ("how we do things in NOAH"). We also act the way we do because we find the configuration of relationships in particular settings that form and shape our actions.

A *setting* for Lichterman is closely related to Bourdieu's field theory. A field is a configuration, a network of relationships that is "simultaneously a space

---

[37] Crucial to this analysis would be quantitative and qualitative data concerning each BBCO affiliate. The closest thing we have is the large-scale 2011 National Study of Community Organizing Coalitions. See Wood and Fulton, *A Shared Future*, ch. 1.
[38] Eliasoph and Lichterman, "Culture in Interaction"; Lichterman, "Religion in Public Action."

of conflict and competition."[39] Position-takings that occur in a field are enabled by the relation an agent's position has in regard to other relations. Similarly, a setting, for Lichterman, is "the social and material coordinates of an interaction scene."[40] Settings turn our attention to the "social and spatial framework for interaction."[41] Settings are inhabited and impacted by group style: "Sets of understandings about what constitutes appropriate participation in a setting, or group styles, are sometimes shared by many groups across a society. Group style is what gives settings their power to shape interaction and identity, in ways potentially different from how they would unfold outside the setting."[42] This point is crucial: the "social and material coordinates" can help us think in terms of group and grid aspects of social identity, as well as in terms of position-taking within the organization and position-taking in relation to larger fields.

The setting of NOAH is a site of convergence of multiple fields, primarily religious and political. But NOAH itself is its own setting, and its own group identity is collectively and dialogically established as the political culture develops over time and as its meeting places move around the city of Nashville. In this way it makes practical sense to speak of a "style" of action that pertains to NOAH. Rev. James and Rev. Mary are able to make an argument about the "style" of NOAH's group identity—that the role of clergy are crucial to the group identity. John and Shannon can contest this from their own positions and make alternative claims about NOAH's collective identity. Settings help us think about the material and social environment of the deeply relational aspect of position-takings in BBCO and the impact of other fields on a particular setting. Rev. James and Rev. Mary are not only making religious and institutional arguments and stances; they see the clergy caucus as a way to shore up the economic power of NOAH by building its institutional base. They seek to organize certain people—clergy—as a way to help organize money for NOAH and thus build its power.

Let's return to a story I first told in chapter 1, regarding an exchange at a NOAH board meeting. What I did not say in chapter 1 was that in 2016, a public action was held in that sanctuary, where close to seventeen hundred people turned out. Key "targets" such as metro council members and mayoral candidates were present. Throughout my time with NOAH, that public

---

[39] Bourdieu and Wacquant, *An Invitation to Reflexive Sociology*, 17.
[40] Lichterman, "Religion and Social Solidarity," 249.
[41] Lichterman, "Religion in Public Action," 20.
[42] Lichterman, "Religion and Social Solidarity."

action was often referred to with pride. It positioned NOAH as a powerful organization in Nashville and is a crucial episode in NOAH's public story of itself.

When the small group conversations began, which I related earlier, people started by credentialing. Credentialing involves position-taking in the field. Typically, when someone engages in an act of credentialing, they demonstrate their self-interest in the organization. Then the action happens: someone says she believes the issue of affordable housing is a "moral issue," which is a phrase that gets picked up by the group. The middle-aged white man says, "A lot of us have said that this is a moral issue, and I don't think it is a moral issue. It is a damn political issue! And the city government and mayor aren't going to do a thing about it!" Tim, NOAH's lead organizers responds with, "Unless what?" and the older man gets the point: "Unless we do something about it!"

Then, a pastor brings the conversation to a close: "Like my friend here, I think this is a political issue, but it is a political issue with a moral imperative. The political issue has to be driven by a moral imperative."

Finally, when the group is back together a Jewish leader says with a smile: "This is a damn political issue with a moral imperative." The work of NOAH, she says proudly, is fundamentally about "what kind of city we want to be."[43]

BBCO is a collective practice: it involves stance-taking in relation to others in a setting that shapes the group style. People take stances that demonstrate how social regularities and norms are internalized and embodied. Organizing is a practice in that it has a particular habitus, and so organizing as a practice is primarily characterized by style and use of time.

Habitus is a system of "transposable dispositions . . . as principles of the generation and structure of practices and representation which can be objectively 'regulated' and 'regular' without in any way being the product of obedience to rules."[44] Habits function as "embodied history, internalized as second nature and so forgotten history."[45] For Bourdieu, "habitus" is best expressed in terms of "disposition," which "designates a *way of being*, a *habitual state* (especially of the body) and, in particular, a *predisposition, tendency, propensity*, or *inclination*."[46] Habitus and field need to be taken together, as the habitus

---

[43] Reconstructed from field notes, August 8, 2017.
[44] Bourdieu, *Outline of a Theory of Practice*, 72.
[45] Bourdieu, *The Logic of Practice*, 56.
[46] Bourdieu, *Outline of a Theory of Practice*, 214n1, italics in original.

is "embodied history, internalized as a second nature and so forgotten history."[47] Making history is a relational process, whereby new experiences and unforeseen circumstances are appropriately adapted to by the dispositions one is predisposed to in one's environment.

There are important similarities between habitus and the sense of habit I explored in chapter 4.[48] Individuals are habituated into the customs, mores, and norms of groups. Habits of thought and action, like social norms, discipline and shape individuals, but they are equally sites of critical revision and targets of movements for social change. Democracy as a habitual way of life has to do with what democracy looks like—the "emotional habituations and intellectual habitudes" that each public instills in its members.[49] As one scholar has written, habitus is Bourdieu's way of capturing the "generative foundations of all patterns of social practice."[50] The regularities of the field, its social norms and values are inhabited and enacted in deeply relational ways. Critical revisions of such norms is possible, but the work of such revision needs to make practical sense in the broader setting and is characterized by a scene style. Change does not just happen, but is created and possible through the practical life of the group.

Practice is a matter of time, urgency, and style.[51] In contrast to the scientific, analytic, and rational game theorists, practice has its own "temporal structure."[52] In the example I just recounted, NOAH's organizer Tim acted quickly and in time. By doing so Tim took a particular stance in relation to the middle-aged man. He called the him to account, taking him

---

[47] Bourdieu, *The Logic of Practice*. For an account of Bourdieu's sense of "second nature," which sides with Wittgenstein, yet seeks to save what Lovibond views as exemplary in Bourdieu's theory of habitus, see Lovibond, "Second Nature, Habitus, and the Ethical."

[48] For Bourdieu on "habit," see Bourdieu and Wacquant, *An Invitation to Reflexive Sociology*, 122. On connections between Dewey and Bourdieu, see 122–23; Ostrow, "Culture as a Fundamental Dimension of Experience."

[49] Dewey, *The Public and Its Problems*, 192.

[50] Ostrow, "Culture as a Fundamental Dimension of Experience," 282: "The real brilliance of his text [*Outline of a Theory of Practice*] is showing how historically developed social formations—that is the meaning of socio-culture itself—are grounded in the collective functional meanings and rhythms of everyday life."

[51] At one point in explaining the relationship of practice and time, Bourdieu says, "Practice unfolds in time and it has all the correlative properties, such as irreversibility, that synchronization destroys. Its temporal structure, that is, its rhythm, its tempo, and above all its directionality, is constitutive of its meaning.... In short, because it is entirely immersed in the current of time, practice is inseparable from temporality, not only because it is played out in time, but also because it plays strategically with time and especially with tempo" (*The Logic of Practice*, 81).

[52] As Bourdieu says, practice is "caught up in 'the matter in hand,' totally present in the present and in the practical functions that it finds there in the form of objective potentialities, practice excludes attention to itself (that is, to the past). It is unaware of the principles that govern it and the possibilities they contain; it can only discover them by enacting them, unfolding them in time" (ibid., 92).

as an epistemic authority and responsible for his claims. The leader was not anticipating Tim's question and so took a beat to respond. It was not a scripted conversation; Tim's question makes practical sense. It placed Tim and the leader in a relationship of accountability in a particular setting and scene. Tim took the leader to be entitled to responding to her own analysis. This example demonstrates the enactment of the radically democratic political culture of NOAH in time and with a particular style.

Time and tempo are crucial because the logic of practice is not that of the analyst which can construct theories of practice outside of the conditions that give rise to the practice itself. That sort of logic of practice, which is decontextual, ahistorical, and atemporal, does not make practical sense. Practice is "entirely immersed in the current of time."[53]

Broad-based community organizing is also immersed in the current of time: organizing has a temporal structure, a rhythm, a directionality embodied and enacted in the larger field. The radically democratic political culture of NOAH is best conceived as an ethical way of life. As an ethical way of life, the stances leaders take in relation to one another, the social norms and regularities are learned in time. The political culture of NOAH is founded on democratic individuality and self-interest and as such is concerned with the kinds of individuals formed in NOAH. One's self-interest is the value-laden and relational stake one has in the organizing; this is the directionality of the practice.[54] The temporality of organizing calls attention to Tim's timely response to the leader's complaint, but it also calls attention to the larger calendar of the organizing process: organizing is always a process of disorganizing and reorganizing. The listening campaign itself is an iterative effort that occurs every three to four years. Practice is concerned with the matter at hand; it answers the demand of things to be done and is caught up in the heat of the moment. To talk of the practice of organizing requires attention to the settings of NOAH and the scenes of action; such practical logic would not make sense without the position-taking and relational network in particular material conditions. In a different setting and scene, with different fields of relationship and stances taken, the leader might have rejected Tim's question as offensive and out of place. Tim's question plays with time in a way that makes sense only in NOAH, in an ethical culture and form of

---

[53] Ibid., 81.
[54] Bourdieu's own thoughts on "interest" expand beyond reductionist Marxist economism to a broader notion of interest (Bourdieu and Wacquant, *An Invitation to Reflexive Sociology,* 116). See also Stout, *Blessed Are the Organized,* 41, 216–18.

social practical reasoning of holding each other accountable and responsible for our judgments and actions and those future actions and concerns such actions commit or entitle us to.

The deep relationship between practice and time is such that practical logic is governed by directional urgency. Urgency has less to do with speed than it does with priority. In the "heat of the moment" practices are urgent in the sense that actions are exercised with a sense of priority. As Marshall Ganz has written, "An urgent need to complete a problem set due tomorrow supplants the important need to decide what to do with the rest of life. . . . The urgent need to attend to a critically ill family member supplants the important need to attend a long postponed business meeting (or ought to?)."[55] The directionality of practice stems from the values and interests (broadly speaking) of the habitus. Ganz's aside "or ought to?" highlights the disjuncture between competing values in social practices and returns us to the familiar conversation on sacred values: those evaluative attitudes that are not on the same scale; family and money are not comparable, Ganz is telling us. Similarly, in the NOAH example above, the clergy's response of seeing political issues with "moral imperatives" frames the work in a larger narrative. I doubt the pastor was thinking in terms of Kantian categorical imperatives. Instead, he seems to be expressing a sense of responsibility and accountability toward his fellow neighbor grounded in his broader Christian tradition. He cares about affordable housing not because it is politically lucrative but because this is what his tradition requires of him.

Talk of organizing as a practice helps us see how style and stylistically playing with time (tempo, rhythm) are aspects of organizing. Different actions in different settings and scene styles have different meanings. The importance of style in practice theory highlights the illogical logic of practice itself and the urgent and strategic playfulness with time that is captured in the phrases "the heat of the moment," "the twinkling of an eye," "on the spot," all of which Bourdieu uses in describing the "current of time" in which practice is entirely immersed.

The question Tim posed to the leader betrays this use of time and urgency. As such, it is agitational. Agitation is a crucial part of the broader BBCO tradition: it is a matter of style and of relationship. One cannot agitate out of relationship. Tim's question "Unless what?" was curt. He did not mince words because he did not need more. BBCO is well-known for its style of agitation,

---

[55] Ganz, "Leading Change," 10.

most especially in one-on-one meetings. But this exchange highlights how agitation is part of the broader political culture of NOAH and BBCO generally. Recall the exchange regarding the clergy caucus; that was certainly an agitational, tension-filled scene.

Agitation is meant to wake people up, to stir people into action and relationship. To be agitated is to be unsettled, to experience self-reflexive or social tension. In relational meetings, agitation occurs when someone probes into why we care about the things we do and how we are fighting for the things we hold most dear. Agitation is done with intention and directionality—in this case, to connect their story to the story of BBCO. Agitation makes practical sense only in relationship.[56] Agitation outside of relationship or in a nondemocratic relationship tends toward bullying, shaming, and domination. Agitation involves tending to the presence of another, holding their stories and presence with care. Organizers and leaders agitate by asking questions that cause people to reflect on their commitment to or responsibility for their values and interests.

In this sense, Tim's question is not the only work of agitation in this scene: the leader's claim is also an attempt at agitation, but it tends toward despair and despondency. The leader splits "moral" and "political" issues and by doing so gives the elected officials too much power over NOAH: "I don't think it is a moral issue. It is a damn political issue! And the city government and mayor aren't going to do a thing about it!" Tim's question brings NOAH back in relationship to the issue, to those elected officials, reminds those in the task force of their own position in NOAH, and NOAH's public position to those elected officials. His question helps the leader recognize that he has the power to act and he embraces it: "Unless we do something about it!"

It is crucial to see, however, that this style of agitation was complemented by the pastor's explicit recognition of the values at play in organizing. Organizing is not merely a political game. Organizing is grounded in value-laden relationships. Organizing is first and foremost relational and value-based practice. In my estimation, the leader's comments express despondency and exasperation for two reasons: first, he gives too much power to elected officials and so fails to see the nature of the political relationships as grounded in accountability and responsibility, and thus NOAH's own commitment and entitlement to having a value-laden stake in political life. But second, by attempting to isolate politics from "moral issues" he fails to see

---

[56] Cf. Chambers and Cowan, *Roots for Radicals*, ch. 2.

morals and values as foundational to politics, and so disregards the care and concern his fellow leaders have in organizing. Tim and the pastor correct this by waking him up to the value-laden, radically democratic political culture of NOAH.

Follow the Action

Grasped in this broader frame, the practice of broad-based community organizing requires attention to the relational, dynamic process that involves taking stances (position-takings in a field) in settings. Organizing is not a set of tools or a craft, because that would isolate the agent apart from the broader political culture, social norms, and sacred values at play in the setting. Settings are ambiguous, where multiple narratives and traditions are at play.

Seeing organizing as a practice helps us to also grasp how the practice itself is influenced and shaped by racial capitalism. This is an issue that I will address head-on in the next chapter, but it merits a comment here, too. BBCO, at its best, is about building relational power for working people by working people for their communities. *How* this practice happens needs to attend to the power structures within and beyond the BBCO affiliate. We need to attend to the way power operates in the converging fields, the setting, and in the scene styles of organizing itself. I have attempted to demonstrate that here in this chapter. If unaddressed, the logic of racial capitalism can pervert the attempt to build relational power—it can twist the very practice itself. Instead of a practice grounded in social practical reasoning and mutual recognition, it becomes an instrumental, transactional from of politics under the grip of racial capitalism. BBCO itself then tends to becomes exploitative and expropriative. BBCO needs to double down on the relational and value-laden nature of the practice and recommit to the ethical life of radical democracy in order to shore up economic, political, and religious power to counter racial capitalism in its own ethical life and in the broader contexts in which it organizes. People protect and fight for what they hold most dear; sacred values are at the heart of this practice. The role of counterpublics, and especially counterpublic churches, is especially important in this task.

6
On Black Organizing
Capitalist Exploitation, Racial Expropriation

Any account of radical democracy that cannot adequately grapple with the tentacles of capitalist exploitation and racial expropriation in the U.S. political landscape is fundamentally flawed. This is a weakness in both John Dewey's and Sheldon Wolin's versions of radical democracy. My account of social practical reasoning and radical democracy are deeply inspired by BBCO, but I also draw deeply from a tradition of radical social gospelers and Christian democratic socialists like Cornel West and Rev. George Washington Woodbey, who will feature largely in the next chapter. The vocation of this sort of prophetic Christianity is to negate concrete evils such as racial, gender, and economic domination and exploitation and to transform social and political conditions toward still greater individual and social freedom.

Some religious scholars and theologians are less convinced that BBCO is the right example for the kind of radical democracy I am after. Most recently, Vincent Lloyd has argued that BBCO manipulates the expression of race and theology in the practice of organizing.[1] Rather than grapple with the tangles of race, Lloyd argues, BBCO tends to assimilate racial and religious difference into white Protestantism. Lloyd sees much more promise in a kind of organizing that returns to Lloyd's distinct reading of the origins of a Black theology that has not fallen victim to the secular ideology of neoliberal multiculturalism.

I find Lloyd's claims provocative and helpful in amplifying an already ongoing internal critique of BBCO. Since the 1990s organizers and scholars of organizing have written about how the BBCO model has been dominated by white, Christian, heterosexual men.[2] Mark Warren's and Richard Wood and

---

[1] Lloyd, *Religion of the Field Negro*.
[2] See Sinclair, "Re-examining Community Organizing"; Warren, *Dry Bones Rattling*. For a more recent account, see Wood and Fulton. *A Shared Future*.

Brad Fulton's respective ethnographic studies of the Texas IAF and the Pacific Institute for Community Organizing national network illustrate how various BBCO networks have taken steps to address the critique that it manages the differences of race and religion in the frame of neoliberal white Protestantism (a frame that, for Lloyd, is secularist).[3] In his first book, Wood carried out a comparative analysis between the BBCO approach to organizing and "race-based organizing."[4] Charlene Sinclair deepens critiques like Lloyd's by arguing that BBCO does not take seriously the hegemonic cultural forces of racial capitalism in the practice of organizing. Sinclair writes, "Embedded in Alinsky's method is the moral ideal of the worker as defined by participation within industrialized wage-granting constructs. . . . Alinksy's method discourages direct engagement with questions of race, gender, and sexuality."[5] Simply put, this critique argues that BBCO cannot adequately address the deep cultural and systemic injustices in the United States caused by class exploitation and racial expropriation.

Lloyd's and Sinclair's critiques of BBCO get right to the heart of one of my main concerns with BBCO by forcefully asking: Can BBCO actualize the radically democratic power it purports to build? It is possible to read Lloyd's and Sinclair's work as invectives against BBCO, but I hear an invitation; a more nuanced reading of Lloyd's and Sinclair's work could reveal deep convergences with BBCO as I've experienced it. The first section of this chapter gets Lloyd's critique up and running, supplementing it with work done by Sinclair. I begin with Lloyd in part to be clear on what is at stake: the critique is that BBCO is politically, economically, and theologically deficient; indeed, Lloyd suspects that BBCO has a sinister theological grounding, which turns out not to be theological at all, but instead is secularist. Lloyd begins with a certain definition of "secularism" which he identifies in BBCO, turns his attention to role of the organizer in BBCO, and then presents his alternative of Black organizing and Black theology. I find Lloyd's work, supplemented with Sinclair's, helpful in articulating a crucial challenge for BBCO: How does it understand race expropriation and class exploitation to be shaping up in the United States, and how can BBCO build political and economic power to counter the violent forces of racial capitalism?

---

[3] Wood and Fulton conducted their research for *A Shared Future* before PICO was renamed Faith in Action.
[4] Wood, Faith in Action, ch. 3. Wood's chapter focuses specifically on the Center for Third World Organizing.
[5] Sinclair, "Let the Dead Speak!," 6.

In the next section, I build on Lloyd's work by drawing in political and social theorists to argue that capitalism moves by exploitation and expropriation that depends on "hidden abodes" not entirely encompassed within the economy. Capitalism's "conditions of possibility" lie in certain social, economic, and political relations of power that violently exploit and expropriate. Lloyd's and Sinclair's work invites us to image how BBCO might look if it adequately contends with not only the violent reality of racial capitalism's exploitation but also the conditions of possibility that expropriate peoples, lands, and societies, which Nancy Fraser calls capitalism's "hidden abodes."[6]

The first two sections set up and extend Lloyd's and Sinclair's invitation. The third section explores how BBCO organizes against racial capitalism in a nonsecularist fashion. This section picks up an example I presented in an earlier chapter from NOAH when an unarmed Black person was murdered by the Nashville Metropolitan Police. I explore how the Spirit of radical democracy in BBCO can build relational power against racial capitalism's violent processes of exploitation and expropriation. The narrative and example I draw from here help illustrate how the power of radical democracy in BBCO can be a nonsecularist response to racial capitalism. But BBCO is certainly not a perfect model; improvements need to be made, as is patently clear in Lloyd and Sinclair. The final section argues that by centering the political role of sacred value, in this specific case the sacred value of Black life, BBCO can more adequately build relational power that grasps the role of race expropriation and class exploitation in contemporary racial capitalism.

The Challenge of Black Organizing to BBCO

Lloyd has powerfully argued that BBCO manipulates the expression of race and theology in the practice of organizing. According to Lloyd, organizers center white Christianity by managing expressions of race and theology.[7] BBCO, it turns out, is not the place to find radical democracy that confronts white supremacy, but is in fact another site of toothless secularist politics that actually reduces all differences into a bland unity in difference (whiteness). Rather than grapple with the tangles of race, BBCO tends to assimilate

---

[6] Fraser, "Expropriation and Exploitation in Racialized Capitalism"; Fraser, "Behind Marx's Hidden Abode"; Dawson, "Hidden in Plain Sight."

[7] Lloyd, *Religion of the Field Negro*. See also Lloyd, *Black Natural Law*, esp. "Afterword: Beyond Secularism and Multiculturalism."

racial and religious difference into white Protestantism. "Unmanageable dimensions of difference are muzzled," Lloyd writes.[8] Lloyd sees much more promise in a kind of organizing that returns to his distinct reading of the origins of a Black theology which has not fallen victim to the secular ideology of neoliberal multiculturalism. In what follows, I specify Lloyd's critique by focusing first on the role of the organizer in BBCO, which Lloyd finds problematic. Second, I analyze the alternative of Black organizing. But before I jump in, I need to briefly highlight some of Lloyd's crucial theoretical moves in affiliating BBCO with a "secular ideology" and opposing BBCO to his version of Black theology. For Lloyd, theology's proper work is idolatry critique and social criticism, and the primary idol today is secularism.

Secularism, as Lloyd understands it, is the exclusion and management of religion; in secular logic nothing exists except the ways of this world. These aspects of Lloyd's critique of secular logic ring true with Tracy Fessenden's and Joan Scott's critiques, outlined in chapter 1, but it leaves out Scott's and Fessenden's feminist insights. In my account, drawing from Scott and Fessenden, religious and secular are mutually constructing categories. Secular*ism* refers to the political conditions of a public where no religion is dominant. This differs from an ideologically informed sense of "the secular" or "secular*ist*" that baptizes certain expressions of religious and civic culture and practices as normative for public life. It is to this ideological sense of the secular that Lloyd's critique of BBCO refers. The secular in this sense turns out to be a vague form of heteropatriarchal Protestantism supporting racial capitalism. In this ideological sense of the secular, religion is "compatible with the status quo; often this means that religion is confined to the heart, treated as a personal choice, entailing only those normative claims that match ambient values."[9]

For Black theology, secular ideology is particularly dangerous because it threatens Black theology's revolutionary impulse—thereby defining the political ends of Black theology in terms set by the white world. Black theologians under the lure of secularist logic eventually end up leaving their religious radicalism behind altogether, believing the secular's lie that Black theology has nothing to say that cannot be said in secularist terms.[10] Black theology is best exemplified in the early work of James Cone, who

---

[8] Lloyd, *Religion of the Field Negro*, 114.
[9] Ibid., 4.
[10] Ibid.

emphasizes the paradox and tradition of Black theology. Black theology refuses the "wisdom" of the white world and refuses to follow secularist multicultural logic by attempting to "pluralize" theology. Black theology is *the* orthodox theology: "All theology, properly understood, is black theology. All social criticism, properly understood, is theological. Black theology is social criticism; social criticism is black theology."[11] Black theology as social criticism is iconoclastic and idolatry critique in a world ridden with white idols and secularist icons. Lloyd's aim here is to "reterritorialize" transcendental claims into theology as Black theology.[12] What matters for Lloyd is the project of social criticism and idolatry critique that is inherent in his version of Black theology.

I am quite sympathetic to Lloyd's critique of the secular as an ideology. However, I want to slow down Lloyd's moves from a first opposition between Black theology and the secular to a final opposition between BBCO and Black theology. Lloyd's larger argument against BBCO is built on four central claims: (1) the opposition between Black theology and secularist logic, which I just laid out; (2) the identification of the secular with liberalism/pluralism; (3) the identification of BBCO with liberalism/pluralism; and (4) the opposition between Black theology and BBCO.[13] It is not entirely clear to me that secularist ideology can be identified with liberalism/pluralism. Nor is it clear that BBCO can be reduced with liberalism/pluralism and thus secular ideology. Indeed, in Lloyd's most recent work on prison abolition, the examples given align with my own experience in BBCO as a value pluralist, radically democratic, nonsecularist version of BBCO. At the core of my argument is the assumption that to pluralize theology is not to adopt a secularist theology and so to follow the wisdom of the white world. Religious cultural criticism can emphasize constructivism, pluralism, and liberation from racial capitalist exploitation and expropriation. Indeed, I read Lloyd as uplifting certain forms of organizing, including types of BBCO. So what do we make of his critique?

One answer might be that Lloyd wants BBCO to tear down its own idols and embrace Black theology as social criticism—a project that shares some similarity with my own in the call to center sacred values and theology. Such a move changes how we organize and how we think and theologize about

---

[11] Ibid., 5.
[12] Clark, "Book Review."
[13] Thanks to Toni Alimi and Brian Lee for helping me see these aspects of Lloyd's argument more clearly.

organizing. For Lloyd, BBCO as it is currently practiced sees religion only as a vague sense of values rather than a deep tradition and language of paradox embodied in the wisdom of Black people. Similarly, BBCO employs a secularist multiculturalist model for handling racial difference: "In this way, proper racial difference is difference that can be submerged in unity, presumably in something like the affirmation of common humanity to which religious difference is reduced."[14] All racial and religious difference is subsumed into a vague unity-in-difference, what Lloyd calls a theology of neoliberal multiculturalism.[15] When Lloyd introduces this classification of BBCO as a theology of neoliberal multiculturalism, he notes that it is assumed to be self-evident and not accountable to any other tradition. A number of other scholars would disagree and note that four broad traditions most often feed the practice of organizing in BBCO, notably Catholic social teaching, Black liberation theology, Protestant social gospel, and Latin American liberation theology.[16] Lloyd's point, however, is relevant for my own argument that seeks to center sacred values and the radical social gospel in the practice of organizing.

Take, for example, Lloyd's critique of the BBCO organizer. Lloyd claims that BBCO needs to take racial difference seriously. Blackness is not one identity category among others; it is a way of seeing and being in the world. BBCO organizers, with their theology of neoliberal multiculturalism, have fallen under the guise of "false consciousness." "As outsiders entering a community," Lloyd writes, organizers "[see] themselves as possessing the formula for organizing success," when really "the key players and relationships they chart out overlook the already strong and potentially fecund bonds between women and families in that community."[17] Black organizing takes place within the Black community, without help from an outsider organizer who "artificially" weaves new relationships that overlook already established relationships "often begun over a coffee table in the home." The organizer is an extra human "catalyst" bringing in tow "rigid procedures, slogans, and technical jargon" that ignore "deep relationships, [which] unlike the artificially cultivated relationships of Alinsky-style organizing, are capable of sustaining an organizing effort over the long haul."[18] Lloyd's problem with BBCO organizers is that they impose their theology of neoliberal multiculturalism

---

[14] Lloyd, *Religion of the Field Negro*, 119.
[15] Ibid., 121.
[16] Warren, *Dry Bones Rattling,* ch. 2; Wood, *Faith in Action*, ch. 5, esp. 188.
[17] Lloyd, *Religion of the Field Negro*, 124.
[18] Ibid.

on the Black community's organic relationships that foster the wisdom and power of the poor.

Lloyd's point is not merely that organizers are outsiders to local communities, but also that the style of organizing is white: its discourse and habits of thought and action seek to manage Black theology's wisdom into secularist neoliberal multiculturalism. Black organizing "trusts the grassroots, trusts the wisdom of ordinary black people to continue doing what they have been doing for generations: working together, listening to each other's stories, consulting with community elders, and collectively confronting what strikes them as unjust."[19] This tradition of organizing is rooted in the Black community's quest for liberation. This sort of organizing does away with BBCO's unnecessary "processes and structures of organizing," the very habits that contain its whiteness. Recently BBCO networks like Faith in Action and the Gamaliel Foundation have begun to admit the truth of Lloyd's point and to transform their processes of organizing. Black organizing, by contrast, is grounded in "raw anger and emotion leading to action." Black organizing is liberation "without content, liberation that means overturning the table, radically reconfiguring the social world in a way unimaginable from the perspective of the present. Any content attributed to liberation evinces optimism and so false consciousness, a refusal to acknowledge the depths of racial injustice in America."[20]

Sinclair speaks about these matters from experience, being a trained Alinsky-style organizer herself, and her contribution sharpens and deepens this line of thought. She grounds her understanding of BBCO as a democratic practice that seeks to place power back in the hands of ordinary people in order to achieve "conditional justice."[21] But this approach fails to do the "deep work" of reckoning with how racial capitalism structures and rationalizes its domination in the political economy and the broader culture.[22] It is at this point that Sinclair's argument dovetails with my own criticisms of BBCO, when she states, "Alinsky's approach argues that the utilization of an analysis of race and or gender creates a wedge between people and thus does not enable the development of the large-scale people power needed to resist the exploitation of large corporations or within workplaces."[23] As I have argued,

[19] Ibid., 129.
[20] Ibid., 128.
[21] Sinclair, "Let the Dead Speak!," 5.
[22] Sinclair, "Interventions Forum on Privilege and Power in the Capitalocene."
[23] Ibid.

BBCO dismisses sacred values on the grounds that they divide the constituency. In a similar manner, Sinclair tells us, BBCO dismisses race and gender analysis. Alinsky's very theory of change, Sinclair argues, is premised on a conception of conflict grounded in an exchange of reasons, "which will result in rational adjustments of interest and power."[24] Sinclair's work introduces crucial additions to Lloyd's important critique of BBCO: besides the claim that BBCO manages and manipulates differences of race and religion, BBCO misunderstands the basic nature of capitalism's exploitative and, more important here, *expropriative* structure.

Lloyd and Sinclair offer an invitation to BBCO, not a dismissal. This is a calling back of BBCO to the true work of radical democracy. Lloyd's own agitation of BBCO even uses the practice's tools on itself: he agitates in order to unearth what is really at stake for BBCO. Lloyd's claim that BBCO is bourgeois has standing; in a similar vein, I want to hold BBCO accountable to its radically democratic core. He wants BBCO to criticize its own idols. Rather than reading Lloyd and Sinclair as rejecting BBCO, I hear them inviting those who support broad-based organizing to further develop its capacity to resist the secular idols and instead tap into the theological, economic, and political forces of BBCO to resist racial capitalism. Put differently, Lloyd and Sinclair are pointing out the theological limits of BBCO as it is currently practiced—something I agree with. By eschewing and marginalizing theology and sacred values in the practice of BBCO, its political theological imagination remains desiccated, dried up, fallow. BBCO needs to center the theological work of relational power-building in its practices and especially the political role of sacred values. The sort of relational power that results strengthens counterpublics that build economic and political power. To build that sort of power, however, we need to understand what we're up against: how racial capitalism exploits and expropriates.

Racial Capitalist Exploration and Expropriation

Capitalism exploits. As an economy, *simpliciter,* its basic mode consists of workers entering the capitalist market to sell their labor so that they may get access to the basics of life. But in a capitalist economy, these same workers have no right to the surplus value of the product they have produced. The

---

[24] Sinclair, "Let the Dead Speak!," 6.

capitalist market is not an arena of equal exchange. Workers are compensated only what is socially necessary to continue capitalist accumulation and are denied access to the means of production that might allow them to appropriate its surplus, inevitably leading to the emergence of two classes locked in conflict: capitalists and everyday people who have to work for a living.[25] But capitalism is more than an economy; it is an "institutionalized social system" that uses hegemony to rationalize its violent reality.[26] Issues of gender, ecology, and political power are central here. Capitalism depends on several "hidden abodes" behind the two-story (base and superstructure) structure that is the house of orthodox Marxism: capitalism as it shapes up today depends on background conditions that infiltrate our social reproductive lives, our very conception of nature, and our understanding of political power.[27]

Capitalism also expropriates. Not every human has equal access to the market or is considered a "worker." There are those under capitalism who are considered less than "workers" and those not granted the status of human, and history shows that capitalist expropriation is integrally connected to racial oppression. In the Black radical tradition, historians have highlighted the depths to which fifteenth-century slavers went in order to rationalize their human cargo as commodities.[28] Expropriation is "accumulation by other means" and works by "confiscating capacities and resources and conscripting them into capital's circuits of self-expansion."[29] Reckoning not only with capitalism's exploitative nature but also its expropriative nature unveils how deeply racialized capitalism is as an institutionalized social order. We need to contend not only with class exploitation that shapes up primarily in the labor relationship, prototypically imaged as the worker entering the capitalist market, selling "his" labor to gain his subsistence; we also need to contend with how expropriation moves through power relationships that often shape up in the form of sociopolitical status (the nonhuman, the nonworker, the noncitizen, etc.).[30] To speak of capitalism is to speak of a racialized economic

---

[25] Fraser, "Expropriation and Exploitation in Racialized Capitalism." The phrase "people who have to work for a living" is from Joerg Rieger's *Theology in the Capitalocene*.
[26] Fraser, "Behind Marx's Hidden Abode." But the claims on hegemony build from Sinclair's work, who draws from Manning Marable's use of Antonio Gramsci's notion of hegemony. See Marable, *How Capitalism Underdeveloped Black America*.
[27] Fraser, "Behind Marx's Hidden Abode."
[28] Smallwood, *Saltwater Slavery*.
[29] Fraser, "Expropriation and Exploitation in Racialized Capitalism," 166.
[30] This move toward an adjustment of class as including a Weberian notion of status is indebted to Nancy Fraser's work. See Fraser and Honneth, *Redistribution or Recognition?* I add "sociopolitical"

order whose expropriation continues to haunt the very life of its institutionalized social order, whether through housing or labor markets, access to healthcare, or schooling, to name a few arenas where capitalism's expropriation continues to mutate.[31] Class exploitation and racial expropriation are two crucial foundations of capitalism today, along with the domains of social reproduction, ecology, and political power. To adequately contend with how race and class power shape up, BBCO needs to build class power *and* contend with white supremacy.

The sort of radical democracy and the form of social practical reasoning that I advance in this book and as I see it taking shape in BBCO need to be able to address capitalism's exploitation and its expropriation. In its ideal form, my account of social practical reasoning is radically democratic. Domination occurs when someone is in a position to *arbitrarily* exercise their will. Capitalist societies are dominating because many workers cannot prevent employers from arbitrarily exercising their power over them; this is why battles over labor laws and unions are so crucial today, but also why racial domination in capitalism is so amplified, because it operates primarily by expropriation rather than exploitation. We must cut out domination at the root; in social practices like the one-on-one, BBCO cultivates a radically democratic culture that requires people to be held responsible for their reasons and accountable to the community and tradition that normatively formed them. Reason-giving acts as a constraint against the arbitrary exercise of the will. The social practice of reasoning is a political practice because it is a social, historical, normative practice, depending on norms and the sociopolitical status of reasoners. Communities of reasoning, over time, have institutionalized these practices; institutions are collections of social practices. Radically revising capitalism's expropriative structure requires building a new democratic culture that depends on a form of mutual recognition that is political in nature—that is, political recognition of each agent as an epistemic authority. This is not a call for an interpersonal panacea to racial bias. To build radically democratic political and economic cultures, you need to transform the structures of society. But structures are constituted by practices grounded in norms; changing structures requires engaging sacred

---

here to denote how status is a political and social institutional relationship, not one of self realization that might be found in other literature on recognition.

[31] For Fraser, these are matters not only of redistribution but also of recognition as a political relationship of status.

values in our political and economic practices. That work starts by building political and economic power from the ground up. Sacred values play a political role in our social practice of reasoning; they are key in identity and community formation; individual and communal agents build practices and institutions on such norms and values in a way that defines their lives apart from others. Democratic politics is the collective pursuit and contestation of the common good. Sacred values and their coincident social practices have a political role in our democratic life together.

Counterpublics like BBCO do not always (or, arguably, even often) engage in social practices like the relational meeting and listening campaign in a radically democratic way. The social practical reasoning is radically democratic *ideally*. Our social practical reasoning presumes radically democratic conditions and is always situated in relationships of power. But those political conditions can be infiltrated by white supremacy and capitalism. To contend with how BBCO can respond to Lloyd's critique and how exploitation and expropriation shape up, I want to return to the example I used in a previous chapter of NOAH's organizing response to the murder of Daniel Hambrick by a police officer.

Sacred Values, Black Life, and Broad-Based Organizing

On July 26, 2018, a police officer fatally shot Daniel Hambrick in the back as he was fleeing for his life after the police illegitimately stopped his car. A few days later, NOAH held a press conference issuing their demands: the dismissal of the chief of police, the establishment of a Community Oversight Board, and the implementation of body and dash cameras throughout the Metropolitan Nashville Police Department (MNPD).

NOAH's organizing takes place in conditions of white supremacy, which concretizes the violence of capitalism's expropriation of Black people. The MNPD operates with little accountability. The MNPD and the metro government delayed implementing body and dash cameras for over a year, and the metro government consistently refused to hold the chief of police accountable for Hambrick's murder, while continuing to implement racist police practices. The state legislature continually upholds the status quo by threatening to overrule any democratic movement by the public. The MNPD and state legislature arbitrarily influence the lives of their citizens insofar as they fail to track citizens' relevant interests, needs, or concerns. In this way, the political conditions are dominated by governmental and state powers that enshrine capitalism's exploitative and expropriative nature. Lloyd claims that any organizing that is not Black organizing cannot but adopt these conditions, and so NOAH's actions in fact further entrench racial capitalism.

But NOAH acted publicly because it decided that a sacred value of the group had been violated. The dialogical process of NOAH members agreeing to the public statement and list of demands includes a politics of tending, of attending to relevant differences, rooted in sacred values. Tending to these sacred values fosters individual and collective self-interest and involves reference to the group and grid aspect of identity by contestation and disagreement.[32] By issuing these demands, NOAH is saying that in light of the horrendous violation that has taken place, *these* are NOAH's demands; *we* stand here. This boundary drawing included the exit of one influential member of a NOAH congregation and complaints by several congregations. Crucially, this democratic dialogical process depends on clarity of self-interest within NOAH's membership. Self-interest is one's value-laden stake in a common good; one's self-interest and what we hold most dear are deeply connected. Individual members have to come up with their own reasons for supporting these demands. Differences have to be tended to. Self-interest is an important part of the shared understanding of NOAH's internal order. Blackness as a unique, nonreducible identity category had to be tended to in these discussions, by all parties.

Angela, a Black organizer I spoke with during this organizing season, addressed this point: "In a lot of what I do in this job, I put my Blackness first. I think that's part of what attracted me to organizing."[33] Angela and Tim, NOAH's lead organizer, both said that the tension in the room was palpable as NOAH was deciding what action to take in response to Hambrick's murder. But "to be in the room around a lot of nonwhite people who are looking for a very intentional response to the shooting was very refreshing," Angela said.

Lloyd warns BBCO of its idols, secularism being the most tempting. He invites us to imagine how organizing might look different if Blackness is not reduced to one difference among others. But in order to contest exploitation and expropriation, BBCO needs to build relational power—a sort of relational power that depends on a form of recognition that can be achieved

---

[32] My account of group and grid identity formation is indebted to Mary Douglas; see chapter 4.
[33] Interview with author, March 4, 2019.

in the one-on-one and listening campaign. This form of recognition is political in the sense of political institutions conferring adequate status as a member of society in the relevant ways. This is not about identity politics or a politics of recognition in terms of self-realization. Instead it is about building a democratic culture that consists of counterpublic institutions that recognize one as a member of the sociopolitical community. When members of the political community are violated, dominated, exploited, or expropriated, they are not granted adequate status, and so the BBCO constituency enters the process of deciding and then acting to hold such injustices accountable.

NOAH's pluralism contributes to its relational power. Because NOAH is constituted by sixty-three member institutions—religious congregations, labor unions, and other community organizations—the grid and group aspects of NOAH's identity are informed by the various publics that form and shape its members in different ways. The democratic process of NOAH's decision-making is generative of relational power because it involves people engaging in social practical reasoning on issues and problems that affect their lives. This process is grounded in the self-interest of each member and the self-interest of NOAH as a group. Insofar as a member's self-interest or sacred value is continually and arbitrarily sacrificed, NOAH teeters toward domination and is undemocratic. Exit and protest are valid in this case because NOAH then would not be what it claims: a group constituted by an ethical way of life known as radical democracy.[34]

NOAH is a prime example of a counterpublic consisting of other publics, whose dialogical decision-making process is radically democratic only when it embraces *parrhesia*, democratic individuality (which crucially depends on self-interest), a politics of tending, and is generative of relational power. Such an ethical way of life of radical democracy is grounded in values held sacred. NOAH arrives at the values it holds sacred through radically democratic social practical reasoning. Its pluralist social practice of radical democracy is generative of relational power that can be leveraged against capitalist exploitation and expropriation. Social practical reasoning confers political recognition that can help build relational power crucial to building class power to contest exploitation. Organizing is about building democratic relational power for working people and their communities. For this to be radically

---

[34] Toleration might be another option, but in the sentence referenced I have considered differences that are continually and arbitrarily sacrificed, making the group dominating. For a consideration of toleration as a virtue, see Bowlin, *Tolerance among the Virtues*.

democratic, in the sense of recognizing all members of the counterpublic, it will need to build power to contest the way that capitalism as an institutional social order is integrally racialized. This same argument could be made, and should be made, for how capitalism exploits and expropriates our gendered and sexed relations of social reproduction. NOAH illustrates how this radically democratic process of social practical reasoning can center sacred values like Black life. This is a point I think Lloyd would embrace; this is a kind of organizing that refutes secular worldly logic while building iconoclastic political and economic power. The plural character of BBCO affiliates does not identify BBCO with secularist ideology.

NOAH acted against the modern violence of the state and its police by claiming that a fundamental sacred value of Black life was horrendously violated. In this case, NOAH's actions are not so much concerned with the political wins or losses. NOAH acted because the group decided this is what it means to be a member of NOAH. NOAH acted because to act otherwise would require reasons that deny the reality of the death-dealing violence against Hambrick. NOAH members saw their self-interest as deeply connected to all those impacted and effected by Hambrick's murder. The group acted out of relational power and called to account those authorities responsible for this brutality.

Notice in my account I have not yet mentioned the role of the organizer as an "outside catalyst." I agree with some of Lloyd's critique of the organizer. Too often, however, in broad-based organizing coalitions and among those who study it, the distinction between the organizer and leaders is emphasized. The social practice of radical democracy needs to be viewed in the entire life of the group. Organizing is a practice; it takes place in relationships of power that entice or restrict certain actions.[35] Such critiques of the professional organizer operate with too strict a difference between organizers and leaders within a BBCO affiliate. The primary job of an organizer is to identify and connect leaders, who are already organizing their communities. Lloyd's critique of Alinsky-style organizing jargon and foreign logic seems to be directed not at the social practice of radical democracy as it is found in BBCO. Instead, its true target seems to be the legacy of charisma associated with organizing since the rise of President Barack Obama and other organizers of notoriety like Alinsky, Ed Chambers, and Ernie Cortez.

---

[35] Chapter 5 expands on this understanding of organizing as a practice, as compared to organizing as an art or science.

So far as Lloyd's critique of the charisma of organizing goes, I agree with it. Some hierarchy in organizing groups is inevitable. This seems to be the root of the distinction in BBCO between organizers and leaders, or in Lloyd's case young Black organizers and community elders. In both cases the hierarchy does not need to be unaccountable, unearned, or dominating, and both are grounded in a social practice of radical democracy.

Lloyd might grant that NOAH acted out of a concern for sacred value, but the action still plays the same political game as the MNPD. Lloyd's Black organizing is found in the kind of revolutionary action by urban uprisings in the 1960s that combined "pure rebellion and pure liberation as linked, with both receiving divine sanction."[36] Even when BBCO takes action on race-distinct matters, it fails to even gesture toward Black liberation.

As Lloyd and Sinclair show, BBCO constituencies can and should be pushed to act in accordance with the sacred value of Black life, and they need to stay vigilant against choosing conventionalism and the status quo over more tension-raising actions. Lloyd has not given many empirical examples of what he imagines as Black organizing.[37]

That is, until his most recent coauthored work on abolitionism.[38] But even there, as he writes about abolitionist organizing, he does two things that connect his work to the tradition of radical democracy I find in BBCO and advance here. First, he conceives of abolitionism as an idea *and* a set of practices; second, it has a revivalist *spirit*.[39] In this sense, abolitionism is a set of organizing practices that arise from particular individuals engaged in specific struggles to end the prison-industrial complex. Attuned to these struggles, abolition sounds and looks like the complicated reality of "practical politics."[40] Abolition and Black organizing share a certain sort of pessimism, but abolitionism is characterized by a hope that "careens back up in the form of righteous fury."[41] Abolitionists contest elections and work on legislation; abolition practice starts at the local level, focusing on ridding communities of state violence.[42]

---

[36] Lloyd, *Religion of the Field Negro*, 128.
[37] Lloyd cites a few in "Of Puzzles and Idols."
[38] Dubler and Lloyd, *Break Every Yoke*. I will continue my engagement directly with Lloyd and not with Dubler's work, which is primarily concerned with prison abolition, not Black organizing as Lloyd articulated it in his previous work.
[39] Ibid., esp. introduction and ch. 5: "The Spirit of Abolition."
[40] Ibid., 35: "[Prison abolition] is the leveraging of principle and moral clarity in the service of practical politics."
[41] Ibid., 46.
[42] Ibid.

But abolition is also a spirit, an ethical way of life that is imbued with abolitionist faith.[43] For Lloyd and Joshua Dubler, spirit may or may not have much to do with religion. Much depends on the sort of religion found in the spirit of abolition. Abolitionist spirit has a certain faith, but that does not mean it has religion. The abolitionist spirit is similar to and distinct from how I have referred to "Spirit" throughout this book. In my post-Hegelian account, Spirit refers to our social practice of reasoning that is grounded in social practices of mutual recognition and determinate negation. Spirit in this sense refers to the normative structure and the inferential practice of determining the meaning of our concepts. But for me, Spirit is more than an ethical way of life. Practices of the Spirit build relational power through an experience of love and grace, of God's Spirit bringing us together, transforming us, and helping us see what's possible. This sort of relational power is basic to the life of radical democracy. The ethical life of radical democracy is always oppositional to the institutionalized social order of racial capitalism and its practices of exploitation and expropriation. For Lloyd, the spirit of abolition is an ethical faith—a faith concerned with ridding our world of carceral norms, practices, and institutions that systemically and violently govern our lives, and replacing them with an ethical way of life that is more like abolition democracy.[44] The abolitionist spirit has an abolitionist theology, and Lloyd gets concrete as he explicates this, referring to examples of organizers and organizations using religion pragmatically—even liturgically—to abolitionist ends.[45]

As he writes about them, Black organizing and abolition seem to share several crucial aspects with radical democracy as I find it in BBCO. All include a minimal hierarchy of elders, elements of dialogue and consensus building, and acting out of relational power. It is certainly the case that BBCO is not abolitionist; it is gradualist, to use Lloyd's terminology. But if it is the case that the spirit of abolition and the Spirit of radical democracy share a radically democratic ethos and are driven by prophetic commitment to rid the world of racial capitalism's exploitation and expropriation, then they share a common ethical spirit.[46]

---

[43] In speaking of the prison abolitionist work of Bryan Stevenson, Lloyd and Dubler write, "Even if not explicitly marshaled under the banner of abolitionism, in Stevenson one may rightfully pinpoint the abolition spirit: politically charged religious ideas put in service of a high justice, precipitating desperate[ly] needed legal services and public education" (ibid., 219).

[44] Ibid., 49–53.

[45] Ibid., ch. 5, esp., 213–15.

[46] I have left "spirit" lowercase here to specify the relation between abolition and BBCO.

The unique role of BBCO is to be a space where the social practice of radical democracy is lived out amid a variety of publics within a specific counterpublic group identity. It cannot be every kind of organizing. BBCO is one practice of politics that fits within a broader ecology of political practice and ethical life of radical democracy that can contain both abolitionist and BBCO as strategies to end racial capitalism's exploitation and expropriation as it takes shape as an institutionalized social order. At its best, BBCO is irreducibly plural and generative of relational power; at its worst, BBCO assimilates all of these values into a unity in difference.

Organizing has always been about a political culture and the values therein. A radically democratic culture can be fostered in BBCO that builds relational power to contest racial capitalism. In order to create such a political culture organizing needs to be seen as a *practice*, not a craft or a set of political tactics. We need to focus on the tensions in the practice and the urgency and priorities that guide strategic action. In the end, Lloyd might say that the culture of BBCO is too often tempted by the idol of a theology of multicultural neoliberalism. BBCO as I have found it is characterized by a plurality of values, some sacred values, that hold relationships and are generative of relational power and a social practice of radical democracy. I see much commonality between what I am calling for in BBCO and what Lloyd is encouraging of BBCO. But Sinclair's point, that BBCO needs to account for the way racial capitalism infiltrates the practice itself, helpfully deepens BBCO's radically democratic core. Too often, broad-based organizers and those who study BBCO turn away from the foundational aspects of its relational practice out of fear that sacred values and racial or gender analysis are wedge issues. Doubling down on the relational nature of BBCO can help organizing counterpublics build power against racial capitalism's exploitation and expropriation.

The Invitation

The account of radical democracy and social practical reasoning as I have developed it in conversation with BBCO is pluralist and constructivist and outlines a social practical account of the political role of sacred values in BBCO. This social practical account helps us grasp how BBCO political culture is grounded in a social practice of radical democracy as an ethical way of life infused with sacred values. Humans are reasoning creatures and construct narratives and practices around such values. BBCO needs to be pushed by democratic theories that emphasize critiques of capitalist exploitation and racial expropriation. It needs to incorporate those insights into the practice of organizing.

Lloyd's and Sinclair's work invites us to intentionally consider the last point: BBCO needs to adequately contend with the way that class and racial power shape up today. Avoiding racial and gender analysis—along with avoiding talk of sacred value—because we fear such analysis might divide the constituency avoids "carefully analyz[ing] the ways in which the Black human body has been racialized and deployed as an integral part of the means of production."[47] Racial expropriation in capitalism is not just an additional factor, but it is indeed one of its conditions of possibility.

Organizing is about rebuilding our democratic culture so that it ensures freedom and the flourishing of all. Churches have been and can still be crucial resources for cultivating, articulating, and achieving economic, political, and social freedom. Communities of faith can incubate, support, and themselves be sites of organizing political economic power against racial capitalism. But to reclaim this tradition that is exemplified within the radical social gospel, congregations need to deepen their political imagination of how we organize sacred values for radical democracy. It is the sad case that the radical social gospel has been neglected in the literature on BBCO, but its deep tradition of prophetic justice against racial capitalism's exploitation and expropriation is ripe for use in today's struggles. The next and final chapter offers an ecclesiology for such an account.

---

[47] Sinclair, "Interventions Forum on Privilege and Power in the Capitalocene."

7
On Churches

Radical democracy would be weaker without churches. But this does not mean Christians are at all clear on how or why they should organize their churches in radically democratic organizing efforts like BBCO. Today calls for churches to organize typically mean little more than creating spaces for dominated, expropriated, or exploited people or speaking out against social justice issues. Such calls often lack examples for what is supposed to be done once those spaces are created or the statements released. This lack of concrete examples leaves unexplored the underlying power relations that uphold structures of power and leave people uncertain as to what organizing actually means and how to do it well. Yet we are not without examples to emulate. In crafting a counterpublic political ecclesiology of organizing, we can learn from and extend the lessons from the founders of the radical social gospel. By organizing in BBCO, churches today can again pick up the work of the radical social gospel.

Organizing strengthens congregations. This adage has long been and continues to be noted by professional organizers and those scholars who study organizing. In order to have a strong broad-based organizing constituency, so the logic continues, you need to have strong member institutions. Now, on the one hand, when sociologists and political scientists and theorists take up the question of religious institutions in BBCO they tend to speak in terms of "religious cultural strategies" or "social capital."[1] This is one approach to the question on churches in organizing, but from the opposite direction. Such accounts are interested in how congregations or religious institutions as certain sorts of groups contribute to the success of BBCO. These accounts do not offer anything specific about churches as theologically normed communities formed around a certain mission and vocation. On the other hand, when theologians and theological ethicists speak of organizing, they tend to look for the individual practices in organizing that

---

[1] Cf. Swarts, *Organizing Urban America*; Wood, *Faith in Action*; Wood and Fulton, *A Shared Future*.

are characteristic of Christian life or the life of churches; I spend some time in this chapter addressing some contemporary accounts. More seldom, however, are counterpublic political ecclesiologies that offer theological reasons for local churches to get involved as theologically normed groups in BBCO. This chapter's goal is to provide such a counterpublic political ecclesiology for local churches to join BBCOs.

The theological points I make are drawn from experiences of Christians organizing in churches who are called to a certain sort of work that they hold true to their mission. This will lead to the claim that Christian identity is best described as a task. To make this case, I draw from the historical example of the radical social gospel. Radical social gospelers understood the social gospel primarily as a movement, as a way of life, not merely as a set of ideas or beliefs. This approach places me on one side of a fundamental tension that lies at the heart of all ecclesiological investigations: a tension between investigating the church normatively or concretely.[2] The starting point for my ecclesiology is the historical existence of counterpublic churches. For these reasons, my account sticks to offering a counterpublic political ecclesiology of churches.

Second, this chapter's argument returns to a thread running throughout the book: the role of counterpublics in BBCO. On both this point and the one above the life and work of Rev. George Washington Woodbey is crucial in fleshing out this political ecclesiology of counterpublics. Woodbey was formed and shaped in Black counterpublics. Long before he joined the Socialist Party of America (SP) as its first Black organizer, and for many years after he left the SP, he was a committed churchman. After a brief caveat in the first section, this chapter's second section dives into Woodbey's life, seeking to draw out three key themes and principles of a counterpublic political ecclesiology: cooperation, dialogue, and agitation. Each of these principles leads to a deep entanglement between religion and politics and economics. For Woodbey, socialist politics were enactments of biblical principles. Today we can read Woodbey's works and about his life and construct our own counterpublic political ecclesiology.

---

[2] Cf. Neiman and Haight, "On the Dynamic Relation between Ecclesiology and Congregational Studies," 14: "Ecclesiology is presently responding to two sources of pressure from opposite directions.... The foci of these two pressure points are addressed by two distinct subdisciplines of ecclesiology, the one pursuing a normative concept of the church, the other studying its historical manifestations, most concretely in congregational studies." See also Ormerod, "Social Science and Ideological Critiques of Ecclesiology," 554: "What then is the object of theological investigation, the concrete reality or its normative form?"

We need to do some updating of Woodbey's nascent political ecclesiology, and as I explore his life and writing I work dialogically to develop my counterpublic political ecclesiology. In the third section, I briefly review theologians and theological ethicists who have written about social practices of recognition, political ecclesiology, or churches in organizing. This leads to the final section, which sums up my argument and addresses the reality that a counterpublic political ecclesiology of churches in BBCO takes place in religiously plural constituencies.

My work throughout this chapter is not so much history or historiography. Rather, I turn to Woodbey as a social ethicist, reading him as a source of social ethical, political theological insight of the crucial aspects of a counterpublic political ecclesiology. As I make constructive claims I build on the social practical reasoning and socially constructed conception of religious identity I advanced in chapter 3. A church's identity is deeply connected to its task, which I understand to be a specific sort of work: Christians are gathered by God and sent into the world to do the Spirit's work of establishing relationships of liberation and love.

Counterpublic churches can be many different sizes, and their members have a number of different positions of political, racial, gender, class, and status power. However, "counterpublic" picks out a specific sort of power relationship with the broader political and economic context. Counterpublics are groups whose members are on the lower end of the political, economic, and status power relationship, but not all members of counterpublic churches need to personally experience exploitation, expropriation, or domination. That is the importance of solidarity within counterpublics.

Relations of liberation and love consist positively in political conditions of radical democracy and mutual recognition as an intersubjective Spirit that characterizes our ethical life. Spirit in this sense refers to normative structure and the inferential practice of determining the meaning of our concepts. But mutual recognition can also be an experience of love, of grace, of God's Spirit transforming how it is we are with each other and how we are in the world. God's Spirit beckons us, moves us toward ethical practices that more accurately live out this sense of liberation and love. This is another way of saying that the radical social gospel is a movement, an ethical, Spirit-filled way of life. Being brought together by God's Spirit, the life of Christians is distinct insofar as their lives and relational bonds are transformed in the Spirit's grace and love. Woodbey believed there was power in the churches to build the cooperative commonwealth. That power is still there in the people of God. Insofar as God calls together and sends churches, the identity of the people of God is best conceived as a task: to serve God and the world by working for and establishing relationships of liberation and love. Christian churches are called to this particular work of building relational power and do so by the Spirit's graceful movement in the world. Claiming that God's Spirit calls churches to build relational power characterized by particular kinds of relationships is a political and economic claim—a radically democratic claim enacted in particular kinds of political and economic relationships found in BBCO, where individuals enact radical democracy and a politics of tending.

Approaching Rev. George Washington Woodbey: A Caveat

This chapter is not a work in history or historiography, but rather an exercise in Christian social ethics, wherein I turn to a figure from the past for social ethical and political theological insights for contemporary questions. Woodbey had clear theological and ethical reasons for organizing for socialist politics. We can learn from him principles and themes in constructing our own counterpublic political ecclesiology of organizing. Beginning with Woodbey helps situate my argument as continuing the work of the radical social gospel tradition of which Woodbey was a part. From Woodbey we can better understand what resources a counterpublic political ecclesiology can summon to counter the exploitative and expropriative power of racial capitalism.

After he officially stopped stumping for the Socialist Party in 1915, Rev. Woodbey continued speaking in churches and race organizations across the country. He was a Baptist pastor until 1912, resigning because of a theological disagreement; at least that is how Woodbey tells the story.[3] Woodbey's ministry and theology charged him to build economic power for Black Americans. Socialist organizing was the surest road because it is simply the implementation of biblical principles. Woodbey is not a case study in secularist theology; he did not give up his faith for socialist politics. Rather than saying that Woodbey used his faith and theology toward

---

[3] Woodbey, untitled article. Philip Foner first reported that Woodbey was forced out of his congregation due to his socialism (Woodbey, *Black Socialist Preacher*, 35n57).

socialist ends, it is more accurate to say it the other way around: his socialist politics were used to the ends of his faith and theology. First formed in Black counterpublic institutions in the post-Reconstruction South, Woodbey's radical social gospel grounded his socialist organizing in the Socialist Party, Black churches, and new abolitionist racial justice organizations, like the Afro-American League, the National Association for the Advancement of Colored People, and the United Negro Improvement Association.[4]

Woodbey keenly understood Christianity's spiritual and ethical power for democratic socialist movements against racial capitalism, though he most likely wouldn't put it in those terms. Woodbey was part of a small, crucial movement of Christian radical social gospelers, who, in the late nineteenth and early twentieth century, argued that churches are key to building radically democratic movements.[5] Without the churches, they argued, democratic movements in the United States were not only weaker but theologically and ethically adrift.

From Woodbey we can draw out a counterpublic political ecclesiology of organizing. A Baptist preacher, he was the SP's first Black organizer and an adept strategist in organizing churches for economic democracy. My own reading of Woodbey's life and work is informed by my position as a white scholar far removed from the experience of slavery and Jim Crow, which Woodbey experienced his whole life.[6]

One thing is clear: there is much to learn from the Woodbey, especially in his analysis of churches organizing against racial capitalism. One of the important lessons Woodbey's writings demonstrate is that race and class are not static concepts but relational ones that capture material dynamics of power and that evolve together. As such, they must be examined and explained together. As I aim to show in the next section, however, there are at least three crucial principles of a counterpublic political ecclesiology: cooperation, dialogue, and agitation. Each of these concepts has rich political theological, social ethical values for churches living out their Christian call to build relationships of liberation and love.

---

[4] For a recent account of the new abolitionist movement as the Black social gospel, see Dorrien, *The New Abolition*; Dorrien, *American Democratic Socialism*, esp. 121–41.
[5] Cf. Dorrien, *The New Abolition*; Dorrien, *Breaking White Supremacy*; Dorrien, *Social Ethics in the Making*.
[6] See Kelley, "Winston Whiteside and the Politics of the Possible."

Woodbey in Dialogue: A Counterpublic Political Ecclesiology

Born into slavery in 1854 to Charles and Rachel Woodbey in Mountain City, Tennessee, George Washington Woodbey's earliest memories of his childhood include the time he spent in the white Baptist church that baptized him, where whites and Blacks worshiped. In the rural, mountainous, and sparsely populated region of East Tennessee, white and Black people lived in close proximity, but the class, race, and status hierarchy was patently obvious and violently enforced. Woodbey knew well the violence of racial expropriation, witnessed its transformation in the rise of the sharecropping system, and abhorred its afterlife in racial capitalism.

For Woodbey, the evils of slavery and those of capitalism have a common root of capitalist exploitation and expropriation. In the dedication of his first book, *What to Do and How to Do It or Socialism versus Capitalism*, published in 1903, he describes himself as "one who was once a chattel slave freed by the proclamation of Lincoln and now wishes to be free from the slavery of capitalism."[7] Woodbey understood that a Christianity that didn't assert practical economic and political action could not bring about social equality between Black Americans and whites, let alone political or economic equality. This is the starting point for any counterpublic political ecclesiology inspired by the radical social gospel: the significance of Christian faith is found as much in the concrete expression and enactment of the belief as it is in the coherence of its concept.

Woodbey's brand of socialism was deeply indebted to exposure early in his life to the Black churches as counterpublic spaces of economic, political, social, as well as religious freedom. Education was crucial to Woodbey's sense of social, economic, and political freedom. Woodbey himself had the luxury of attending only two terms in the log shanty that hosted the first school for Black Americans in Johnson City, Tennessee. The three oldest Black churches in Johnson City also emerged from that one-room shanty. Woodbey's mother helped start one of them—Thankful Baptist Church, the first Black Baptist church in Johnson City, and Woodbey himself preached his first sermon to that community in 1864 in his mother's house.[8] It wasn't until the early

---

[7] Woodbey, *Black Socialist Preacher*, 40.
[8] *Omaha Guide*, "Ex-Slave, 83, Interesting Minister"; Daniels, "The Formative Years of Johnson City, Tenn.," 63–64.

1870s that Thankful Baptist Church—which still exists today—gained independence from that collective, cooperative space of schooling and faith and purchased its own land.[9] One of the leaders of this church was a farm laborer and well-respected Baptist minister, Rev. William Jobe. Woodbey writes later that it was Rev. Jobe who gave him his first New Testament, apparently telling Woodbey as he placed his hands upon Woodbey's head, "My Boy the Lord has a great work for you to do."[10] Indeed, the New Testament serves as an example for Woodbey of the deep connection between religion and education. Many years later he said, "The New Testament was the only book I could get aside from my two school books. I read it over and over, and it seemed so wonderful to me."[11]

The community of Thankful Baptist Church from its humble beginnings in the one-room schoolhouse deeply formed and shaped Woodbey. Despite tremendous odds, Black Americans paid for their own teachers, books, and buildings when they could, with the aid of the Freedman's Bureau and Northern missionary societies.[12] Like many other Black Americans, the experience of education was deeply connected to Woodbey's lived reality as a Black Christian in post-Reconstruction Tennessee.[13] The church house and the schoolhouse were literally the same place. For Woodbey, both education and religion are key tools with which to overcome domination from the capitalist white world.

For Woodbey being a Christian always involved the contemporary concrete experiences of the lived faith in racial capitalism. These are lessons for us, too. As liberation theologians have taught us, the task of co-laboring with God in God's liberating love requires historical concreteness.[14] Likewise, people of faith who are members of church communities can—and should— think creatively about how to organize themselves to build deeper economic democracy, and the broader political economy has a deep relevance for the public expression of Christian faith today. Indeed, racial capitalism

---

[9] Daniels has the date as 1875, but Shaffer follows the data offered by Thankful Baptist Church itself, which provides an 1872 date: "Thankful Baptist Church."
[10] Excerpt from 1918 unpublished piece from Charles Holm.
[11] *Omaha Guide,* "Ex-Slave, 83, Interesting Minister."
[12] David Phillips, "Education of Blacks in Tennessee during Reconstruction."
[13] Kickler, "Black Children and Northern Missionaries, Freedmen's Bureau Agents, and Southern Whites in Reconstruction Tennessee," 179–217.
[14] As James Cone put it, "If the reality of a thing was no more than its verbalization in a written document, the black church since 1966 would be a model of the creative integration of theology and life, faith and the struggle for justice. But we know that the meaning of reality is found *only* in its historical embodiment in people as structured in societal arrangements" ("Black Theology and the Black Church," 352, emphasis in original).

incentivizes and de-incentivizes—even using force to do so—certain expressions of religious identity. Churches need to think practically about how to build—from the ground up—political economies that center the power and agency of workers and everyday people. Political and economic power—just like political and economic democracy—need to be built together. Enacting a religious identity that pushes back on racial capitalism presumes an alternative political economy. For Woodbey, being a Christian required enactment of the biblical principles of the cooperative economy through practicable socialist policies. His radical social gospel emerged from counterpublic Black churches.

Counterpublics are social arenas that contest dominating interpretations of a subjugated group's identities by inventing discourses to help people build economic and political power despite racial capitalism. Counterpublic churches are dialogical spaces, wherein discursive practices contest and challenge each other as they seek to build political economic power. In counterpublics, relationships are woven together, including between people who may or may not belong to a particular subjugated group, to form a constituency as the group strives for collective goals. To call churches counterpublics is to put them in a particular economic and political power relationship with the broader society. Counterpublics like the church that Woodbey grew up in are made up of people experiencing—or in solidarity with those experiencing—exploitation and domination. This political ecclesiology blurs reified categories of, say, religion versus secular and is charged with political, economic, and religious passion. For Woodbey, this passion is grounded in the counterpublic life of the Black church of Thankful Baptist Church.

These brief reflections on Woodbey's early life bring us to the first principle: *cooperation*. In Woodbey's vision of the cooperative commonwealth, religious, political, and economic democracy are deeply connected. Woodbey believed that there was great potential for the socialist cause in counterpublic churches. The problem, he believed, was that too many pastors were separating "morals and religion from economics."[15] The spirit of brotherhood taught in the Bible and enacted in socialist politics seeks to establish a "cooperative commonwealth," which he first came to know at Thankful Baptist Church. Put theologically, the cooperative commonwealth is a vision of society wherein God invites us into covenantal relationships that

---

[15] Woodbey, *Black Socialist Preacher*, 93.

are economically, politically, and morally significant, relationships that enhance our agency as producers and co-constructors of the world with God. This sort of cooperative community is characterized by radically democratic institutions and a distribution of power in all areas of life such that human agents have control over their own productive and reproductive labor.

Churches today are still unique spaces of economic, political, and religious power, and the potential for carrying forward the radical social gospel is still great. Many places of faith use their property for self-perpetuation or in creative ways to carry out their vocation and mission to build deeper democratic cultures to realize religious, political, economic, and social freedoms. Mainline denominations today hold vast wealth in their property, and ecclesiastical and theological education institutions often survive by selling off these properties. Some churches, more in harmony with Woodbey's first experience, use their properties as incubators for worker cooperatives, spaces where workers organize and run their own democratically governed businesses.[16]

Churches are historical institutions and theologically normed communities.[17] They should not be reduced to merely human institutions, but neither should they be subjected to theological reductionism, abstracting away from Christian practice and lived religion. As theologically normed communities, churches constantly engage in acts of self-interpretation, whereby they make theological claims about their identity. As a communion of disciples who recognize Jesus Christ as God's incarnate Word, Christians are inspired and brought together by God's Spirit and sent to work for God's purposes.[18] Churches' identities are deeply connected to their task: gathered by God and sent into the world. As a historical community churches are part of the world and cannot be understood except as part of the world. Being brought together by God's Spirit, the life of Christians is distinct insofar as their lives and relational bonds are transformed in the Spirit's grace and love. Insofar as God calls together and sends churches, the identity of the people of God is best conceived as a task: serve God and the world by building

---

[16] See Southeast Center for Cooperative Development, "Faith and Co-ops" for a thorough introduction to worker cooperatives and their relevance to the Christian church.

[17] Cf. Neiman and Haight, "On the Dynamic Relation between Ecclesiology and Congregational Studies"; Haight, *Christian Community in History*. For an earlier version of this that demonstrates Haight's roots in liberation theology, see his *An Alternative Vision*, esp. ch. 9.

[18] For a Schleiermacherian interpretation of how such an account of the church exists by the Spirit's inspiration and attuning of social practices to the relevant precedent within the historical community, see Hector, *Theology without Metaphysics*, esp. ch. 2. For a more contemporary example of my political ecclesiology, see Muelder, *The Ethical Edge of Christian Theology*, esp. 347ff.

relationships of love and liberation.[19] The church cannot be understood apart from this communing, the cooperative embodied and material living out of this task.[20]

Political ecclesiologies quickly drift into pneumatologies, where descriptions of the work of churches blends into descriptions of the work of the Holy Spirit.[21] There is good doctrinal and scriptural bases for this overlap between ecclesiology and pneumatology.[22] Pneumatologies, however, have the tricky challenge of reckoning with the variety of Christian experience.[23] This challenge is relevant to ecclesiologies, too, raising the question not only of what the church is, but where. Beginning with the historical experience of each gathering of God's people does not solve the question of definition, but instead helpfully historicizes it and broadens our vision to include the social political situation and the experience of the Spirit moving in the world (not only in the "church" qua church). Theological reflection on how the Spirit is moving God's people turns us to Christian social practices, without asking us to place undue weight on social practices because of the relevant and obvious reality of human fallibility, corrigibility, and need for correction.[24] Christians live, make theological claims about God's movement, and take action collectively in history; it is fitting that our ecclesiologies begin there, too.[25] God's Spirit calls churches to build relations of liberation and love—and to do this Christians need to engage in certain social practices of mutual recognition under conditions of radical democracy like the relational meeting and the listening campaign. This is why ecclesiology needs to focus as much on the

---

[19] For two examples of Christian identity as a task, see Tanner, *Theories of Culture*, esp. 154–55; Tanner, *Christ the Key*, ch. 6; Migliore, *Faith Seeking Understanding*, ch. 11.

[20] "The church must exist for others, not for its own self-preservation. It must focus on service not survival. The fellowship of the Eucharist demands fellowship and denounces exploitation. Without a commitment to the struggle against oppression and marginalization the Eucharist is empty" (Maldonado, "Liberation Ecclesiologies with Special Reference to Latin America," 585–86).

[21] As an example, see Hauerwas and Tran, "Ecclesiology and Politics."

[22] Volf and Lee, "The Spirit and the Church."

[23] Zahl, *The Holy Spirit and Christian Experience*.

[24] Muelder, *The Ethical Edge of Christian Theology*, 353–54: "The Spirit was to lead the church into deeper insights into truth and love than the disciples had been aware of when Jesus was with them. Hence Christians are called on always to practice *openness* to fresh disclosures of love and truth in the church and in the world." See also Tanner, *Theories of Culture*, ch. 6.

[25] This claim presumes a certain stance on the relationship between theology and social sciences that others would disagree with—namely, that social sciences have theological import. Broadly this debate is between postliberals and adherents of radical orthodoxy, who claim that the church qua church has its own social ethic and polis, and social gospelers, liberals, and liberationists who claim social sciences serve theological purposes. I stand with the latter group. On this debate, see Gutiérrez, *Essential Writings*; Petrella, *The Future of Liberation Theology*; Muelder, *The Ethical Edge of Christian Theology*; Deats and Muelder, *Toward a Discipline of Social Ethics*; Tanner, *Theories of Culture*; Dorrien, *Social Ethics in the Making*.

local congregation and Christian social practice and social practical reasoning as on general ecclesiologies, Scripture, or doctrine.[26] The Spirit moves in mundane ways through ordinary practices, despite our frail, at times clumsy human condition.[27] As some theologians have long recognized, the normative strength of theological concepts like liberation gain significance and materiality in the lived reality of Christians experiencing and wrapped up in relations of exploitation, domination, expropriation, and oppression.[28]

Woodbey knew the importance of theological concreteness. Again and again throughout the pages of his first book, *What to Do*, and then in his 1905 pamphlet, *The Bible and Socialism*, Woodbey makes the connection between the domination of chattel slavery and capitalist domination. Both slavery and capitalism violate the fundamental biblical truth of humanity's sacred value. Woodbey's Bible teaches that God stands with the oppressed and the poor; socialism, and the spirit of brotherhood it teaches, is just another name for the golden rule.[29]

Woodbey never conflated his Christian faith with socialism, but he was aware this question could easily creep into his readers' minds. To address it, Woodbey works dialogically in his writings. And here we encounter our second and third principle: *dialogue* and *agitation* are important political theological concepts for Woodbey.

He frames *What to Do* as a *dialogue* with his mother, where she poses seemingly innocent yet persistent questions about divisions between Black Christians and socialism, only to have Woodbey show how Christianity and socialism share much more than she assumes. Throughout the conversation he outlines a socialist vision for what a society might look like built upon the biblical spirit of brotherhood. Dialogue, for Woodbey, is about voice and presence, but it is also about listening to his interlocutor and listening for the Spirit. Dialogue is about mutual recognition for Woodbey. Dialogue and cooperation go hand in hand in his political ecclesiology.

Woodbey *agitates* his readers through dialogue. He seeks to wake them up to the Spirit's movements. In *The Bible and Socialism* (1905), Woodbey frames his book as a dialogue, but this time with his mother's pastor, who has more pressing questions. This is Woodbey's chance to speak preacher to

---

[26] Neiman and Haight, "On the Dynamic Relation between Ecclesiology and Congregational Studies," 17–19, 23–26.
[27] Tanner, *Christ the Key*, ch. 6.
[28] Cf. Gutiérrez, *Essential Writings*, esp. ch. 1.
[29] Woodbey, *Black Socialist Preacher*.

preacher and address some of the failings he saw in churches and in the SP broadly in its antireligion stance. He claims the mantle of socialism for the Black social gospel and with fiery prose encourages his readers and fellow pastors to do the same. Countering the secularist logic that splits religion and politics, he writes, "We Socialists stand with the prophet, in this case, and say that on earth is the place to begin doing right and that the courts have been turning the judgement of the poor into the bitterness of wormwood long enough.... What you need to do, Pastor, is to get your mouth open in behalf of the needy."[30] One can hear Woodbey's patience wearing thin with preachers who protest that religion and politics have little to do with each other, and with socialists who dismiss religion as irrelevant.

The dialogical structure of Woodbey's writing pervades nearly all of his smaller pieces. Dialogue lends itself to agitation because Woodbey instigates, challenges, stirs, and probes into the thought of his dialogue partner, whether it be his mother or his mother's pastor. He meets them as equals engaging in conversation with them, recognizing them as epistemic authorities. He presents an alternative view meant to break open their perspective, allowing the Spirit to move through his words. His writings are not diatribes; Woodbey did not believe that the SP was wholly right on all things. But he found that as a Christian the SP best enacted the morals and religious teachings of the Bible. It offered the best enactment of the values that were the foundation of his Christianity: the spirit of brotherhood and the cooperative commonwealth.

It is important for Woodbey that the spirit of brotherhood and the cooperative commonwealth are established through dialogue, while always allowing for dissent and influence from others. Cooperation, dialogue, and agitation characterized his nascent political ecclesiology. In Woodbey's dialogue one can sense the ethical way of life of radical democracy, grounded in social practical reasoning and practices of mutual recognition. His dialogical style contributes to his vision of radical democracy and helps us focus on important epistemic conditions of radical democracy. And yet, because he uses dialogue as a way to agitate toward the cooperative commonwealth, what we have here is not a form of dialogical democracy but a radically democratic, grassroots form of democracy as an ethical way of life that is ripe with tension and conflict. Woodbey certainly writes pamphlets to persuade, but he does not mean to dominate the conversation. Here again, we see that

---

[30] Ibid., 147.

reason-giving acts as a constraint against arbitrary use of power and thus domination. Dialogue and agitation are methods of communicating the message of socialism, which is in harmony with Christ's message of the cooperative commonwealth in the Bible. In socialism, Woodbey sees a social and political set of morals already expressed in Christianity. Woodbey took his dialogue partners as epistemic authorities, responsible and accountable for the norms that governed their conversation. Dialogue and cooperation are crucial to the Spirit of radical democracy.

But Woodbey can guide us only so far. He failed to see how capitalism commodifies social reproduction or how kinship and the family are concepts ensconced in the violent history of racial capitalism.[31] Woodbey's view of women's unique struggle in capitalism is closer to what Sally Miller calls the "carbon copy" view of men.[32] And like the man who attracted him to socialism in the first place, Eugene Debs, Woodbey believed that the race problem would be solved with the arrival of socialism.[33] His reductionism aside, his experience as a Black American socialist provides for us important insights.

Woodbey stood for all workers' rights and he put his body on the line for it; he took to the national stage four times at the SP's 1908 national convention, speaking powerfully in favor of Asian immigration. He was eulogized as "an outstanding figure in the battle for women's rights, fighting side by side with Susan B. Anthony and others."[34] Spurring reform movements, economic and political freedom could come only through socialism. This line of argument drew him to the scrappy Industrial Workers of the World (IWW, known as the Wobblies).

In 1912, the IWW and other socialists took on San Francisco, when the city, encouraged by the city's elite, banned all street meetings and speeches in the central business district (called "soapbox row").[35] During that violent and bloody Free Speech Fight, Woodbey was badly beaten by the police and vigilantes and jailed.[36] For the first weeks of protesting, the city authorities and police didn't know how to respond, but eventually they started arresting

---

[31] The problem of the revolutionary subject haunts Woodbey's own radical social gospelism. For an account of this in Woodbey, see Dorrien, *American Democratic Socialism*, 121–41. On racial capitalism, kinship, gender, and slavery, see Morgan, *Reckoning with Slavery*.
[32] Miller, *Race, Ethnicity, and Gender in Early Twentieth-Century American Socialism*, 16–26.
[33] Dorrien, *American Democratic Socialism*, 135.
[34] *California Eagle*, "Passing of the Old Guard."
[35] Miller, "The I.W.W. Free Speech Fight."
[36] Dorrien, *American Democratic Socialism*, 137.

protestors. The Wobblies and others decided to flood the prisons with protesters. This led to a violent disaster. The prison was at capacity and local vigilantes took matters into their own hands by brutally beating any protestor or prisoner and welcoming those coming into town by train to support the crowd with bats, guns, and violence. The vigilantes proceeded to remove the prisoners themselves at night, took them north of San Diego, beat them senseless, and sent them on their way.[37] At the beginning of this fight, Woodbey joined the Wobblies as a key speaker during one of their protests.[38] The threat of brutal racist violence against Woodbey never swayed his sense of urgency, but certainly must have chastened it.

Woodbey's sense of sacred value guided his Christian life and ministry in the church. My account is meant to introduce a dynamism, fallibilism, and potential for critical revision within our social practices so that we avoid—as much as possible—unnecessary limitations of our political theological visions by positing a revolutionary subject of history. Political ecclesiologies can be guided by a social practical sense of sacred value without positing a direction to history or a revolutionary subject. Insofar as churches perceive the Spirit to be calling them into organizing, they opt for the margins and stand with the poor, not because they view the poor to be monolithic or that history itself has a direction, but because as they discern God's liberating work in different contexts and contingent times and they embrace the reality that Jesus stands with the marginalized and oppressed.

Experiences of oppression and domination illustrate the significance of the role of dialogue and contestation as it shows up in Woodbey's writings and in our own organizing practices today. Woodbey was an agitator and understood the necessary productivity of discomfort that was often met with brutality and violence. He was formed and shaped in counterpublic institutions, grounded in the neo-abolitionist tradition of the Black social gospel and its unyielding critique of racial capitalism. For Woodbey, the importance of agitation—of discomfort—to a pluralist politics of sacred value is a lesson organizers need to internalize. The politics of sacred value are not comfortable; they compel action, fiery dialogue, and contestation within the counterpublic as it seeks to build relational power through social practices of mutual recognition.

---

[37] Shanks, "The I.W.W. Free Speech Movement"; Miller, "The I.W.W. Free Speech Fight."
[38] Woodbey, *Black Socialist Preacher*, 27–29; West, *Prophesy Deliverance!*, 126–27.

A Political Ecclesiology for Churches Organizing Today

Recognition sits at the heart of this counterpublic political ecclesiology, but a recognition of political status, not only of self-fulfillment. Counterpublic churches can certainly provide a sense of personhood, a powerful sense of "somebodyness," that an individual is a unique and beloved child of God. This somebodyness is at the heart of the Black social gospel.[39] But social practices of recognition presume radically democratic political conditions that do not always obtain. Capitalism's exploitation and expropriation run rampant, so counterpublic communities, like that of Thankful Baptist Church for Woodbey, seek to build relational power that changes the overarching social, political, and economic conditions of racial capitalism. Recognition is a political affair as much as it is social and economic.

Recently, some theologians have also turned to "recognition" and social practices as crucial concepts in ecclesial social practices. Whether explicitly concerned with broad-based organizing and counterpublics or not, recognition tends to function in these accounts as a form of self-fulfillment. In this section, I briefly bring together five contemporary accounts that address recognition, social practices, and political ecclesiology, to then take into account the upshot of the counterpublic political ecclesiology outlined above. This leads to the final section of the chapter, which attends to the reality that a counterpublic political ecclesiology of churches organizing takes place in religiously plural constituencies.

Kevin Hector's "social practical" account of how the Holy Spirit enters into normative social practices is grounded in a reading of Schleiermacherian attunement, whereby practitioners follow Christ's Spirit insofar as they are mutually recognized by the relevant community as doing so. To follow Christ, in Hector's account, is to take "Christ's confirming performances *as* one's own.... On Schleiermacher's account, then, to follow Christ is to intend one's performances to be recognizable as such by those who are recognized as following him, and one intends this by trying to go on in the same way as precedent performances which are recognized as doing so."[40] On this account, recognition functions as a form of normative authority and responsibility, but the larger political conditions of such epistemic authority are left unarticulated, and the primary avenue of critique of such norms are

---

[39] Dorrien, *The New Abolition*; Dorrien, *Breaking White Supremacy*.
[40] Hector, *Theology without Metaphysics*, 87, 94–95.

experiences of disrespect rather than exploitation, expropriation, and domination.[41] Hector's account is similar to my own in its attention to social practical reasoning, but his can lead to a form of recognition politics that tends toward assimilationist cultural politics rather than a counterpublic politics of radical democracy.

Focusing on women organizing in BBCO, Susan Engh's account is noteworthy because of her keen attention to the experience of women organizing in and outside of churches.[42] She carefully examines how "inreach" is a crucial aspect of the organizing process that transforms a congregation's understanding of how one's "pew mate" is and how organizing is an expression of one's faith. Dan Rhodes and Tim Conder argue that the church is constituted by an alternative pattern of life: social practices that are sacramental in nature, meaning that God moves "in, under, over, and through the frailties of human action."[43] The church is distinguished by God's gracious gift of the presence of Christ and is a distinct social body that presents a real political alternative in its existence: the church is a distinct politics and is a distinct social ethic.[44] Bradford Hinze's account accentuates the ecclesial practices of prophetic obedience, which include attending, receiving, and responding to the laments and cries of God's people through dialogue, protest, and negotiation—practices that are found within BBCO. "Obedience," says Hinze, practically looks like "a behavior specified by an act of attention to another person, an act of reception or recognition of the claims of the other, and an act of response."[45] For Hinze, too, recognition has to do more with a capaciousness of self to receive the other's claims on one's life. Ecclesial practices of prophetic obedience are not restricted to BBCO, but they are found there. The Spirit of God is mediated through church practices that lead faith into action in the broader political and economic context of local churches. Practices of prophetic obedience school Christians in attending, recognizing, and acting in response to the movements of the Spirit.

Over the past decade, Luke Bretherton has developed a theologically sophisticated and politically apt account of Christian reasons for engaging in BBCO that argues for such a postsecular context of the church-BBCO relation.[46] The tension between ecclesiology and politics is at the heart of

---

[41] Ibid., 272ff.
[42] Engh, *Women's Work*, esp. ch. 2.
[43] Conder and Rhodes, *Organizing Church*.
[44] Ibid., 16, 26.
[45] Hinze, *Prophetic Obedience*, esp. ch. 5.
[46] Bretherton, *Resurrecting Democracy*. See also Syndicate, "Symposium on Luke Bretherton's Resurrecting Democracy."

Bretherton's work on BBCO. Out of this tension proper Christian political judgment is rendered.[47] For Bretherton, ecclesiology and politics are co-constituting and mutually divulging.[48] He argues that we find ecclesiological concepts in political language and vice versa. In no way, however, is ecclesiology to be reduced to politics, nor politics to ecclesiology. The church qua church might be in the world, but it is certainly not of the world.

Bretherton's turn toward Christian judgment creates the theological space to consider ad hoc relationships between Christians and non-Christians. The church is its own social logic that can be even "oppositional" to non-Christian political social logic. Thus the proper political relationship between Christians and non-Christians is not one of commensuration between rival traditions but ad hoc political action determined by ecclesiological judgment.[49] BBCO mediates the appropriate relationship between ecclesial and nonecclesial institutions and facilitates Christian political judgment as Christians pursue a common life politics with our neighbors.[50]

The church is an ontological category, and it lays claim to a distinct way of being in the world characterized by God's presence.[51] As a *res publica* it is primarily constituted by its worship life that "recapitulates" the reconciling work of Christ in its common life together as Christians.[52] In and through the reconciling work of Christ the church is presented with the possibility of being a truly public and political community of justice. The church's social practices are imperfect examples of a distinctive way of being led by the Spirit. The church's vocation is the proclamation of the Gospel expressed through its liturgical practices, the eucharist being a prime example.[53] Bretherton worries that politics can tend to instrumentalize worship and reduce worship and the church to merely a "resource" for BBCO.[54] The church

[47] "The richer, more concrete and deeper one's engagement and immersion in particular forms of the relationship between ecclesial and political life, the richer and deeper one's conceptions of what it means for a church practice of the political and the political conditions of the church" (Bretherton, "Coming to Judgment," 173).

[48] In *Christ and the Common Life*, Bretherton turns from postsecularism to secularity without secularism, as I will outline below.

[49] "Ad hoc" in Bretherton, *Hospitality as Holiness*, esp. chs. 4–6; for "Christian judgement," see Bretherton, "Coming to Judgement."

[50] As Bretherton says, "In short, [BBCO] is a way for churches to relate acts of political judgement and realize obligations of neighbor love in the public sphere" (*Christianity and Contemporary Politics*, 94).

[51] Bretherton, *Hospitality as Holiness*, 101.

[52] Bretherton, *Christianity and Contemporary Politics*, 95. Bretherton's ecclesiology is inspired by figures like Oliver O'Donovan, William Cavanaugh, and Dietrich Bonhoeffer; "recapitulates" in Bretherton, *Hospitality and Holiness*, 104.

[53] Bretherton, *Christianity and Contemporary Politics*, 95.

[54] Ibid., 98; Bretherton, *Resurrecting Democracy*, 159–60, 372n23.

needs to maintain its roots in the proclamation of the Gospel. The gift of the Word to the church and its liturgy account for the church's distinctiveness.

Bretherton's recent work marks important shifts, however. In previous work he was concerned with the ontological and eschatological nature of the church. In *Christ and the Common Life*, he turns to the pneumatological and eschatological nature of the people of God. The people of God is a spatiotemporal reality that is enacted and thus as lived is distinct from other forms of sociality.[55] Here we have the emphasis on context-sensitive judgment, enabled only by the movement of the Spirit. Bretherton prefers the "people of God" over other terms of cultural politics, like "race," "class," "gender," and "sexuality," that bring people together based on preestablished commonalities. Here, again, is Bretherton's aversion to language and frames of counterpublics. Politics is the art of forming, norming, and sustaining a common life, and so "the people" is best thought of in terms of "peopling." The people of God is formed and shaped out of a politics of the common life and the free movement of the Spirit; it is never arrived at, and is always in formation. The starting place for peopling is the relationships between the people. Attending to these relationships enables wily wisdom and proper judgments that are context-sensitive.

My account is distinct from these five in several ways. In starting with Woodbey's experience of Thankful Baptist Church as a counterpublic, my ecclesiological lens follows what some theologians have called an "ecclesiology from below."[56] I begin with the concrete experience of Christians gathered together in their social, political, economic, and religious reality. As many scholars of Black churches since Du Bois have realized, these counterpublic spaces have long understood their political, economic, and religious lives as deeply entangled.[57] Counterpublic churches are spaces of economic cooperation and education; Woodbey's experience here is representative of a larger reality continuing today. Christians who gathered in such counterpublics interpreted the Spirit as moving them to fight for religious, political, economic, and educational freedom. They were called as a local community to build relational power in concrete ways. A political ecclesiology of organizing, then, begins with the Spirit's call to Christian churches to build relationships of liberation and love, and this mission is concretized in the

---

[55] Bretherton, *Christ and the Common Life*, 406, 408.
[56] Cf. Haight, *Christian Community in History*.
[57] Du Bois, *Economic Co-operation among Negro Americans*.

experience of counterpublic churches like Woodbey's, building relational power for political, economic, and racial justice.

God's Spirit calls churches to build relational power that is grounded in Christian social practices of reciprocal recognition of liberation and love. This recognition, however, is about political status, countering capitalist expropriation, and building an ethical life characterized by the movement of the Spirit as we build relational power. To claim Christian identity, on my account, is to participate in a practical, discursive, material tradition and its normative ethical life. Christians, as Christian, have reason to take certain things as sacred. As they engage in social practical reasoning and the Christian tradition's normatively established ethical life, they can engage in deep critical revision of it because fallibility and corrigibility sit at the heart of social practical reasonings. As we narrate our religious identity into the broader tradition, we rightly feel passionately about what we hold most dear, and so we often seek to protect and fight for those things and people. Christian identity, then, is best identified with a task, a life to be lived characterized by a certain ethical life of the Spirit.

This claim deepens—in a post-Hegelian and radical social gospel way—recent work in liberal and liberationist theology.[58] The Spirit of God moves individual Christians and churches to live out this task. One way to do this is through the one-on-one and the listening campaign. For some Christians, and because of the role of sacred value, such practices are religious practices. Now we can see the role these practices play ecclesiologically in the life of counterpublic churches. These social practices are grounded in a form of social practical reasoning that attends to how the Spirit of God in Christ brings us closer together, reweaving the relational fabric of our institutions, to build relational power to protect what it is that we hold most dear. By starting with Woodbey, we can see that such an ethical life of counterpublic churches is grounded in Scripture and draws on a deep and wide tradition of radical social gospelers, engaged in and deeply committed to social practical reasoning and radical democracy.

Christian churches do not claim to be the center of God's activity; God and God's liberating love are the focus of the people of God. In this sense the church is "uncentered" and focuses instead on co-laboring with God and the task of "radical service."[59] Churches are called to be a co-laborer with God in

---

[58] Cf. Tanner, *Theories of Culture*; Tanner, *Christ the Key*; Muelder, *The Ethical Edge of Christian Theology*; Dorrien, *In a Post-Hegelian Spirit*.

[59] On the "uncentered" nature of the church, see Gutiérrez, *Essential Writings*, 243ff. See also Haight, *An Alternative Vision*.

God's liberating work in the world. This political ecclesiology of organizing might be summed up in one simple claim: people organize to protect and fight for what they hold sacred. The "cooperative commonwealth" was a well-traded term among social gospelers. For Woodbey, the cooperative commonwealth and the socialist adage the "spirit of brotherhood" rang in harmony and were the foundation of his counterpublic political ecclesiology. Today, movements for economic democracy and the cooperative economic movement in BBCO are the contemporary of the radical social gospel's "cooperative commonwealth." As these efforts are expressed in BBCO they give expression to a counterpublic political ecclesiology. By building economic and political democracy, by fighting heteropatriarchal racial capitalism's exploitation and expropriation, churches today can take up the call of the radical social gospel.

Moving Together: Plural Constituencies

An ecclesiology from below affirms that churches have Holy work to do, moved by the Spirit through their practices, in BBCO. The Spirit moves churches in surprising places so that the people of God may gather with non-Christian others to join in God's liberating work. The BBCO affiliate is not the church, because by my account the church is a historical entity communing in response to the Spirit's movement. When Christians engage in religious practices of radical democracy and reciprocal recognition, the Spirit can move us and transform our ethical life together, and we can freely work out the task of liberation and love. Other members of the affiliate who hold different religious and nonreligious commitments and values (some sacred values, some not) are just as equal and important members of the affiliate. This can place churches in relations of tension and conflict with others. What is left to do but engage in the tensive practice of social practical reasoning between the sacred values of one's religious tradition and another. If some of those commitments of sacred value conflict with others in the affiliate, then organizers and leaders will have to attend to the variety of values present in the coalition. The group will have to make judgments about which are the most pressing and urgent, and how to build power and protect those values in a democratic way—that is, without continually sacrificing other sacred values or preventing contestation and influence from all parties. What they should not do—I have been arguing—is exclude these values due to fear of splintering the group or marginalize such values by saying that they raise "unwinnable" issues.

My post-Hegelian approach to Spirit might raise the fear that I unwittingly introduce a dangerous progressivist teleology into the practice of organizing. Am I providing a frame for BBCO that excludes non-Christian religious voices and expressions of sacred value? I think not. If anything, my post-Hegelian account of social practical reasoning encourages the expression and enactment of determinate difference in the relational fabric of BBCO counterpublics. The solidarity of a counterpublic is hard won, not to be taken lightly, built through religious political practices of mutual recognition like the relational meeting and listening campaign, and can be leveraged against racial capitalism. This potential objection, however, takes for granted a reading of Hegel's own understanding of the category of "religion" that is now being questioned.[60] This important question goes beyond my project here, but the best examples of this sort of theologies of religious diversity encourage social practices of determinate difference, mutual recognition, and, if Christian, commitment to the church's task as that of building relationships of love and liberation against racial capitalism.[61]

Christian social practices are theologically normed and grounded in the Christian community's experience throughout history. The work of liberation pulls churches into coalitions with nonecclesial entities and non-Christians who do more than teach the church how to be a better church. They have roles to play in the liberating movement of the Spirit. Churches, as theologically normed social and historical communities, are practicing their faith through organizing. A social practical account of sacred value opens the possibility for us to see Woodbey's own socialist organizing and socialist commitments as one example of the work of the church, while never reducing the two. Woodbey was not searching for salvation in the SP. He joined the Party because that is where he found the ethics of Jesus most fully enacted. This was not a politics of salvation; it was part of his Christian identity.[62] To be Christian for Woodbey was to engage in the Christian activity of organizing and building radical democracy to end racial capitalism. So it can be for churches today.

---

[60] Lewis, *Religion, Modernity, and Politics in Hegel*; Stewart, *Introduction to Hegel's Lectures on the Philosophy of Religion*; Williams, "Art, Logic, and the Human Presence of Spirit in Hegel's Philosophy of Absolute Spirit"; Farneth, *Hegel's Social Ethics*.
[61] Cf. Muelder, *The Ethical Edge of Christian Theology*; Dorrien, *A Darkly Radiant Vision*; Thatamanil, *Circling the Elephant*; Rieger, "Religion, Labor, Class, and Justice."
[62] For the critique of a politics of salvation, see Bretherton, *Resurrecting Democracy*, 216.

Fallibilism, constructivism, and pluralism are crucial in this endeavor and enable churches to build relationships freely with nonecclesial entities. Because churches do not claim to be the unique presence of God's Spirit in the world, counterpublic churches do not pretend to be in control of God's Spirit. Nor does this political ecclesiology limit the task of Christians to that of BBCO, but instead affirms it as one avenue to faithfully listen to the Spirit. The Spirit moves as churches listen and act.

Woodbey's politics of sacred value was driven by the theological claim that the Spirit moves us into and through these moments of discomfort: that God calls us to the implementation of a practical cooperative economics and radical democracy as Woodbey saw it exemplified in the cooperative commonwealth. Dialogue and the possibility of contestation were crucial to Woodbey and he lived them out in protest and organizing with the SP, Black churches, and racial justice organizations. He sought to hold counterpublic constituencies to their ideals: to the brotherhood of man and to building the cooperative commonwealth that enacts the ethics of the Bible. Woodbey's example depends on epistemic conditions that are free in the sense of nondomination, where individuals are free to engage in debate and dialogue without fear of reprisal. If anything, his is an example of the importance of freedom to think and feel with integrity and to freely voice those concerns, cares, and values in public. Democracy, to Woodbey, was so much more than political conditions; it included the political status of being recognized as a member of the political community who could influence and contest the political life of a group. He sought to be heard and to hear his interlocutors. Debate, dialogue, and contestation are only as good as a group's political life cultivates habits of nondomination and allows free and full expression of our evaluative attitudes. Woodbey helps us gesture to the epistemic and political qualities of democracy as radical democracy—radical because it goes to the qualitative roots of life; it starts with our relationships and values.

It is undeniable that Woodbey organized in the midst of racial capitalism. The violence, exploitation, and expropriation of racial capitalism were only too familiar to him as a Black man in the post-Reconstruction U.S. South. Woodbey's commitment to socialism was fundamentally grounded in his Black Christian faith and in the counterpublic spaces of Black churches and socialist organizations. They provided the sacred values—the cooperative commonwealth and the biblical spirit of brotherhood—that kept him going, pulled him through, and carried him on.

A counterpublic political ecclesiology affirms with Woodbey that Jesus instructed his followers to pray and act for such improvement of earthly conditions.[63] Christ's message to the poor concerns itself with practical, cooperative economic conditions here on earth. For Woodbey, the spirit of brotherhood, the golden rule, and the cooperative commonwealth all ring in harmony—and they all call back to his early experiences being raised in a counterpublic church that provided for its own education and religious worship, a church that supported its members' own economic efforts by cooperative efforts in that one-room schoolhouse.

[63] Woodbey, *Black Socialist Preacher*, 163.

Bibliography

Adams, Robert Merrihew. *Finite and Infinite Goods: A Framework for Ethics*. New York: Oxford University Press, 2002.

Ahn, Ilsup, and Kao, Grace, eds. *Asian American Christian Ethics: Voices, Methods, Issues*. Waco, TX: Baylor University Press, 2015.

Alcoff, Linda. *Visible Identities: Race, Gender, and the Self*. New York: Oxford University Press, 2006.

Ali, Omar H. *In the Balance of Power: Independent Black Politics and Third-Party Movements in the United States*. Athens: Ohio University Press, 2008.

Alinsky, Saul David. *Rules for Radicals: A Practical Primer for Realistic Radicals*. New York: Random House, 1971.

Anderson, Elizabeth. "Practical Reason and Incommensurable Goods." In *Incommensurability, Incomparability, and Practical Reasoning*, edited by Ruth Chang, 90–109. Cambridge, MA: Harvard University Press, 1997.

Anderson, Elizabeth. *Value in Ethics and Economics*. Cambridge, MA: Harvard University Press, 1993.

Asad, Talal. *Formations of the Secular: Christianity, Islam, Modernity*. Stanford, CA: Stanford University Press, 2003.

Asad, Talal. *Genealogies of Religion: Discipline and Reasons of Power in Christianity and Islam*. Baltimore: Johns Hopkins University Press, 1993.

Banner, Michael C. *The Ethics of Everyday Life: Moral Theology, Social Anthropology, and the Imagination of the Human*. Oxford: Oxford University Press, 2014.

Bender, Courtney. *Heaven's Kitchen: Living Religion at God's Love We Deliver*. Chicago: University of Chicago Press, 2003.

Bender, Courtney. *The New Metaphysicals: Spirituality and the American Religious Imagination*. London: University of Chicago Press, 2010.

Bender, Courtney. "Things in Their Entanglements." In *The Post-Secular in Question: Religion in Contemporary Society*, edited by Philip Gorski, 43–76. New York: New York University Press, 2012.

Berlin, Isaiah. *Liberty: Incorporating Four Essays on Liberty*. Edited by Henry Hardy. Oxford: Oxford University Press, 2002.

Bilgrami, Akeel. *Secularism, Identity, and Enchantment*. Cambridge, MA: Harvard University Press, 2014.

Bourdieu, Pierre. "The Force of Law: Toward a Sociology of the Juridical Field Essay." *Hastings Law Journal* 38, no. 5 (1987): 814–54.

Bourdieu, Pierre. "Forms of Capital." In *Handbook of Theory of Research for the Sociology of Education*, edited by J. E. Richardson, translated by Richard Nice, 241–58. New York: Greenwood Press, 1986.

Bourdieu, Pierre. "Genesis and Structure of the Religious Field." *Comparative Social Research* 13 (1991): 1–44.

Bourdieu, Pierre. *The Logic of Practice*. Translated by Richard Nice. Stanford, CA: Stanford University Press, 1990.

Bourdieu, Pierre. *Outline of a Theory of Practice*. New York: Cambridge University Press, 1977.

Bourdieu, Pierre. "What Makes a Social Class? On the Theoretical and Practical Existence of Groups." *Berkeley Journal of Sociology* 32 (1987): 1–17.

Bourdieu, Pierre, and Loïc Wacquant. *An Invitation to Reflexive Sociology*. Chicago: University of Chicago Press, 1992.

Bowlin, John R. *Tolerance among the Virtues*. Princeton, NJ: Princeton University Press, 2016.

Brandom, Robert. "Freedom and Constraint by Norms." *American Philosophical Quarterly* 16, no. 3 (1979): 187–96.

Brandom, Robert. *Making It Explicit: Reasoning, Representing, and Discursive Commitment*. Cambridge, MA: Harvard University Press, 1994.

Brandom, Robert. *Reason in Philosophy: Animating Ideas*. Cambridge, MA: Belknap Press of Harvard University Press, 2009.

Brandom, Robert. "Some Pragmatist Themes in Hegel's Idealism." In *Tales of the Mighty Dead: Historical Essay in the Metaphysics of Intentionality*, 210–34. Cambridge, MA: Harvard University Press, 2002.

Brandom, Robert. *Tales of the Mighty Dead: Historical Essays in the Metaphysics of Intentionality*. Cambridge, MA: Harvard University Press, 2002.

Braunstein, Ruth. *Prophets and Patriots: Faith in Democracy across the Political Divide*. Oakland: University of California Press, 2017.

Braunstein, Ruth, Todd Nicholas Fuist, and Rhys H. Williams, eds. *Religion and Progressive Activism: New Stories about Faith and Politics*. New York: New York University Press, 2017.

Bretherton, Luke. *Christ and the Common Life: Political Theology and the Case for Democracy*. Grand Rapids, MI: William B. Eerdmans, 2019.

Bretherton, Luke. *Christianity and Contemporary Politics: The Conditions and Possibilities of Faithful Witness*. Malden, MA: Wiley-Blackwell, 2010.

Bretherton, Luke. "Coming to Judgment: Methodological Reflections on the Relationship between Ecclesiology, Ethnography and Political Theory." *Modern Theology* 28, no. 2 (April 2012): 167–96.

Bretherton, Luke. "Congregation and Demos." *Syndicate* (blog). Accessed November 12, 2019. https://syndicate.network/symposia/theology/resurrecting-democracy/.

Bretherton, Luke. *Hospitality as Holiness: Christian Witness amid Moral Diversity*. Burlington, VT: Ashgate, 2006.

Bretherton, Luke. *Resurrecting Democracy: Faith, Citizenship, and the Politics of a Common Life*. New York: Cambridge University Press, 2015.

Brubaker, Rogers. "Social Theory as Habitus." In *Bourdieu: Critical Perspectives*, edited by Craig Calhoon, Edward LiPuma, and Moiche Postone, 212–34. Chicago: University of Chicago Press, 1993.

Burley, Justine, ed. *Dworkin and His Critics*. Malden, MA: Blackwell, 2004.

Bush, Stephen S. "Horribly Wrong: Moral Disgust and Killing." *Journal of Religious Ethics* 41, no. 4 (2013): 585–600.

Bush, Stephen S. *Visions of Religion: Experience, Meaning, and Power*. New York: Oxford University Press, 2014.

Bush, Stephen S. *William James on Democratic Individuality*. New York: Cambridge University Press, 2017.

California Eagle. "Passing of the Old Guard." October 7, 1937.

Casanova, José. *Public Religions in the Modern World*. Chicago: University of Chicago Press, 1994.

Casanova, José. "Rethinking Secularization: A Global Comparative Perspective." In *Religion, Globalization and Culture*, edited by Peter Beyer and Lori Beaman, 101–20. Leiden: Brill, 2007.

Cavanaugh, William T. *Torture and Eucharist: Theology, Politics, and the Body of Christ*. Malden, MA: Blackwell, 1998.

Certeau, Michel de. *The Practice of Everyday Life*. Translated by Steven Rendall. Berkeley: University of California Press, 1984.

Chambers, Edward T., and Michael Cowan. *Roots for Radicals: Organizing for Power, Action and Justice*. New York: Continuum, 2003.

Clark, Adam. "Book Review: Lloyd, Vincent: Religion of the Field Negro: On Black Secularism and Black Theology." *Theological Studies* 82, no. 2 (June 1, 2021): 377–79. https://doi.org/10.1177/00405639211019800d.

Coles, Romand. *Beyond Gated Politics: Reflections for the Possibility of Democracy*. Minneapolis: University of Minnesota Press, 2005.

Coles, Romand. *Visionary Pragmatism: Radical and Ecological Democracy in Neoliberal Times*. Durham, NC: Duke University Press, 2016.

Coles, Romand, and Hauerwas, Stanley. *Christianity, Democracy, and the Radical Ordinary: Conversations between a Radical Democrat and a Christian*. Cambridge, UK: Lutterworth Press, 2008.

Coles, Romand, and Stanley Hauerwas. "Of Tensions and Tricksters." In *Christianity, Democracy and the Radical Ordinary*, 277–308. Cambridge, UK: Lutterworth Press by Cascade Books, 2008.

Coles, Romand. "Moving Democracy: Industrial Areas Foundation Social Movements and the Political Arts of Listening, Traveling, and Tabling." *Political Theory* 32, no. 5 (2004): 678–705.

Conder, Tim, and Daniel Rhodes. *Organizing Church: Grassroots Practices for Embodying Change in Your Congregation, Your Community, and Our World*. Ashland, MO: Chalice Press, 2017.

Cone, James H. "Black Theology and the Black Church: Where Do We Go from Here?" In *Black Theology: A Documentary History*, edited by James H. Cone and Gayraud S. Wilmore, 266–78. Maryknoll, NY: Orbis Books, 1993.

Cone, James H. *A Black Theology of Liberation*. 20th anniversary ed. Maryknoll, NY: Orbis Books, 2006.

Cortes, Ernesto, Jr. "All Organizing Is Constant Re-organizing." *Shelterforce* (blog), 1996. https://shelterforce.org/1996/01/01/all-organizing-is-constant-re-organizing/.

Crenshaw, Kimberlé. "Mapping the Margins: Intersectionality, Identity Politics, and Violence against Women of Color." In *Critical Race Theory: The Key Writings That Formed the Movement*, edited by Kimberlé Crenshaw, Neil T. Gotanda, Gary Peller, and Kendall Thomas, 357–83. New York: New Press, 1995.

Curl, John. *For All the People: Uncovering the Hidden History of Cooperation, Cooperative Movements, and Communalism in America*. Oakland, CA: PM Press, 2012.

Daniels, Ophelia Cope. "The Formative Years of Johnson City, Tenn. 1885–1890: A Social History." Tennessee Agricultural and Industrial State College, 1947.

David Phillips, Paul. "Education of Blacks in Tennessee during Reconstruction, 1865–1870." *Tennessee Historical Quarterly* 46, no. 2 (1987): 98–109.

Davidson, Donald. "How Is Weakness of the Will Possible?" In *Moral Concepts*, edited by Joel Feinberg, 93–113. Oxford: Oxford University Press, 1969.

Dawson, Michael C. *Black Visions: The Roots of Contemporary African-American Political Ideologies*. Chicago: University of Chicago Press, 2001.

Dawson, Michael C. "Hidden in Plain Sight: A Note on Legitimation Crises and the Racial Order Debate." *Critical Historical Studies* 3, no. 1 (2016): 143–62.

Davaney, Sheila Greeve. "Theology and the Turn to Cultural Analysis." In *Converging on Culture: Theologians in Dialogue with Cultural Analysis and Criticism*, edited by Delwin Brown, Sheila Greeve Davaney, and Kathryn Tanner, 3–16. Oxford, UK: Oxford University Press, 2001.

Day, Keri. *Azusa Reimagined: A Radical Vision of Religious and Democratic Belonging*. Stanford, CA: Stanford University Press, 2022.

Deats, Paul, ed. *Toward a Discipline of Social Ethics: Essays in Honor of Walter George Muelder*. Boston: Boston University Press, 1972.

Decosimo, David. "Intrinsic Goodness and Contingency, Resemblance and Particularity: Two Criticisms of Robert Adams's Finite and Infinite Goods." *Studies in Christian Ethics* 25, no. 4 (November 1, 2012): 418–41.

Decosimo, David. "Killing and the Wrongness of Torture." *Journal of the Society of Christian Ethics* 36, no. 1 (June 17, 2016): 181–98.

Deloria, Vine. *God Is Red: A Native View of Religion*. Golden, CO: North American Press, 1992.

Dewey, John. "Creative Democracy—The Task before Us." In *John Dewey: The Later Works 1925–1953*, vol. 14: *1939–1949*, edited by Jo Ann Boydston, 224–31. Carbondale: Southern Illinois University Press, 1988.

Dewey, John. "Emerson: The Philosopher of Democracy." *International Journal of Ethics* 13, no. 4 (1902): 405–13.

Dewey, John. "The Ethics of Democracy." In *John Dewey: The Early Works, 1882–1898*, vol. 1, edited by Jo Ann Boydston, 227–52. Carbondale: Southern Illinois University Press, 1969.

Dewey, John. *The Public and Its Problems: An Essay in Political Inquiry*. Athens, OH: Swallow Press, 2016.

Diggins, John Patrick. "The Godless Delusion." *New York Times*, December 16, 2007. https://www.nytimes.com/2007/12/16/books/review/Diggins-t.html.

Dorrien, Gary J. *American Democratic Socialism: History, Politics, Religion, and Theory*. New Haven, CT: Yale University Press, 2021.

Dorrien, Gary J. *Breaking White Supremacy: Martin Luther King Jr. and the Black Social Gospel*. New Haven, CT: Yale University Press, 2018.

Dorrien, Gary J. *A Darkly Radiant Vision: The Black Social Gospel in the Shadow of MLK*. New Haven, CT: Yale University Press, 2023.

Dorrien, Gary J. *Economy, Difference, Empire: Social Ethics for Social Justice*. New York: Columbia University Press, 2010.

Dorrien, Gary J. *In a Post-Hegelian Spirit: Philosophical Theology as Idealistic Discontent*. Waco, TX: Baylor University Press, 2020.

Dorrien, Gary J. *Kantian Reason and Hegelian Spirit: The Idealistic Logic of Modern Theology*. Malden, MA: Wiley-Blackwell, 2012.

Dorrien, Gary J. *The Making of American Liberal Theology: Imagining Progressive Religion, 1805–1900*. Louisville, KY: Westminster John Knox Press, 2001.

Dorrien, Gary J. *The New Abolition: W. E. B. Du Bois and the Black Social Gospel*. New Haven, CT: Yale University Press, 2015.

Dorrien, Gary J. *Social Democracy in the Making: Political and Religious Roots of European Socialism*. New Haven, CT: Yale University Press, 2019.
Dorrien, Gary J. *Social Ethics in the Making: Interpreting an American Tradition*. Malden, MA: Wiley-Blackwell, 2009.
Dorrien, Gary J. *Soul in Society: The Making and Renewal of Social Christianity*. Minneapolis, MN: Fortress Press, 1995.
Douglas, Mary. "The Effects of Modernization on Religious Change." *Daedalus* 111, no. 1 (1982): 457–84.
Douglas, Mary. *Natural Symbols: Explorations in Cosmology*. New York: Routledge, 1996.
Dressner, Richard B. "William Dwight Porter Bliss's Christian Socialism." *Church History* 47, no. 1 (March 1978): 66–82.
Du Bois, W. E. B. *Black Reconstruction in America*. New York: Free Press, 1998.
Du Bois, W. E. B. *Economic Co-operation among Negro Americans*. Atlanta University Publications, no. 12. New York: Russell & Russell, 1969.
Dubler, Joshua, and Vincent Lloyd. *Break Every Yoke: Religion, Justice, and the Abolition of Prisons*. New York: Oxford University Press, 2020.
Duke, David Nelson. *In the Trenches with Jesus and Marx: Harry F. Ward and the Struggle for Social Justice*. Tuscaloosa: University of Alabama Press, 2003.
Dunbar, Anthony P. *Against the Grain: Southern Radicals and Prophets, 1929–1959*. Charlottesville: University Press of Virginia, 1981.
Dworkin, Ronald. *Life's Dominion: An Argument about Abortion, Euthanasia, and Individual Freedom*. New York: Vintage Books, 1994.
Dworkin, Ronald. "Objectivity and Truth: You'd Better Believe It." *Philosophy & Public Affairs* 25, no. 2 (1996): 87–139.
Dworkin, Ronald. "The Concept of the Sacred: A Response to My Critics." In *Is Nothing Sacred?*, edited by Ben Rogers, 138–43. New York: Routledge, 2004.
Dykstra, Craig R. *Growing in the Life of Faith: Education and Christian Practices*. Louisville, KY: Westminster John Knox Press, 2005.
Dykstra, Craig, and Dorothy C. Bass. "A Theological Understanding of Christian Practices." In *Practicing Theology: Beliefs and Practices in Christian Life*, edited by Miroslav Volf and Dorothy C. Bass, 13–32. Grand Rapids, MI: Eerdmans, 2002.
Eliasoph, Nina, and Paul Lichterman. "Culture in Interaction." *American Journal of Sociology* 108, no. 4 (2003): 735–94.
Elisha, Omri. *Moral Ambition: Mobilization and Social Outreach in Evangelical Megachurches*. Berkeley: University of California Press, 2011.
Elmer, Don. "Community Organizer Genealogy Project: Cortes, Ernesto Jr." 2010. https://repository.library.brown.edu/studio/item/bdr:420367/.
Emirbayer, Mustafa, and Victoria Johnson. "Bourdieu and Organizational Analysis." *Theory and Society* 37, no. 1 (2008): 1–44.
Engh, Susan. *Women's Work: The Transformational Power of Faith-Based Community Organizing*. Lanham, MD: Lexington Books/Fortress Academic, 2019.
Evans, Christopher Hodge. "Historical Integrity and Theological Recovery: A Reintroduction to the Social Gospel." In *The Social Gospel Today*, edited by Christopher Hodge Evans, 1–16. Louisville, KY: Westminster John Knox Press, 2001.
Farneth, Molly B. "Constructivism in Ethics: A View from Hegelian Semantics." In *Religious Ethics and Constructivism: A Metaethical Inquiry*, edited by Kevin Jung, 63–81. New York: Routledge, 2018.
Farneth, Molly B. *Hegel's Social Ethics: Religion, Conflict, and Rituals of Reconciliation*. Princeton, NJ: Princeton University Press, 2017.

Farneth, Molly B. "'The Power to Empty Oneself': Hegel, Kenosis, and Intellectual Virtue." *Political Theology* 18, no. 2 (March 2017): 157–71.

Fessenden, Tracy. *Culture and Redemption: Religion, the Secular, and American Literature*. Princeton, NJ: Princeton University Press, 2007.

Fraser, Nancy. "Behind Marx's Hidden Abode." *New Left Review* 86, no. 86 (April 1, 2014): 55–72.

Fraser, Nancy. "Expropriation and Exploitation in Racialized Capitalism: A Reply to Michael Dawson Debate." *Critical Historical Studies* 3, no. 1 (2016): 163–78.

Fraser, Nancy. "Rethinking the Public Sphere: A Contribution to the Critique of Actually Existing Democracy." In *Habermas and the Public Sphere*, edited by Craig Calhoon, 109–42. Cambridge, MA: MIT Press, 1994.

Fraser, Nancy, and Axel Honneth. *Redistribution or Recognition? A Political-Philosophical Exchange*. New York: Verso, 2003.

Fulkerson, Mary McClintock. *Places of Redemption: Theology for a Worldly Church*. New York: Oxford University Press, 2007.

Fulkerson, Mary McClintock. "Receiving from the Other: Theology and Grass-roots Organizing." *International Journal of Public Theology* 6, no. 4 (2012): 421–34.

Ganz, Marshall. "Leading Change: Leadership, Organization, and Social Movements." In *Handbook of Leadership Theory and Practice: A Harvard Business School Centennial Colloquium*, edited by Nohria Nitin and Khurana Rakesh, 527–68. Boston: Harvard University Press, 2010.

Garrison, Joey. "Nashville MLS Ownership Reaches Terms on Community Benefits Agreement for Stadium Project." *The Tennessean*, August 27, 2018. https://www.tennessean.com/story/news/2018/08/27/nashville-soccer-stadium-mls-fairgrounds/1115093002/.

Gates, Henry Louis. *The Black Church: This Is Our Story, This Is Our Song*. New York: Penguin Press, 2021.

Gerteis, Joseph. *Class and the Color Line: Interracial Class Coalition in the Knights of Labor and the Populist Movement*. Durham, NC: Duke University Press, 2007.

Glaude, Eddie S. "Of the Black Church and the Making of a Black Public." In *African American Religious Thought: An Anthology*, edited by Cornel West and Eddie S. Glaude, 338–65. Louisville, KY: Westminster John Knox Press, 2003.

Gordon Nembhard, Jessica. *Collective Courage: A History of African American Cooperative Economic Thought and Practice*. University Park: Pennsylvania State University Press, 2014.

Gordon Nembhard, Jessica. "Economic Justice as a Necessary Component of Racial Justice." The Wendland-Cook Program in Religion and Justice. Accessed August 16, 2021. https://www.religionandjustice.org/interventions-forum-coops.

Greene, Alison Collis. "Southern Christian Work Camps and a Cold War Campaign for Racial and Economic Justice." In *Working Alternatives: American and Catholic Experiments in Work and Economy*, edited by Christine Firer Hinze and John C. Seitz, 253–79. Catholic Practice in North America. Baltimore: Project Muse, 2020.

Gregory, Eric. "Christianity and the Rise of the Democratic State." In *Political Theology for a Plural Age*, edited by Michael Kessler, 99–106. New York: Oxford University Press, 2013.

Gregory, Eric. "Social Anthropology, Neighbor-Love, and the Ethics of Humanitarianism." In *Everyday Ethics: Moral Theology and the Practices of Ordinary Life*, edited by Michael Lamb and Brian A. Williams, 120–51. Washington, DC: Georgetown University Press, 2019.

Griffith, Ruth Marie. *God's Daughters: Evangelical Women and the Power of Submission.* Berkeley: University of California Press, 1997.

Gutiérrez, Gustavo. *Essential Writings.* Edited by James B. Nickoloff. Maryknoll, NY: Orbis Books, 1996.

Hacking, Ian. *The Social Construction of What?* Cambridge, MA: Harvard University Press, 1999.

Haight, Roger. *An Alternative Vision: An Interpretation of Liberation Theology.* New York: Paulist Press, 1985.

Haight, Roger. *Christian Community in History.* 3 vols. New York: Continuum, 2004.

Hall, David D., ed. *Lived Religion in America: Toward a History of Practice.* Princeton, NJ: Princeton University Press, 1997.

Harris, Cheryl I. "Whiteness as Property." *Harvard Law Review* 106, no. 8 (1993): 1707–91.

Harrison, Beverly Wildung. "The Power of Anger in the Work of Love: Christian Ethics for Women and Other Strangers." *Union Seminary Quarterly Review* 36 (1980): 41–58.

Hart, Stephen. *Cultural Dilemmas of Progressive Politics: Styles of Engagement among Grassroots Activists.* Chicago: University of Chicago Press, 2001.

Haslanger, Sally Anne. *Resisting Reality: Social Construction and Social Critique.* New York: Oxford University Press, 2012.

Haslanger, Sally Anne. "What Is a Social Practice?" *Royal Institute of Philosophy Supplement; London* 82 (July 2018): 231–47.

Hauerwas, Stanley. *After Christendom?* Nashville, TN: Abingdon Press, 1991.

Hauerwas, Stanley, and Jonathan Tran. "Ecclesiology and Politics." In *T&T Clark Handbook of Ecclesiology*, edited by Kimlyn J. Bender and D. Stephen Long, 404–18. New York: T&T Clark, 2020.

Hector, Kevin. *Theology without Metaphysics: God, Language, and the Spirit of Recognition.* New York: Cambridge University Press, 2011.

Hegel, Georg Wilhelm Friedrich. *Lectures on the Philosophy of Religion: The Lectures of 1827.* Vol. 1. Edited by Peter Crafts Hodgson. Oxford: Clarendon Press, 2006.

Hegel, Georg Wilhelm Friedrich. *Phenomenology of Spirit.* Translated by Arnold V. Miller. Oxford: Clarendon Press, 1977.

Henrich, Dieter. "Hegel and Hoelderlin." *Idealistic Studies* 2 (January 1, 1972): 151.

Herdt, Jennifer A. *Forming Humanity: Redeeming the German Bildung Tradition.* Chicago: University of Chicago Press, 2019.

Higginbotham, Evelyn Brooks. *Righteous Discontent: The Women's Movement in the Black Baptist Church, 1880–1920.* Cambridge, MA: Harvard University Press, 1993.

Hinze, Bradford E. *Prophetic Obedience: Ecclesiology for a Dialogical Church.* Maryknoll, NY: Orbis Books, 2016.

Hirschkind, Charles. *The Ethical Soundscape: Cassette Sermons and Islamic Counterpublics.* New York: Columbia University Press, 2006.

Hodgson, Peter Crafts. *Hegel and Christian Theology: A Reading of the Lectures on the Philosophy of Religion.* Oxford and New York: Oxford University Press, 2005.

Hodgson, Peter Crafts. "Editorial Introduction." In *Lectures on the Philosophy of Religion: The Lectures of 1827.* Vol. 1, edited by Peter Crafts Hodgson, 1–72. Hegel Lectures Series. Oxford: Clarendon Press, 2006.

Hooker, Juliet. *Theorizing Race in the Americas: Douglass, Sarmiento, Du Bois, and Vasconcelos.* New York: Oxford University Press, 2017.

Horwitt, Sanford D. *Let Them Call Me Rebel: Saul Alinsky, His Life and Legacy.* New York: Random House, 1989.

Hurd, Elizabeth Shakman. *Beyond Religious Freedom: The New Global Politics of Religion*. Princeton, NJ: Princeton University Press, 2015.

Isasi-Díaz, Ada María. *La Lucha Continues: Mujerista Theology*. Maryknoll, NY: Orbis Books, 2004.

Isenberg, Sheldon R., and Dennis E. Owen. "Bodies, Natural and Contrived: The Work of Mary Douglas." *Religious Studies Review* 3, no. 1 (January 1977): 1–17.

Jackson, Timothy P. *Political Agape: Christian Love and Liberal Democracy*. Grand Rapids, MI: William B. Eerdmans, 2015.

Jacobsen, Dennis A. *Doing Justice: Congregations and Community Organizing*. Minneapolis, MN: Fortress Press, 2017.

Johnston, Mark. "Constitution Is Not Identity." *Mind* 101, no. 401 (January 1992): 89.

Johnston, Mark. "Manifest Kinds." *Journal of Philosophy* 94, no. 11 (1997): 564–83.

Johnston, Mark. "Objectivity Refigured: Pragmatism without Verificationism." In *Reality, Representation, and Projection*, edited by John Haldane and Crispin Wright, 85–132. Mind Association Occasional Series. New York: Oxford University Press, 1993.

Jordan, Candance. "Bearing Witness to Testimonies of Antiblackness." *The Immanent Frame*, January 21, 2021. https://tif.ssrc.org/2021/01/21/bearing-witness-to-testimonies-of-antiblackness/.

Jung, Moon-Ho. *Coolies and Cane: Race, Labor, and Sugar in the Age of Emancipation*. Baltimore: Johns Hopkins University Press, 2006.

Kahn, Paul W. *Political Theology: Four New Chapters on the Concept of Sovereignty*. New York: Columbia University Press, 2011.

Kamm, F. M. "Ronald Dworkin's Views on Abortion and Assisted Suicide." In *Dworkin and His Critics*, edited by Justine Burley, 218–39. Malden, MA: Blackwell, 2004.

Kelley, Robin D. G. *Hammer and Hoe: Alabama Communists during the Great Depression*. 25th anniversary ed. Chapel Hill: University of North Carolina Press, 2015.

Kelley, Robin D. G. "The Roots of Anti-Racist, Anti-Fascist Resistance in the US." CounterPunch.org, March 11, 2020. https://www.counterpunch.org/2020/03/11/the-roots-of-anti-racist-anti-fascist-resistance-in-the-us/.

Kelley, Robin D. G. "Winston Whiteside and the Politics of the Possible." In *Futures of Black Radicalism*, edited by Gaye Theresa Johnson and Alex Lubin, 277–86. London: Verso, 2017.

Kickler, Troy Lee. "Black Children and Northern Missionaries, Freedmen's Bureau Agents, and Southern Whites in Reconstruction Tennessee, 1865–1896." PhD diss., University of Tennessee–Knoxville, 2005.

Korsgaard, Christine M. *Creating the Kingdom of Ends*. New York: Cambridge University Press, 1996.

Kripke, Saul A. *Naming and Necessity*. Cambridge, MA: Harvard University Press, 1980.

Kukla, Rebecca, and Mark Lance. "Intersubjectivity and Receptive Experience." *Southern Journal of Philosophy* 52, no. 1 (March 2014): 22–42.

Lakein, Meir. "On Gathering." *Political Theology*, May 19, 2021, 1–7.

Lamb, Michael, and Brian A. Williams, eds. *Everyday Ethics: Moral Theology and the Practices of Ordinary Life*. Washington, DC: Georgetown University Press, 2019.

Lambelet, Kyle. "A One-to-One on the Road to Emmaus." *Daily Theology* (blog), May 5, 2017. https://dailytheology.org/2017/05/05/a-one-to-one-on-the-road-to-emmaus/.

Landes, Joan B. *Women and the Public Sphere in the Age of the French Revolution*. Ithaca, NY: Cornell University Press, 1988.

Lewis, Thomas A. *Freedom and Tradition in Hegel: Reconsidering Anthropology, Ethics, and Religion*. Notre Dame, IN: University of Notre Dame Press, 2005.
Lewis, Thomas A. *Religion, Modernity, and Politics in Hegel*. New York: Oxford University Press, 2011.
Lichterman, Paul. *Elusive Togetherness: Church Groups Trying to Bridge America's Divisions*. Princeton, NJ: Princeton University Press, 2005.
Lichterman, Paul. *How Civic Action Works: Fighting for Housing in Los Angeles*. Princeton, NJ: Princeton University Press, 2021.
Lichterman, Paul. "Religion and Social Solidarity: A Pragmatist Approach." In *Religion and Volunteering: Complex, Contested and Ambiguous Relationships*, edited by Lesley Hustinx, Johan von Essen, Jacques Haers, and Sara Mels, 241–61. Cham: Springer International, 2015.
Lichterman, Paul. "Religion in Public Action: From Actors to Settings." *Sociological Theory* 30, no. 1 (2012): 15–36.
Link, Eugene P. *Labor-Religion Prophet: The Times and Life of Harry F. Ward*. Boulder, CO: Westview Press, 1983.
Lloyd, Vincent W. *Black Dignity: The Struggle against Domination*. New Haven, CT: Yale University Press, 2022.
Lloyd, Vincent W. *Black Natural Law*. New York: Oxford University Press, 2016.
Lloyd, Vincent W. "Human Dignity Is Black Dignity." *Church Life Journal*, June 16, 2020. https://churchlifejournal.nd.edu/articles/human-dignity-is-black-dignity/.
Lloyd, Vincent W. "Of Puzzles and Idols." Accessed July 2, 2022. https://syndicate.network/symposia/theology/resurrecting-democracy/.
Lloyd, Vincent W. *Religion of the Field Negro: On Black Secularism and Black Theology*. New York: Fordham University Press, 2018.
Lofton, Kathryn. *Consuming Religion*. Chicago: University of Chicago Press, 2017.
Loomer, Bernard. "Two Conceptions of Power." *Process Studies* 6, no. 1 (Spring 1976): 5.
Lovibond, Sabina. "Second Nature, Habitus, and the Ethical: Remarks on Wittgenstein and Bourdieu." *Ethical Perspectives* 22, no. 1 (March 2015): 131–49.
Lowe, Lisa. *The Intimacies of Four Continents*. Durham, NC: Duke University Press, 2015.
Luker, Ralph E. "Interpreting the Social Gospel: Reflections on Two Generations of Historiography." In *Perspectives on the Social Gospel: Papers from the Inaugural Social Gospel Conference at Colgate Rochester Divinity School*, edited by Christopher Hodge Evans, 1–13. Lewiston, NY: Edwin Mellen Press, 1999.
Lukes, Steven. "Comparing the Incomparable: Trade-Offs and Sacrifices." In *Incommensurability, Incomparability, and Practical Reason*, edited by Ruth Chang, 184–95. Cambridge, MA: Harvard University Press, 1998.
Lumsden, Simon. "The Rise of the Non-Metaphysical Hegel." *Philosophy Compass* 3, no. 1 (2008): 51–65.
MacIntyre, Alasdair C. *After Virtue: A Study in Moral Theory*. Notre Dame, IN: University of Notre Dame Press, 2007.
MacIntyre, Alasdair C. *Ethics in the Conflicts of Modernity: An Essay on Desire, Practical Reasoning, and Narrative*. New York: Cambridge University Press, 2016.
MacIntyre, Alasdair C. *Whose Justice? Which Rationality?* Notre Dame, IN: University of Notre Dame Press, 1988.
Mahmood, Saba. *Politics of Piety: The Islamic Revival and the Feminist Subject*. Princeton, NJ: Princeton University Press, 2005.

Maldonado, Michelle Gonzales. "Liberation Ecclesiologies with Special Reference to Latin America." In *The Oxford Handbook of Ecclesiology*, edited by Paul D. L. Avis, 573–94. Oxford: Oxford University Press, 2018.

Manigault-Bryant, LeRhonda S. *Talking to the Dead: Religion, Music, and Lived Memory among Gullah-Geechee Women*. Durham, NC: Duke University Press, 2014.

Marable, Manning. *How Capitalism Underdeveloped Black America: Problems in Race, Political Economy and Society*. Boston: South End Press, 1983.

Marable, Manning. *W. E. B. Du Bois: Black Radical Democrat*. New updated ed. London: Routledge, 2016.

Marsh, Charles, Peter Slade, and Sarah Azaransky, eds. *Lived Theology: New Perspectives on Method, Style, and Pedagogy*. New York: Oxford University Press, 2017.

McAlevey, Jane. *No Shortcuts: Organizing for Power in the New Gilded Age*. New York: Oxford University Press, 2016.

McDannell, Colleen. *Material Christianity: Religion and Popular Culture in America*. New Haven, CT: Yale University Press, 1995.

Migliore, Daniel L. *Faith Seeking Understanding: An Introduction to Christian Theology*. Grand Rapids, MI: William B. Eerdmans, 2014.

Milbank, John. "On Complex Space." In *The Word Made Strange: Theology, Language, and Culture*, 268–92. Cambridge, MA: Blackwell, 1997.

Milbank, John. *Theology and Social Theory: Beyond Secular Reason*. Malden, MA: Blackwell, 2006.

Miller, Grace L. "The I.W.W. Free Speech Fight: San Diego, 1912." *Southern California Quarterly* 54, no. 3 (1972): 211–38.

Miller, Sally M., ed. *Race, Ethnicity, and Gender in Early Twentieth-Century American Socialism*. Vol. 1. Garland Reference Library of Social Science. Labor in America, vol. 880. New York: Garland, 1996.

Morgan, Jennifer L. *Reckoning with Slavery: Gender, Kinship, and Capitalism in the Early Black Atlantic*. Durham, NC: Duke University Press, 2021.

Muelder, Walter George. *The Ethical Edge of Christian Theology: Forty Years of Communitarian Personalism*. New York: E. Mellen Press, 1983.

Neiman, James, and Roger Haight. "On the Dynamic Relation between Ecclesiology and Congregational Studies." In *Explorations in Ecclesiology and Ethnography*, edited by Christian Scharen, 9–33. Grand Rapids, MI: W. B. Eerdmans, 2012.

Nussbaum, Martha Craven. "Plato on Commensurability and Desire." In *Love's Knowledge: Essays on Philosophy and Literature*, 106–24. New York: Oxford University Press, 1990.

Nussbaum, Martha Craven. *Upheavals of Thought: The Intelligence of Emotions*. New York: Cambridge University Press, 2001.

O'Donovan, Oliver. *Finding and Seeking*. Vol 2. Ethics as Theology. Grand Rapids, MI: William B. Eerdmans, 2014.

O'Donovan, Oliver. *Self, World, and Time: An Induction*. Vol 1. Ethics as Theology. Grand Rapids, MI: William B. Eerdmans, 2013.

Omaha Guide. "Ex-Slave, 83, Interesting Minister: Ran against Bryan for Senator in Nebr. on Prohibition Ticket." January 30, 1937.

Ormerod, Neil. "Social Science and Ideological Critiques of Ecclesiology." In *The Oxford Handbook of Ecclesiology*, edited by Paul D. L. Avis, 553–72. Oxford: Oxford University Press, 2018.

Orsi, Robert A. *Between Heaven and Earth: The Religious Worlds People Make and the Scholars Who Study Them*. Oxford: Princeton University Press, 2005.
Orsi, Robert A. *History and Presence*. Cambridge, MA: Belknap Press of Harvard University Press, 2016.
Orsi, Robert A. *The Madonna of 115th Street: Faith and Community in Italian Harlem, 1880–1950*. London: Yale University Press, 2010.
Ortner, Sherry B. *Making Gender: The Politics and Erotics of Culture*. Boston: Beacon Press, 1996.
Ortner, Sherry B. "Theory in Anthropology since the Sixties." *Comparative Studies in Society and History* 26, no. 1 (1984): 126–66.
Osterman, Paul. *Gathering Power: The Future of Progressive Politics in America*. Boston: Beacon Press, 2002.
Ostrow, James M. "Culture as a Fundamental Dimension of Experience: A Discussion of Pierre Bourdieu's Theory of Human Habitus." Edited by Edmund Husserl, James S. Churchill, and Karl Ameriks. *Human Studies* 4, no. 3 (1981): 279–97.
Oyakawa, Michelle. "'Turning Private Pain into Public Action': The Cultivation of Identity Narratives by a Faith-Based Community Organization." *Qualitative Sociology* 38, no. 4 (December 1, 2015): 395–415.
Payne, Charles M. *I've Got the Light of Freedom: The Organizing Tradition and the Mississippi Freedom Struggle*. London: University of California Press, 2007.
Petrella, Ivan. *The Future of Liberation Theology: An Argument and Manifesto*. Burlington, VT: Ashgate, 2004.
Pettit, Philip. *Republicanism: A Theory of Freedom and Government*. Oxford: Oxford University Press, 1997.
Pinkard, Terry. "What Is a 'Shape of Spirit'?" In *Hegel's Phenomenology of Spirit: A Critical Guide*, edited by Dean Moyar and Michael Quante, 112–29. Cambridge: Cambridge University Press, 2008.
Political Theology Network. "Perspectives on Asian Americans and the Spirit of Racial Capitalism." December 23, 2021. https://politicaltheology.com/symposium/perspectives-on-asian-americans-and-the-spirit-of-racial-capitalism/.
Putnam, Hilary. *Mind, Language, and Reality*. New York: Cambridge University Press, 1979.
Rawls, John. *Political Liberalism*. New York: Columbia University Press, 2005.
Rawls, John. *A Theory of Justice*. Oxford: Clarendon Press, 1972.
Rhodes, Daniel P. "Virtue and Power: The Narrative of Reason and the Reasoning of Public Narratives in the Construction of a New Politics of the Collective Good." *Political Theology*, October 24, 2022, 1–21.
Rieger, Joerg. "Religion, Labor, Class, and Justice: Buddhist—Christian Dialogue in Fresh Perspective." *Buddhist-Christian Studies* 39 (2019): 133–46.
Rieger, Joerg. *Theology in the Capitalocene: Ecology, Identity, Class, and Solidarity*. Minneapolis: Fortress, 2022.
Robinson, Cedric J. *Black Marxism: The Making of the Black Radical Tradition*. Totowa, NJ: Biblio Distribution Center, 1983.
Rogers, Mary Beth. *Cold Anger: A Story of Faith and Power Politics*. Denton: University of North Texas Press, 1990.
Rogers, Melvin L. "Democracy, Elites and Power: John Dewey Reconsidered." *Contemporary Political Theory* 8, no. 1 (February 2009): 68–89. http://dx.doi.org.ezproxy.cul.columbia.edu/10.1057/cpt.2008.25.

Rogers, Melvin L. *The Undiscovered Dewey: Religion, Morality, and the Ethos of Democracy.* New York: Columbia University Press, 2009.

Roll, Jarod. *Spirit of Rebellion: Labor and Religion in the New Cotton South.* Urbana: University of Illinois Press, 2010.

Rorty, Richard. *Philosophy and Social Hope.* New York: Penguin Books, 1999.

Ryan, Mary. "Gender and Public Access: Women's Politics in Nineteenth Century American." In *Habermas and the Public Sphere*, edited by Craig Calhoon, 259–88. Cambridge, MA: MIT Press, 1994.

Salomon, Noah. *For Love of the Prophet: An Ethnography of Sudan's Islamic State.* Princeton, NJ: Princeton University Press, 2016.

Salvatierra, Alexia, and Peter Goodwin Heltzel. *Faith-Rooted Organizing: Mobilizing the Church in Service to the World.* Downers Grove, IL: InterVarsity Press, 2014.

Scharen, Christian. "Learning Ministry over Time: Embodying Practical Wisdom." In *For Life Abundant: Practical Theology, Theological Education, and Christian Ministry*, edited by Dorothy C. Bass and Craig R. Dykstra, 265–89. Grand Rapids, MI: William B. Eerdmans, 2008.

Scott, Joan Wallach. *Sex and Secularism.* Princeton, NJ: Princeton University Press, 2018.

Shaffer, Donald. "Thankful Baptist Church," email to author, October 30, 2021.

Shanks, Rosalie. "The I.W.W. Free Speech Movement: San Diego, 1912." *Journal of San Diego History* 19, no. 1 (1973). https://sandiegohistory.org/journal/1973/january/speech/.

Sigurdson, Ola. "Beyond Secularism? Towards a Post-Secular Political Theology." *Modern Theology* 26, no. 2 (April 2010): 177–96.

Sinclair, Charlene. "Interventions Forum on Privilege and Power in the Capitalocene: Fraud and Force." *Wendland-Cook Program in Religion and Justice* (blog), June 27, 2022. https://www.religionandjustice.org/interventions-forum-on-privilege-and-power-in-the-capitalocene#contributorfour.

Sinclair, Charlene. "Let the Dead Speak! Black Being-ness as Ground of Resistance." PhD diss., Union Theological Seminary, 2017.

Sinclair, Charlene. "Re-Examining Community Organizing." *Social Policy* 38, no. 4 (Fall 2008/2009): 48–48.

Smallwood, Stephanie E. *Saltwater Slavery: A Middle Passage from Africa to American Diaspora.* Cambridge, MA: Harvard University Press, 2007.

Smith, Michael, David Lewis, and Mark Johnston. "Dispositional Theories of Value." *Proceedings of the Aristotelian Society*, supplement 63 (1989): 89–174.

Smith, Ted. "Theories of Practice." In *The Wiley-Blackwell Companion to Practical Theology*, edited by Bonnie J. Miller-McLemore, 244–54. Chichester: Blackwell, 2012.

Snarr, C. Melissa. *All You That Labor: Religion and Ethics in the Living Wage Movement.* New York: New York University Press, 2011.

Southeast Center for Cooperative Development. "Faith and Co-ops." Accessed March 27, 2022. https://www.co-opsnow.org/tool-kit.

Speer, Paul W., and Hahrie Han. "Re-engaging Social Relationships and Collective Dimensions of Organizing to Revive Democratic Practice." *Journal of Social and Political Psychology* 6, no. 2 (2018): 745–58.

Springs, Jason A. "'Dismantling the Master's House': Freedom as Ethical Practice in Brandom and Foucault." *Journal of Religious Ethics* 37, no. 3 (2009): 419–48.

Springs, Jason, Cornel West, Richard Rorty, Stanley Hauerwas, and Jeffrey Stout. "Pragmatism and Democracy: Assessing Jeffrey Stout's Democracy and Tradition." *Journal of the American Academy of Religion* 78, no. 2 (2010): 413–48.

Stall, Susan, and Randy Stoecker. "Community Organizing or Organizing Community? Gender and the Crafts of Empowerment." *Gender and Society* 12, no. 6 (1998): 729–56.

Stauffer, Aaron. "Attuning the Church, Debating What Lies beyond Racial Capitalism." Political Theology Network, January 6, 2022. https://politicaltheology.com/attuning-the-church-debating-what-lies-beyond-racial-capitalism/.

Stauffer, Aaron. "How Do Christians Practice Democracy?" *Marginalia: An Imprint of the L.A. Review of Books* (blog), February 28, 2020. https://marginalia.lareviewofbooks.org/how-do-christians-practice-democracy/.

Stewart, Jon. *Introduction to Hegel's Lectures on the Philosophy of Religion: The Issue of Religious Content in the Enlightenment and Romanticism*. Oxford: Oxford University Press, 2022.

Stocker, Michael. *Plural and Conflicting Values*. New York: Oxford University Press, 1992.

Stout, Jeffrey. "Adams on the Nature of Obligation." In *Metaphysics and the Good: Themes from the Philosophy of Robert Merrihew Adams*, edited by Samuel Newlands and Larry M. Jorgensen, 368–87. Oxford: Oxford University Press, 2009.

Stout, Jeffrey. *Blessed Are the Organized: Grassroots Democracy in America*. Princeton, NJ: Princeton University Press, 2010.

Stout, Jeffrey. *Democracy and Tradition*. Princeton, NJ: Princeton University Press, 2004.

Stout, Jeffrey. *Ethics after Babel: The Languages of Morals and Their Discontents*. Boston: Beacon Press, 1988.

Sullivan, Winnifred Fallers. *Church State Corporation: Construing Religion in US Law*. Chicago: University of Chicago Press, 2020.

Sullivan, Winnifred Fallers. *The Impossibility of Religious Freedom*. Princeton, NJ: Princeton University Press, 2018.

Swarts, Heidi J. *Organizing Urban America: Secular and Faith-Based Progressive Movements*. Minneapolis: University of Minnesota Press, 2008.

Syndicate. "Symposium on Luke Bretherton's Resurrecting Democracy." Accessed November 13, 2019. https://syndicate.network/symposia/theology/resurrecting-democracy/.

Tanner, Kathryn. *Christ the Key*. Cambridge: Cambridge University Press, 2010.

Tanner, Kathryn. "Theological Reflection and Christian Practices." In *Practicing Theology: Beliefs and Practices in Christian Life*, edited by Miroslav Volf and Dorothy C. Bass, 228–44. Grand Rapids, MI: Eerdmans, 2002.

Tanner, Kathryn. *Theories of Culture: A New Agenda for Theology*. Minneapolis, MN: Fortress Press, 1997.

Taves, Ann. "Feminization Revisited: Protestantism and Gender at the Turn of the Century." In *Women and Twentieth-Century Protestantism*, edited by Margaret Lamberts Bendroth and Virginia Lieson Brereton, 304–24. Urbana: University of Illinois Press, 2002.

Taylor, Charles. "The Diversity of Goods." In *Philosophy and the Human Sciences*. Vol. 2. Philosophical Papers, 230–47. New York: Cambridge University Press, 1985.

Taylor, Charles. *A Secular Age*. Cambridge, MA: Belknap Press of Harvard University Press, 2007.

Teele, Dawn Langan. *Forging the Franchise: The Political Origins of the Women's Vote*. Princeton, NJ: Princeton University Press, 2018.

Thatamanil, John J. *Circling the Elephant: A Comparative Theology of Religious Diversity*. New York: Fordham University Press, 2020.

Thompson, Patricia. "Field." In *Pierre Bourdieu: Key Concepts*, edited by Michael Greenfell, 65–80. New York: Routledge, 2012.

Tran, Jonathan. *Asian Americans and the Spirit of Racial Capitalism*. New York: Oxford University Press, 2022.

Volf, Miroslav, and Maurice Lee. "The Spirit and the Church." In *Advents of the Spirit: An Introduction to the Current Study of Pneumatology*, edited by Bradford E. Hinze and D. Lyle Dabney, 380–407. Milwaukee, WI: Marquette University Press, 2001.

Ward, Ian. "Public Reasoning and Religious Difference." PhD diss., Princeton University, 2008.

Warren, Mark R. *Dry Bones Rattling: Community Building to Revitalize American Democracy*. Princeton, NJ: Princeton University Press, 2001.

West, Cornel. "Afterword." In *Cornel West: A Critical Reader*, edited by George Yancy, 346–62. Blackwell Critical Readers. Malden, MA: Blackwell, 2001.

West, Cornel. *The American Evasion of Philosophy: A Genealogy of Pragmatism*. Madison: University of Wisconsin Press, 1989.

West, Cornel. "Black Theology and Marxist Thought." In *Black Theology: A Documentary History*, edited by Gayraud S. Wilmore and James H. Cone, 409–24. Maryknoll, NY: Orbis Books, 1979.

West, Cornel. *Cornel West on Black Prophetic Fire*. Edited by Christina Buschendorf. Boston: Beacon Press, 2014.

West, Cornel. *The Cornel West Reader*. New York: Basic Civitas Books, 1999.

West, Cornel. *Democracy Matters: Winning the Fight against Imperialism*. New York: Penguin Press, 2004.

West, Cornel. *Prophesy Deliverance! An Afro-American Revolutionary Christianity*. Louisville, KY: Westminster John Knox Press, 2002.

West, Cornel. "Toward a Socialist Theory of Racism." In *Prophetic Fragments*, 97–108. Grand Rapids, MI: Eerdmans, 1988.

Wiggins, David. "Weakness of Will, Commensurability, and the Objects of Deliberation and Desire." *Proceedings of the Aristotelian Society* 79 (1978): 251–77.

Williams, Bernard. "Moral Luck." In *Moral Luck: Philosophical Papers, 1973–1980*, 20–40. Cambridge: Cambridge University Press, 1981.

Williams, Delores S. *Sisters in the Wilderness: The Challenge of Womanist God-Talk*. Maryknoll, NY: Orbis Books, 2013.

Williams, Robert R. "Art, Logic, and the Human Presence of Spirit in Hegel's Philosophy of Absolute Spirit." In *Hegel's Philosophy of Spirit: A Critical Guide*, edited by Marina F. Bykova, 243–66. Cambridge: Cambridge University Press, 2019.

Williams, Robert R. *Hegel's Ethics of Recognition*. Berkeley: University of California Press, 1997.

Williams, Robert R. *Recognition: Fichte and Hegel on the Other*. SUNY Series in Hegelian Studies. Albany: State University of New York Press, 1992. Online.

Winner, Lauren F. *The Dangers of Christian Practice: On Wayward Gifts, Characteristic Damage, and Sin*. London: Yale University Press, 2018.

Wolf, Susan. "A World of Goods." *Philosophy and Phenomenological Research* 64, no. 2 (2002): 467–74.

Wolin, Sheldon S. *Democracy Incorporated: Managed Democracy and the Specter of Inverted Totalitarianism*. Princeton, NJ: Princeton University Press, 2008.

Wolin, Sheldon S. *Fugitive Democracy: And Other Essays*. Princeton, NJ: Princeton University Press, 2016.

Wolin, Sheldon S. *Politics and Vision: Continuity and Innovation in Western Political Thought*. Princeton, NJ: Princeton University Press, 2004.

Wolin, Sheldon S. *The Presence of the Past: Essays on the State and the Constitution.* Baltimore: Johns Hopkins University Press, 1989.

Wolin, Sheldon S. *Tocqueville between Two Worlds: The Making of a Political and Theoretical Life.* Princeton, NJ: Princeton University Press, 2001.

Wolterstorff, Nicholas. "An Engagement with Rorty." In *Understanding Liberal Democracy: Essays in Political Philosophy,* edited by Terence Cuneo, 41–52. Oxford: Oxford University Press, 2012.

Wolterstorff, Nicholas. *Religion in the University.* New Haven, CT: Yale University Press, 2019.

Wood, Richard L. *Faith in Action: Religion, Race, and Democratic Organizing in America.* Chicago: University of Chicago Press, 2002.

Wood, Richard L., and Brad Fulton. *A Shared Future: Faith-Based Organizing for Racial Equity and Ethical Democracy.* Chicago: University of Chicago Press, 2015.

Woodbey, George Washington. *Black Socialist Preacher: The Teachings of Reverend George Washington Woodbey and His Disciple, Reverend George W. Slater, Jr.* Edited by Philip Foner. San Francisco: Synthesis, 1983.

Woodbey, George Washington. Untitled article. *California Eagle,* February 5, 1916.

Zahl, Simeon. *The Holy Spirit and Christian Experience.* Oxford: Oxford University Press, 2020.

Index

For the benefit of digital users, indexed terms that span two pages (e.g., 52–53) may, on occasion, appear on only one of those pages.

abolitionism, 182
abortion, 4, 39–40
Adams, Robert M., 37–47, 89–93
agency, 109–16, 118–30, 192–95
agitation, 56–57, 62–66
Alinsky, Saul, 17, 48
Anderson, Elizabeth, 85–89
anger, 44–45, 59, 63–66
anti-blackness, 64–65, 168–85
assimilationist (politics), 34, 69, 174–75, 200–5

Banner, Michael, 4–6
Baptism, 52–55
Bass, Dorothy, 50–55
Bender, Courtney, 50–55
Black (organizing), 27–31, 168–85
Bourdieu, Pierre, 147–67
Brandom, Robert, 93–104
Braunstein, Ruth, 32
Bretherton, Luke, 32–37, 201–3

capitalism, 7–14, 109–16, 130–42, 168–85, 191–99
Chambers, Edward, 19
Christian (identity), 48–77, 109–16
Church, 9, 27–31, 186–208
class, 11–13, 109–16
coercion, 118–21
Cone, Jame H., 170–75
congregation, 27–31, 186–208
constructivism, 109–16
    See also social construction
cooperation (economic), 27–28, 193–98
    See also cooperatives
cooperatives, 27–28, 152–53
Cortez, Ernesto, 181–82

counterpublic, 17–47, 70–77, 109–16, 117–44, 186–208
credentialing, 162

DART Center, xi
Dawson, Michael, 27–31
debate, 122–27
deliberation, 104–9
democracy, 81–116, 117–44
demos, 130–37
demotic, 130–37
Dewey, John, 118–30
dialectic, 93–104
dialogue, 135
difference, 93–104
disagreement, 69
domination, 11–14
Dworkin, Robert, 37–46
Dykstra, Craig, 52–67

ecclesiology, 27–31, 186–208
economy, 27–31, 147–67
eucharist, 52–53, 202–3
exploitation, 11–12, 168–85
expropriation, 11–12, 168–85

fallibilism, 46–47, 103, 157, 199, 207
feminism, 19–26
field, 147–67
    See also Bourdieu, Pierre
freedom, 117–44
fugitivity, 130–37
fury, 63–66
    See also anger

Gamaliel, xi
gender, 11–12, 22–26, 29–30, 104–9

INDEX

Glaude, Eddie, 27–31

habit(s), 118–30
habitus, 147–67

idealism, 93–104
identity, 109–16
idols, 170–75
incommensurability, 83–89
incomparable, 85–89
individualism, 98–99
individuality, 117–44
Industrial Areas Foundation (IAF), xiv
inferentialism, 15–16
interfaith, xiv, 56, 69, 205–8
intersubjectivity, 93–104

judgement, 104–9
justice, 3–13
  See also social justice

labor, 11–12
leadership, 45, 62
liberalism, 172
liberation, xxvi, 99–100, 102–3, 170–75, 188–89, 191–99, 200–5
liberty. See freedom
listening, xxiv–xxvii, 48, 55–69, 93–104
lived religion, 70–77

mistakes, in organizing, 62–63, 103, 150–51, 157
money, 38, 88–89, 165
monisms, 85–89
morality, social construction of, 4, 109–16
multiculturalism, 168–75

narrative, xxi–xxii
norms, 15–16

objectivity, 37–46, 104–9
organizer, 147–67, 168–85
organizing (practice of), 147–67

Orthodoxy, 109–16, 171–72

pain, xxii, 60–61, 63–64, 69, 88, 101–2
pluralism, 69, 135, 172, 180, 207
pneumatology, 195–96, 200–8
police, 123–44
practical reasoning, xx–xxi, xxiv, 15–16, 81–116
practice, 50–55, 147–67
prayer, 52–53, 55, 71, 72
prophetic, 138–42
public, 20–21

race, 11–12, 27–31, 109–16, 168–85
racial capitalism, 8–13, 168–85
racism, 109–16, 168–85
radical, 9–14
recognition, xx, 81–116

sacred value (theories of), 37–46
secular, xiii–xiv, 17–47
  See also secularism
secularism xiii–xiv
secularization, xiii–xiv
setting, 153–55
social construction, 109–16
social ethics, 3–16
social gospel, 3–4, 10–12
social justice, 3–5, 6–13
socialism, 6–10
spirit, xvi–xvii, xix–xxii

tending, 130–37
  See also democracy
time, 62–65

value, 85–89
virtue, 44–45, 152–53
vocation, 194–95, 200–5

West, Cornel, 138–42
Wolin, Sheldon, 130–37
Woodbey, George Washington, 186–208
working people, 175–78
worship, 88, 107